MASTER PIECES

Richard Ball & Peter Campbell

MASTER

PIECES

Hearst Books · New York

Title page:
St. Joseph at work in his carpenter's shop *by Robert Campin.*
Right panel of the Merode Altarpiece *(detail); Metropolitan*
Museum of Art, New York, The Cloisters Collection, Purchase

Copyright © 1983 by Richard Ball and Peter Campbell

First published 1983

All rights reserved. No part of this book may be reproduced
or utilized in any form or by any means, electronic or
mechanical, including photocopying, recording or by any
information storage and retrieval system, without
permission in writing from the Publisher. Inquiries should
be addressed to Hearst Books, an affiliate of William Morrow
and Company, Inc., 105 Madison Avenue, New York,
NY 10016.

Library of Congress Card Catalog Number: 83-81095

ISBN: 0-688-02488-2

Designed and produced by
Richard Ball and Peter Campbell
16 Newman Passage, London W1

Set by TNR Productions Ltd, London

Printed in Hong Kong by
Mandarin Offset International (HK) Ltd

First U.S. Edition

1   2   3   4   5   6   7   8   9   10

Acknowledgements

We would like to thank the designers and makers who
worked with us on the project and who contributed so much
to its success. Their response to the challenge of making
furniture from paintings was truly impressive, and they were
unfailingly generous with their time and knowledge. We are
proud to have worked with them.

The color illustrations are reproduced by kind permission of
the following:
The Trustees, The National Gallery, London: cover, 15, 51;
The Trustees, The Wallace Collection, London: 10; Mr. and
Mrs. Eric Estorick: 23; The National Gallery of Art,
Washington: 26, 73; SCALA/Firenze: 34, 84, 132; Home
House Society Trustees, Courtauld Institute Galleries
(Courtauld Collection): 42; Philadelphia Museum of Art: 58;
Bildarchiv Preussischer Kulturbesitz: 66; The Tate Gallery,
London: 92; Museum Mayer van den Bergh, Antwerp: 98;
The Trustees of the British Library: 104; The Museum of
Modern Art, New York: 110; Cliché des Musées Nationaux,
Paris: 125; The Archives of Giorgio de Chirico curated by
Claudio Bruni Sakraischik: 140. All color photographs of the
furniture taken by the authors.

The black and white illustrations are reproduced by kind
permission of the following:-
The Metropolitan Museum of Art, New York: title page, 6
(top left), 69, 118; The National Gallery of Art, Washington:
6 (top right); Copyright The Frick Collection, New York: 6
(bottom); The Edward James Foundation: 8, 9;
Rijksmuseum, Amsterdam: 13; National Museum Vincent
van Gogh, Amsterdam: 16 (left); The American Museum in
Britain, Bath: 16 (right); Institute of Agricultural History and
Museum of English Rural Life, University of Reading: 17, 21;
Courtesy, Essex Institute, Salem, Mass.: 32; The Mansell
Collection: 36, 65, 89, 108; Courtesy of the Victoria and
Albert Museum, London: 44, 74, 101 (right); Courtesy of
Browse and Darby, London: 48; Courtesy of the Domoto
Museum, Kyoto: 49 (left); Photographie Bulloz, Paris: 49
(right); Home House Society Trustees, Courtauld Institute
Galleries, London (Princes Gate Collection): 57; from *Where
the Wild Things Are*, story and pictures by Maurice Sendak,
Copyright © 1963 by Maurice Sendak; Reprinted by
permission of Harper & Row, Publishers, Inc: 60; Museo
Civico di Torino: 75; Weidenfeld and Nicolson
Archives/Photo D. Bellon: 80; Cliché des Musées
Nationaux, Paris: 81 (left), 90, 131; Galerie Isy Brachot,
Bruxelles-Paris: 81 (right); Collection, Museum of Modern
Art, New York: 95; The Burrell Collection – Glasgow
Museums and Art Galleries: 100; Courtesy, The Henry
Francis du Pont Winterthur Museum: 101 (left); Stedelijk
Museum, Amsterdam: 112; Fitzwilliam Museum,
Cambridge: 123; Courtesy of the Giorgio de Chirico
Foundation: 144.

Works by de Chirico, Léger, Matisse and Picasso:
© S.P.A.D.E.M. Paris 1982; works by Magritte and Matisse:
© A.D.A.G.P. Paris 1982.

Working drawings by Hayward Art Group (Alison George)

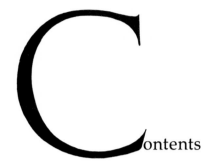

Contents

Introduction   7

1. Foppa: Young Cicero's Stool   10
2. Van Gogh: Vincent's Chair   14
3. El Lissitzky: Tatlin's Table   22
4. Davis: The Limner's Table   26
5. Fra Angelico: Deacon Justinian's Platform Bed   34
6. Cézanne: The Café Table   42
7. Antonello: The Study Furniture   50
8. Duchamp: The Ready-Made Bed   58
9. Bouts: Simon's Trestle Table   66
10. Bosch: The Miser's Chest   72
11. Magritte: The Humanoid Table   78
12. David: Madame Récamier's Bed   84
13. Léger: The Acrobat's Cat's Chair   92
14. Bruegel: The Proverbial Stool   98
15. Crane: Captain Duck's Settee   104
16. Matisse: The Red Studio Chair   110
17. Ghirlandaio: The Madonna's Lectern   116
18. Picasso: Still Life Sideboard   124
19. Carpaccio: Saint Augustine's Armchair   132
20. De Chirico: Chair in the Valley   140

Introduction

Some of the most intriguing pieces of furniture ever designed are trapped in two dimensions, in paintings on the walls of the world's museums. This book began with the question "What would the pieces of furniture which painters have included in their pictures look like if they existed in three dimensions?" The furniture makers and sculptors who took up the challenge and built the twenty pieces described in *Master Pieces* provided an answer. Paintings became their pattern book as they brought furniture out of the flat canvas and into the three-dimensional world.

The question was stimulated by René Magritte, the stern surrealist who painted some awesomely odd furniture. Magritte himself was acutely aware of the great divide between two-dimensional paintings and the three-dimensional world. His well known painting of a pipe bears the legend "This is not a pipe" – which is a fair point, as it is obviously a painting. With this point in mind we looked at the curious table in Magritte's painting *A Difficult Crossing* (illustrated on p. 78); it looks quite normal apart from one leg, which is human in shape. "This is not a table," we thought, "but it most certainly should be". We decided we should drag the painted table out into three dimensions and see if it could stand on its own strange feet in the real world. The sculptor Patrick Daw proved that the scheme could work (p. 78). It became clear that equally appealing pieces of furniture lurked in pictures by other master painters. A complete range of *master pieces* could be built up.

Certain periods are rich sources. Medieval paintings are surprisingly full of furniture. Artists of the time often introduced contemporary furniture into their pictures of biblical scenes. They also received commissions to record major social events, such as baronial feasts, complete with furniture. These paintings supply furniture historians with valuable evidence about the way medieval furniture was used, and offer today's furniture maker simple and satisfying projects.

Top right: The Flemish artists of the 15th century pioneered the painting of contemporary furnished interiors, even in biblical scenes such as Rogier van der Weyden's Christ appearing to His Mother *(detail). Metropolitan Museum of Art, New York, Bequest of Michael Driecer, 1921*

Top left: Giorgio de Chirico's classical landscapes make the most ordinary furniture seem odd. Conversation among the Ruins *(1927) is typical. National Gallery of Art, Washington, Chester Dale Collection*

Opposite: St. Francis's stylish desk is a 15th-century precursor of 20th-century furniture design. See, for example, Rietveld's baby chair illustrated on p. 112. St. Francis in Ecstasy *by Giovanni Bellini. The Frick Collection, New York*

The Renaissance artists of Italy painted many plain and elegant pieces, some of which seem ideal subjects for 3-D reproduction. We chose three – the Foppa (p. 10), Fra Angelico (p. 34) and Ghirlandaio (p. 116). The seventeenth-century Dutch genre painters were prolific painters of interior scenes in Holland's taverns and bourgeois parlors. Their furniture is on the whole a precise and predictable representation of well known styles, real examples of which are easily found in museums of furniture. For this reason we felt that reproduction would not be in the spirit of this project.

The drawbacks which detract from seventeenth-century Dutch paintings are even more marked in the eighteenth century. Moreover, eighteenth-century society loved intricate craftsmanship; most of the period's pieces therefore demand too high a level of skill for the ordinary mortal to emulate.

Country furniture of the nineteenth century is a more fruitful area: its principles of construction are simple and the painters often less slavish in their imitation of the model, either through aesthetic principle or, in the case of many naive painters, lack of formal training. See, for example, Joseph H. Davis's table (p. 26).

The twentieth century is an inexhaustible mine of imaginative furniture. Salvador Dali's Mae West Lips sofa (p. 9) has already been successfully manufactured, but commercial operations have bypassed other wonderful surrealist furniture. Magritte's surreal inventions reign supreme, while de Chirico's landscapes are dotted with enviable seats. Matisse's lovely rooms are filled with appropriately desirable glowing furniture (p. 110), and Léger invented furniture in the style of his "tubist" paintings (p. 95). Making a Picasso piece true to the artist was a challenge we could not refuse (p. 124).

The hunt through the history of art for likely pieces of furniture adds a new dimension to the appreciation of paintings. Working out the design details forces you to spend a long time with the painting, rather than pausing briefly in front of the canvas during an afternoon's drift through the museum. As you scrutinize the paint for clues to construction, materials and finishing, the painter's way of seeing and painting reveals itself.

Our approach to the project was to make each piece of furniture in the spirit of the artist's interpretation rather than to try and reproduce the piece he may have used as a model. The approach demanded close observation of the paintings, and this brought quick rewards. There is often some quirk to be found in what at first seems a straightforward portrayal of a piece of ordinary furniture. For instance, Vincenzo Foppa's simple stool (p. 10) has an intriguing asymmetrical cut-out in the end panel. We kept this feature, although it is unlikely to have

Salvador Dali's Birth of Paranoiac Furniture *(above) and its notorious, full-size, 3-D offspring from 1936 – the Mae West Lips Sofa (opposite), upholstered in Schiaparelli's Shocking Pink satin. Edward James Foundation*

figured in any model Foppa could have used. This cut-out turned an ordinary stool into something interesting and original.

Howard Raybould compared his role as designer and maker of the Cézanne table (p. 42) to that of a detective trying to recreate a crime. There are only a few clues in the painting, and the designer has to build up the whole scene from this. Raybould also articulated a common view among those involved in the project when he found himself at the half-way stage wondering "how strong should I myself be in all this? Am I a model maker or a creative decision maker?" His assumption was that the model maker would feel obliged to make the piece utterly faithful to the plans. In fact he found that his own piece soon took on its own identity. The painter's original decisions do not necessarily reflect the logical world; the maker can also exploit this artistic license, adding and subtracting elements to improve the three dimensional piece.

On the technical side, modern developments need not be discarded in the interests of historical accuracy. Only the obsessive would want to do without the time saving tools and techniques available to today's amateur merely because the Renaissance professional had no electric drill. A fine example of this process in action is the splendid desk designed by John Makepeace (p. 50). Although based on a fifteenth-century painting by Antonello, the piece is made of Medium Density Overlay (MDO) a new material of considerable potential. The chair accompanying the desk is a refined exercise in the use of laminated wood.

Other pieces draw on techniques most amateurs would not consider. Howard Raybould's table (p. 42), for example, has a carved wooden tablecloth, while Floris van den Broecke and Mary Little used wood-graining techniques on their table (p. 26). Both techniques are within the scope of a beginner.

On occasion it seemed important not to force the artist's vision into the routine rectangles which dominate most modern furniture projects. An awareness of the possibilities of asymmetry was the key to certain pieces. Three-dimensional designer Floris van den Broecke's response to the bizarre perspective of Joseph H. Davis's table is a witty and original exercise in non-rectangular geometry. The Matisse and Léger chairs designed by Mark Dunhill (p. 110 and p. 92), or Patrick Daw's version of Van Gogh's famous chair (p. 14), are other examples of the non-rectangular approach. Dunhill and Daw are both sculptors rather than furniture designers.

One of the joys of making "master pieces" lies in the attempt to match the texture of the painting in the three dimensional piece. We decided all modern materials could be exploited to the full, both in construction and finishing. The great painters were themselves constantly exploring the possibilities of new materials and techniques. These considerations suggested on occasion that a sculptor – for whom the awareness of the practical and aesthetic possibilities of many different materials is routine – might enjoy the special problems of a particular project. The plank-like looks of the seat in de Chirico's *Furniture in the Valley* (p. 140), on the other hand, made it a suitable job for furniture maker Jim Partridge, whose own designs ably exploit plank-appeal.

Every project we have chosen is possible, interesting and usable. The text describes how each piece is constructed and finished and why the designer chose to make it the way he did. Working drawings give the dimensions of every element used to make each piece. The measurements in the drawings are taken from the pieces created by the designers. However, the designers did not necessarily make working drawings before starting work, and in some cases took very few measurements. There was a consensus among the designer/makers that the designing of a piece of furniture cannot always be divorced from the activity of making it. Many of them found they saw new elements in the paintings after they began work and adapted their design accordingly.

It is our belief that more people would make their own furniture if they could find designs they like. We are also convinced that paintings can provide the amateur furniture maker with lively and original designs to solve this do-it-yourself dilemma. The history of art is an unrivalled source book of furniture design, and one where the amateur does not risk depressing comparisons with a manufacturer's machine-made alternative or a skilled craftsman's original. There is quite simply no original to compare to. As the painter's piece of furniture is two-dimensional, each person's 3-D creation can lay claim to complete originality.

Above all, the pieces of furniture in *Master Pieces* are attractive, inventive, interesting and, unlike too many do-it-yourself projects and furniture kits, they are fun to design and make. Readers may disagree with our interpretation of the evidence in the paintings and decide to construct the pieces along different lines. We hope this will happen. We also hope readers will find new pieces in other paintings and design their own utterly original master pieces.

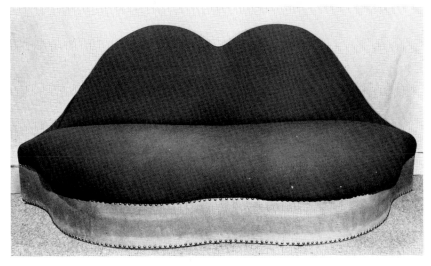

Young Cicero's Stool
by Kevin Jordan
from *Young Cicero Reading* (*c*. 1460) by Vincenzo Foppa (*c*.1430-*c*.1515)
Wallace Collection, London

This simple and appealing fresco of the studious young Cicero was salvaged from a demolition site in nineteenth-century Milan. It is a solid piece of wall cut from the splendid old Medici Bank in Milan's Via de' Bossi. The bank was built and extravagantly decorated in the 1460s by Cosimo de' Medici of the famous Florentine banking family. It was admired as Milan's loveliest building.

Builders were very active in Milan at the time. The wealthy were restoring and modernizing the city's palaces, and craftsmen were in great demand. Vincenzo Foppa was one such artist/craftsman, and he was commissioned to paint a series of frescoes in the new Medici Bank. *Young Cicero Reading* is the only survivor.

For over 400 years young Cicero could be seen on the front of the parapet above the courtyard outside the bank, and for all this time the picture was exposed to dust and weather. Fortunately true fresco – wall-painting on fresh plaster – is one of the most durable of wall coverings. The color becomes part of the plaster as it dries. Thanks to this durability young Cicero survived in remarkably good condition.

After the dramatic salvage job during the demolition, the picture was sold to a Parisian collector and bought by Sir Richard Wallace (of London's Wallace Collection) in 1872.

The Cicero connection comes from the inscription on the bench, M.T.CICERO (*ie* Marcus Tullius Cicero). Cicero was held up as an example to all fifteenth-century schoolboys. Plutarch's *Life of Cicero* asserts that he was the wonder of ancient Rome's schools, and it therefore seems likely that he was placed in the bank's courtyard as an emblem of industry and learning, alongside frescoes of other figures representing the liberal arts.

Vincenzo Foppa is recognized as the founder of the Milanese school of painting, which was later overwhelmed by the arrival of Leonardo da Vinci. The picture has elements typical of the artist, who is known

11

ORDER OF WORK

1 Cut four mortises through top panel. To pierce mortise, mark out with pencil and drill $^{15}/_{16}$ diameter hole through center. Clean out with sharp chisel

2 Cut two mortises and tenons in each end panel. Cut mortises as in top panel. To cut tenon, mark out with pencil, saw along waste side of lines with fine-toothed tenon saw and chisel out waste from center section

3 Cut tenons in side rails

4 Mark out basic shape of cutout in end panels with pencil. Make left leg 1¼ wide at base, right leg ¾ wide. Cut out waste at right angles with saber saw

5 Shape left leg of end panels with spokeshave or shaping tool and sandpaper, beveling it to ¾ outside, 1¼ inside at base, leveling off near top

6 Check all parts fit. Glue and assemble. Clamp together until glue dries

Finish

1 Rub on tinted emulsion by hand
2 Sand lightly
3 Wipe surface with damp tissue
4 Touch up as necessary with poster paint
5 Paint brilliant violet outlines on all edges and on inside faces of end panels
6 French polish
7 Remove shine with fine steel wool

MATERIALS

	No.	Size (ins)
Pine for:		
Top	1	1 × 9½ × 17
End panels	2	1 × 7 × 9½
Side rails	2	1 × 4 × 14½

PVA woodworking adhesive

FINISH

White pigmented primer (emulsion paint) colored with yellow ochre, raw umber, and crimson poster paint; brilliant white poster paint; French polish

DIMENSIONS

End panel

Top panel

Side view

Side panel

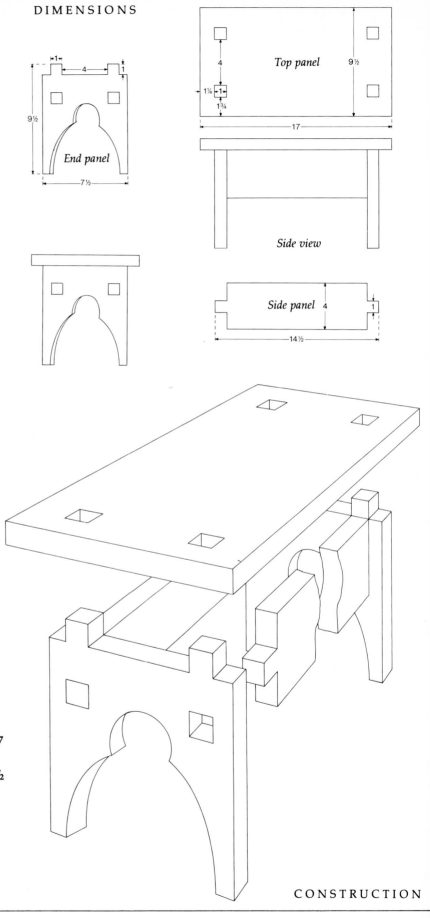

CONSTRUCTION

for a silvery-grey tone and a liking for shimmering effects. The reddish-lilac color of the boy's coat is a Foppa favorite. His outlines are soft and blurred, an effect exaggerated by the chalky texture of the fresco. All these elements influenced the construction and finishing of the stool.

Designing Young Cicero's stool
The stool's shape is a European classic. Similar stools appear in many other paintings of the period, for example Rogier van der Weyden's *Resurrected Christ appearing to the Virgin* in the Metropolitan Museum of Art, New York (p. 6). The same museum owns a real medieval survivor.

Only one face of the stool is visible in the original fresco. The dimensions of this face were decided in relation to the size of the child's leg. The depth was established by looking at other paintings and considering practical use in a modern setting. The shape of the stool's sides was also decided on practical and historical grounds.

No joints are visible in the fresco, and it would be perfectly possible to assemble the stool using only screws and nails. However, mortise and tenon joints were common in Foppa's day and they look good on this type of furniture. They were therefore used to fix the two end panels to the top and to fix two horizontal rails at the sides. PVA adhesive holds the joints in place.

Making the stool

Construction is straightforward, using no rare tools or complex joints. Step-by-step instructions are given alongside the working drawings on p. 12.

Any available timber could be used to construct Cicero's stool. Walnut, oak, poplar and pine were widely used in Italy in Foppa's time. The designer cut the parts for the stool from a century-old plank of pitch pine salvaged from a demolition site. This wood is hard yet easy to work; its age is a guarantee of stability. Like the Foppa fresco, it was grubby after a century of exposure – it was therefore planed clean and sanded smooth before work began.

Perhaps the most delightful feature of the original is the asymmetrical cut-out in the end panel. This was carefully reproduced by removing the basic shape with a saber saw (jigsaw), then bevelling the edges using a spokeshave and sandpaper.

Finishing the stool
The finishing is all-important if the fresco's blotchy paint and rough plaster surface are to be successfully imitated. After sanding the stool smooth, the base paint is rubbed on by hand. The paint is white emulsion colored with three gouaches – yellow ochre, raw umber and a trace of crimson. The first coat is sanded lightly to bring the wood grain through. The surface is blurred to imitate the fresco by wiping it over with a damp tissue. This technique removes more of the paint covering the hard areas of the wood grain.

When the stool has dried, individual areas are painted again by hand until the tones of the original are captured. A violet outline is noticeable on the top of Foppa's stool. This is recreated using brilliant violet gouache. The gouache is applied neat on the edges and inside the end panel cut-outs. It is watered down to paint the shadow cast by the stool top on the panel below. Masking tape can be used to keep a sharp edge.

The finished stool is polished with transparent French polish and rubbed over with fine steel wool to remove the shine.

Young Jesus sits on a stool similar to young Cicero's, but softened by a cushion, in Madonna and Child *by Ambrogio Borgognone (detail), a Milanese painter influenced by Foppa. Rijksmuseum, Amsterdam*

Vincent's Chair

by Patrick Daw

from *Chair and Pipe* (Dec. 1888 – Jan. 1889) by Vincent van Gogh (1853-90)

National Gallery, London

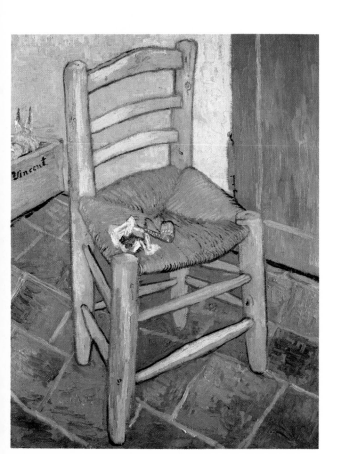

an Gogh's pipe and tobacco pouch lie on an ordinary rush-seated chair, bathed in the yellow light of Provence. This is probably the best-loved of all images of furniture. But the homely country chair has a dark twin in Gauguin's sinister armchair, which Van Gogh painted in red and green, the colors of violence. It was painted at the same time and speaks of breakdown, departure and death.

Both chairs are empty, and empty chairs were a potent negative symbol to Van Gogh. He admired Luke Fildes's engraving of the empty chair in Charles Dickens's study after the writer's death, and he admits to crying like a child at the sight of his own father's empty chair at the end of a visit to Amsterdam in 1878.

Van Gogh arrived in Arles in February 1888 after two miserable years in Paris. He was in poor health, in need of friendship, but full of hope. He wrote enthusiastically to his devoted brother Theo of the "heavenly blues and yellows" of Arles, its dazzling sunflowers and fresh sky. He rented rooms in the Yellow House on the Place Lamartine near the railway station, and the letters joyfully describe the pleasures of furnishing his new home. He chose a dozen chairs and bought two beds. The second was for Gauguin.

Van Gogh dreamed of founding a school of the south, a community of artists in Arles, and he persuaded Gauguin to occupy the room he so carefully prepared for him in October. The two soon quarreled, and Gauguin decided he must leave. The result was Vincent's first major breakdown, which reached a climax on Christmas Eve. *Le Forum républicain* of December 30th reports: "At 11.30pm last Sunday Vincent Vangogh, a painter born in Holland, arrived at House of Tolerance (brothel) number 1, asked for a certain Rachel and offered her – his ear, saying 'Keep this and treasure it'. Then he left. Told of this action, which could only be that of a poor madman, the police went to his address the next morning and found him in bed and giving barely

15

any sign of life. The unfortunate man was admitted to hospital as an emergency case."

Theo arrived to care for his brother. Recovery was slow, but Vincent began painting again. On 27 July 1890, while painting in the fields near Arles, he shot himself in the stomach with a borrowed gun. He died two days later.

Designing Vincent's chair

The chair standing on the red-tiled floor of the Yellow House at Arles must have been brother to the simple rush-seated turned-leg chairs which can still be found in Mediterranean farmhouses and cafes. Van Gogh was uninterested in mere resemblance, he wanted to paint the character of things. In the painting the humble chair has become heavy and solid. The designer felt it was important not only to match the craftsmanship of the original but to keep the distinctive physical presence of the painting.

The strength of many traditional country chairs comes in part from the use of split timber – in which the grain runs true along the entire leg or rung – rather than sawn planks. The rungs would be fitted before the wood was fully seasoned, and the mortises tended to hold them tight. These are not quite the techniques used by Patrick

The slat-back, rush-seated chair is capable of extreme refinement. This American Shaker chair of the 1840s from New Lebanon was for use at a high counter or ironing table

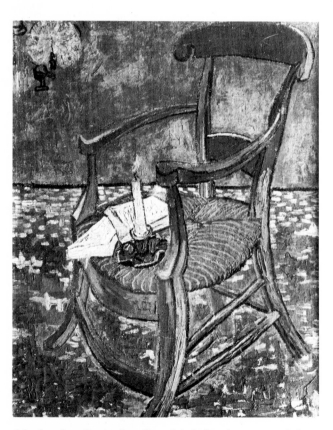

A book and candle stand on Gauguin's dark and empty armchair, painted by Van Gogh at the same time as Chair and Pipe. *National Museum Vincent van Gogh, Amsterdam*

Daw in making the Van Gogh chair, although he took his method of construction from an antique Provençal chair. The shape remains unmistakably Van Gogh.

No wood could match the almost fluorescent glow of Van Gogh's yellow chair with its strong blue outline. In the end a natural disaster gave the designer his material. Dutch elm disease, which has devastated the species in England, made elm wood all too easy to obtain. He decided to look for branches of the right thickness to make each of the parts and to pare these down to size and shape, rather than to cut or split pieces from larger trunks. All the pieces came from the upper branches of the same dead tree, which had in effect been seasoned for four years. He even found pieces with the right curves for the rear posts. All the timber proved to be very stable.

Making the chair

In the whole process of making the chair, the maker measured nothing. The construction sequence is planned so that each new piece is fitted to what has already been made, and in this way a tape measure becomes unnecessary. Technically the job is simple. Indeed the whole chair could be constructed using nothing more than a penknife and a brace and bit. Accuracy is important in drilling the holes in the legs and in cutting the mortises in the back uprights for the slats, but the eye is a more important tool than the rule or square – or book – in achieving a good result. The measurements given below and in the drawings (pp. 18-19) are taken from the finished chair.

First decide the seat height you want – in this case it is 18in. The chair's other dimensions all follow from this initial decision – back height is fractionally less than double, and so on.

Cut the two front legs. They are a little longer than seat height, as they project above the rush seat in the painting. They must now be taken down to the right shape by eye. The traditional tool for paring wood is a draw knife – a two-handled curved blade which the worker pulls towards himself, taking off long shavings from the stave which is held in place against his chest while he sits on a shave horse (straddles a bench). A spokeshave or plane will also do the job. Reduce the front legs from a maximum of 2½in near the top to a minimum of 1¾in at the foot.

In traditional chair-making the pieces were roughly shaped and then turned on a lathe. In the case of the Van Gogh chair it seemed appropriate to keep a rough finish to match the texture of the brushwork in the painting. The pieces are sanded smooth but not made absolutely regular.

Prop the front legs up against a wall, judging the distance between them by eye. If necessary, support them with bricks.

The front rails, including the seat rail, are now measured against the legs, cut to length (allowing 1in at each end for the pegs which hold them in the legs), and shaped. The bottom rails are round in section. They are cut from pieces of the rail's maximum diameter and then shaped to taper away from the center. The ends of the rails are pared down with a chisel and sandpaper to form ¾in diameter dowels 1in long. The top and bottom faces of the front seat rail – like those on the other seat rails – are flat (see drawing on p. 19). It is cut from a rectangular plank of 1 × 2in elm. The front is curved to reproduce the outline of the seat in the painting. The front edges and the top inside edge are all chamfered to prevent

them cutting into the rush seat. A 1in-long cylindrical dowel is chiseled at each end. There should be no sharp shoulder between the rounded pegs at the ends of the seat rails and the main body of the rail. A notch left by a shoulder would distort the shape of the seat when the rush is fitted. The outer face of the rail is therefore tapered next to the peg.

The next step is to drill the holes in the legs. Drilling these at the correct angle is the most difficult part of the construction. Because the chair legs tilt inwards, the holes do not enter the legs at right-angles; drilling is best done with the leg held in a jig – a shallow box into which it can be wedged (see drawing on p. 19). The top of the leg is propped up and wedged so that it is held in the jig the same distance *up* from the horizontal as it leans *in* from the vertical on the finished chair. The angle of tilt from vertical can be checked with an adjustable bevel with the leg propped up. Check the angle of the leg in the jig with the same tool. When the leg is propped up and wedged, holes can be drilled vertically down into the leg. Drill the holes in one leg first and tap home the rails. A rubber mallet is the best tool for this. Elm is an unyielding wood and will not form itself to the hole as softwood will. Hole and dowel must therefore be cut carefully to make a good tight fit.

Place the leg plus rails against the other front leg. Mark where the rails touch the leg and use the adjustable bevel to read off the angles. Drill the holes with the leg held in a jig as before. Tap the leg into place.

Now the front assembly is complete, make the back part of the frame. As well as the sockets for the rails, mortises must be cut on the insides of the two curved uprights to house the three slats. To mark the drilling

The tools of the chair maker's trade – saws, axe, shaving horse and foot-operated lathe – are seen in Silas W. Saunders's 19th-century workshop in Oxfordshire, England

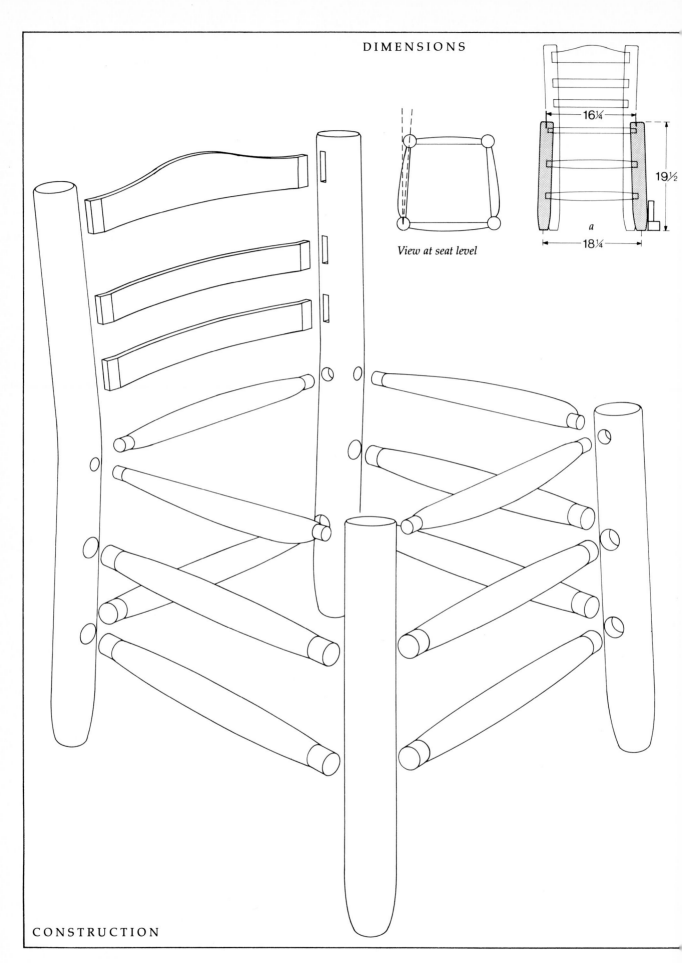

View at seat level

16¼

19½

a

18¼

CONSTRUCTION

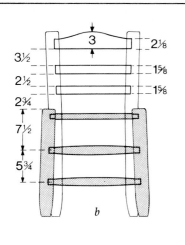
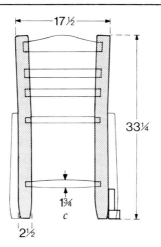
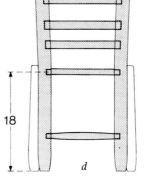
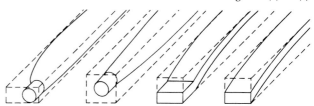
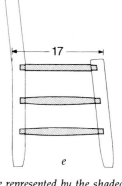

b

c

2½

d

e

33¼

18

17

17½

1¾

Construction sequence, each stage represented by the shaded elements in the diagrams (a) to (e)

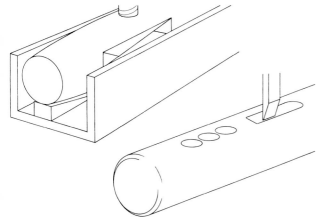

The leg wedged in a jig for drilling

The mortise is finished with a chisel

Above: A seat rail, a rung, and alternative back slats. Below: Sections showing how the alternative slat shapes fit into the rear uprights

ORDER OF WORK

1 Cut and shape the two front legs
2 Prop them up in the correct relative position and take measurements for the 3 front rails
3 Cut and shape the front rails, forming 1in cylindrical dowels at each end
4 Wedge one leg in the jig and drill mortises
5 Assemble front leg and rails without glue
6 Establish entry point of rails in the other front leg
7 Wedge this leg in the jig and drill mortises
8 Assemble front legs and rails without glue
9 Repeat steps 1-8 with the two rear legs, adding mortises for the back slats
10 Take measurements for the 3 rear slats
11 Cut out and assemble slats
12 Prop up front and back assemblies to establish position and length of side rails
13 Cut and shape side rails as before
14 With the legs propped at the right angle in the jig, drill mortises for the side rails
15 Glue the chair together
16 Rush the seat

MATERIALS

	No.	Size (ins)
Elm branches for:		
Front legs	2	2½ × 19½
Upper front rail	1	1¾ × 16¾
Lower front rail	1	1¾ × 17⅜
Front seat rail	1	1 × 2¼ × 15¾
Side seat rails	2	1 × 2¼ × 14¼
Back seat rail	1	1 × 2¼ × 13¼
Back legs	2	2⅝ × 33¼
Back rail	1	1¾ × 13½
Lower back slat	1	1 × 1⅝ × 13¾
Center back slat	1	1 × 1⅝ × 14
Upper back slat	1	1 × 3 × 14½
Upper side rails	2	1¾ × 15⅛
Lower side rails	2	1¾ × 15¾

Woodworking adhesive

For rush seat:
2 bolts of natural rushes; Twine

FINISH

Linseed oil

19

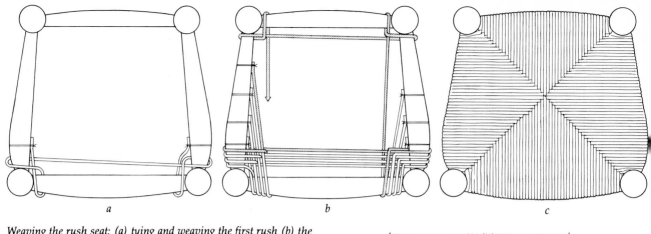

Weaving the rush seat: (a) tying and weaving the first rush (b) the back rail is worked into the pattern (c) the complete seat

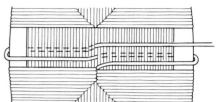

Weaving in a Figure of 8 pattern may be necessary to finish the seat

positions for these, prop the legs up, place a straight edge on top of the uprights from center to center, and mark a pencil line from center to edge on top of the uprights. Use these lines as a drilling guide; the holes are drilled into the legs parallel to the line. Mark out the mortise and with the leg held in a jig or vice at an angle allowing the drill to enter vertically, drill out most of the wood to a depth of 1in and clean up with a chisel.

Do not cut the slats themselves until the seat rail and bottom rung have been cut and tried in position (without glue), so that slat length can be checked against the assembled uprights and rungs. The rung and seat rail are shaped and the sockets drilled in the same way as they were for the front assembly.

The slats are cut from a solid block (see drawing on p. 19) with a saber saw (jigsaw) or bandsaw. The tenons at either end do not continue the line of the curve; they are cut to follow a line parallel to the rails. Angled mortises are an alternative method, illustrated on p. 19.

When the front and back are assembled, prop them up at an appropriate distance apart, altering relative positions until the splay on the front legs looks right. Mark the entry positions of the side and seat rails and measure their length, adding 1in at each end for the tenons. Cut the rails to length and shape them as before. The dowels meet each other inside the legs, and it is therefore necessary to pare a flat face on each pair of dowels until they can be pushed fully home. The side seat rails are wider towards the front of the chair.

Use an adjustable bevel to check the angle at which the rails enter the front and back assemblies. Prop up the legs and uprights at the correct angle in a jig or vise as

before, so that drilling in vertically will cut a mortise at the required angle.

Assemble the whole chair, gluing the rungs, legs and slats in position in a single operation. The joints fit tightly together, so no clamps are needed to hold the chair while the glue sets.

The rush seat
A patient beginner can weave a satisfactory rush seat for Vincent's chair. The job requires two bolts (bundles) of good quality natural rushes. Sea grass or synthetic rush are cheaper than natural rushes and also easier to work: they are sold ready for use and do not have to be twisted together as you weave. However, Vincent's chair seemed to demand the more interesting color and texture of natural materials.

Rushes have to be soaked to make them pliable. On the evening before you want to begin work, select 30 or 40 rushes and soak them in a bath of cold water for three or four minutes. Wrap them in a damp towel and leave them overnight.

The rushes are normally woven in pairs, and it is possible to vary the thickness of the woven rushes by careful selection of individual rushes. Jane McDonald, the weaver of the seat, used thicker rushes as she approached the middle of the seat in order to reproduce the rounded look of the seat in the painting. For the thinner parts of the seat two rushes are twisted together. Four rushes were twisted together for the thicker sections. Twist together as many rushes as you need to reach the desired thickness.

To start work pick two prepared rushes of similar

length. Run your fingers down them from the thin end to the thick to squeeze out any air and excess water. Place the thick end of one rush against the thin end of the other and remove any dust by wiping with a cloth. The rushes should now be supple and silky.

The seat is wider at the front than the back. The first stage of weaving is to fill in the front two corners until the space to be woven is square. Tie the pair of rushes to the inside face of the left-hand side rail using a tight knot. The weaver used upholsterer's twine for this job, but other twines would do. Sea grass or synthetic rush can be tacked to the seat.

Twist the two rushes together to form a smooth coil, always twisting away from the corner. The rushes are only twisted on the top of the seat where they will be seen and used.

Take the twisted rushes over the top of the front rail, then under the front rail, over the left side rail and under the left side rail, keeping as close to the corners as possible. Now take the rushes over to the right hand side rail, over and under this, over and under the front rail and finally tie them off securely to the right side rail directly opposite the fixing on the left rail. Cut off any extra rush.

Repeat the entire operation (see drawing on p. 20) until the gap between the rushes on the front rail is as wide as the rear seat rail. Each time you pick new seat rushes, squeeze them out as before. From now on the back rail can also be worked into the sequence and the entire seat filled.

To do this, tie one end of the next rush to the left side rail just behind the last of the filler rushes, and weave it around the two front corners as before. Instead of tying it off on the right side rail, continue to the back rail, go over and under the back rail at the right, over and under the right side rail, across to the left corner and repeat.

The rushes are no longer tied to the rails; they are tied together to form a single continuous piece. They are joined by tying a reef knot in an inconspicuous place underneath the seat and not too near the corners. To keep the under-side tidy, tuck in knots and loose ends.

When you have worked about one third of the seat the rushes will have formed hollow pockets in the corners. These are stuffed from underneath with broken or short rushes which raise the rushes off the rails to prevent wear and give a firm look to the top.

At this stage allow the seat to dry out for a day. As the rushes dry they will loosen a little – push them together before continuing. Tighter seats look better and last longer. A good natural rush seat can last a hundred years before it becomes brittle.

When you have filled the inside rails there may still be a gap left in the middle of the seat. This is filled by working the rush in a Figure of 8 pattern (see drawing on p. 20) until the center is filled. Such a section is visible in Van Gogh's painting.

Finish off by tying the final rush to an adjacent rush under the seat. Tuck in the ends.

Freshly woven seats tend to be green. As they dry out they take on a more golden color.

English chair "bodgers" in the Chiltern Hills, 1902.
Institute of Agricultural History and Museum of English Rural Life, University of Reading

Tatlin's Table

by Patrick Daw

from *Tatlin Working on the 3rd International Sculpture* (*c.* 1920) by El Lissitzky (1890-1941)

Collection of Mr and Mrs Eric Estorick

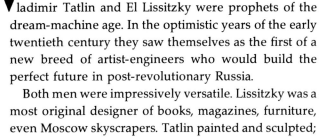

V ladimir Tatlin and El Lissitzky were prophets of the dream-machine age. In the optimistic years of the early twentieth century they saw themselves as the first of a new breed of artist-engineers who would build the perfect future in post-revolutionary Russia.

Both men were impressively versatile. Lissitzky was a most original designer of books, magazines, furniture, even Moscow skyscrapers. Tatlin painted and sculpted; he illustrated children's books and decorated an artists' cafe in Moscow. He designed and built his own stove and his own clothes, and in the onion-domed tower of Novodevichy monastery he constructed his flying machine Letatlin, a sort of hang glider operated by unassisted muscle power.

Tatlin's inspired monument to the 3rd International was to be a celebration of the technological twentieth century. It was to be the world's tallest building, rising 1300 feet to top the Eiffel Tower by 300 feet. Like El Lissitzky's skyscrapers, it was never built, yet it remains an inspiring if monumentally impractical tribute to a squashed ideal. It was commissioned in 1919, two years after the October Revolution, when Tatlin set to work on a model 20-feet tall. The tower was to contain three vast glass chambers, each one rotating at a fixed speed. The lowest level would be a cube housing the legislative assembly; it would turn slowly and symbolically through one revolution a year. Above it a pyramid containing the executive body would turn through one revolution a month. On top, rotating once a day, would be the multi-media information office, capped by radio masts.

Designing Tatlin's table

Both Tatlin and El Lissitzky found machine power seductive, and they encouraged the use of modern, machine-made materials. Patrick Daw's design is faithful to this ideal. He used man-made materials and manufactured fittings to construct a table of extreme simplicity.

The bizarre perspective on the table top makes sizing

No fasteners are visible on the original, but the designer thought subtle woodworking joints would be both alien to the spirit of the piece and difficult to cut satisfactorily in plywood. He therefore chose to use standard block joints to fix the four sides to each other and to the top.

Making the table

Mark out the parts on a sheet of plywood (see diagram on p. 25), using a set-square to keep the all-important right angles. Cut out the twin tops and the eight L shapes. A circular saw will cut the outer edges of each L accurately, but a saber saw (jigsaw) is more suitable for cutting into the inside corners. It is vital to use a sharp saw blade to prevent the ply surface fraying around the saw cut. Even with a sharp blade some fraying is almost unavoidable. The surface where the saw blade exits is the one more likely to splinter; this side should be used on the inside of the assembled table. Wood filler can be used to hide holes.

Stack the twin tops and 8 Ls, with PVA adhesive between alternate layers. Place a heavy weight on top and leave until the glue is set.

Plane the top edge of each L until it is perfectly square. You can check this with a try square.

Joints show clearly in El Lissitzky's drawing. To reproduce this effect sand a slight chamfer on the butting edges of the L shapes.

The components can be painted before assembly.

To assemble the table, place the top, face down, on the workbench and fit the legs using block joints to join the Ls to each other and to the table top. Use a square to check the verticality of the sides.

Finishing the table

Although the paper under the *Tatlin* collage is yellowing now, white remains the only possible color for the table. "I have used black and white as material substance and subject matter," said Lissitzky. The designer tried brilliant white first, but decided it must be toned down with a trace of cream to give it the feel of a relic from the constructivist era.

No grain or brushwork is visible on the table surface. Indeed, El Lissitzky stated forcefully that "the frayed end of a paintbrush is at variance with our notion of clarity." This suggests two solutions – the entire table could be made of plastic-faced boards, or the wood can be spray-painted, building up layer on layer of paint until a tough, flat surface is created. This was Daw's solution. He began by painting on a coat of primer then built up layers of enamel paint, sanding down between coats.

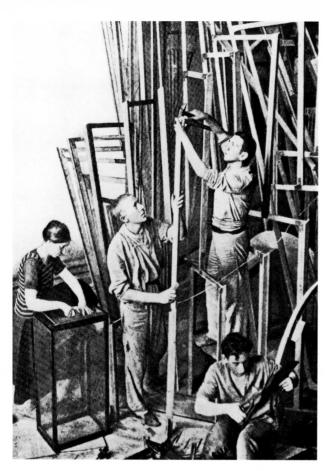

Tatlin and his assistants at work on the model of the Third International monument (1920), in the photograph which formed the basis of El Lissitzky's collage. From left to right: Sophia Dymshits-Tolstaya sands the fittings, Tatlin holds a lath, Shapiro hammers nails and Meyerzon snips out the metal fittings. The collage was an illustration for Six Tales *by Ilya Ehrenburg (1922)*

a problem. We could be looking down steeply onto a dining table; Tatlin could equally be standing on an axonometric drawing of a coffee table. This, the designer decided, is the more likely solution. He also decided that logic demanded a fourth leg to the table.

The constructivists' enthusiasm for standard parts was the major influence on the design. Daw based his construction on the shape of the nearest face of the table; he thought the L shape was a fitting homage to El Lissitzky. The L shapes were cut from a sheet of plywood, exploiting that material's ability to take such a right angle without losing strength. In order to match the sturdy looks of Tatlin's table the designer felt a thickness of 1½in was necessary. To achieve this he cut out eight L shapes and two table tops from a sheet of ¾in plywood and glued them together in pairs. Take care when buying plywood to select a truly flat sheet, as many are warped.

DIMENSIONS

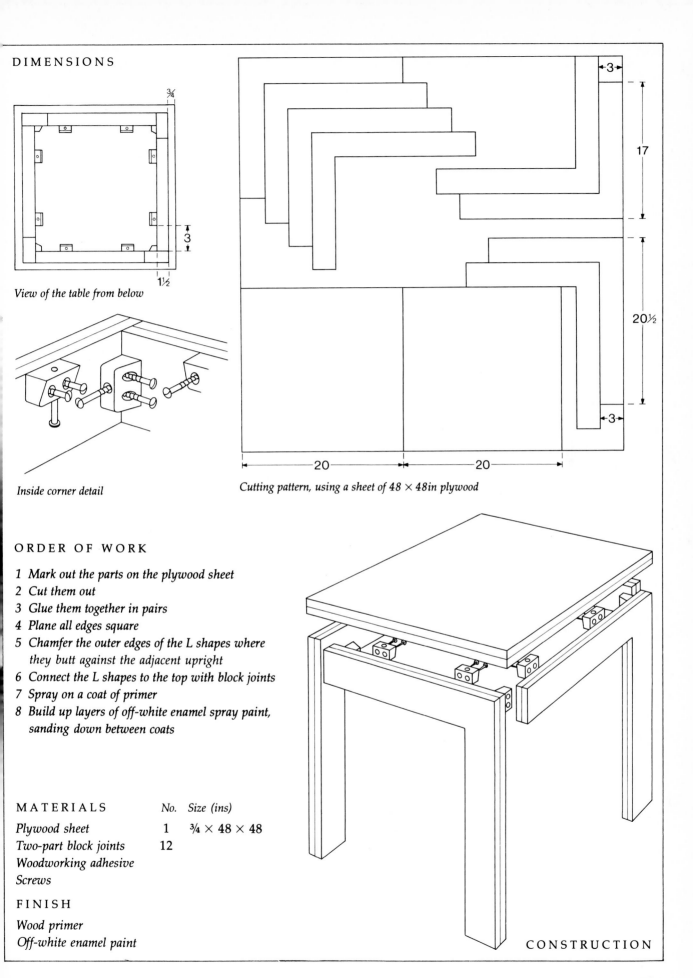

View of the table from below

Inside corner detail

Cutting pattern, using a sheet of 48 × 48in plywood

ORDER OF WORK

1 Mark out the parts on the plywood sheet
2 Cut them out
3 Glue them together in pairs
4 Plane all edges square
5 Chamfer the outer edges of the L shapes where
   they butt against the adjacent upright
6 Connect the L shapes to the top with block joints
7 Spray on a coat of primer
8 Build up layers of off-white enamel spray paint,
   sanding down between coats

MATERIALS	No.	Size (ins)
Plywood sheet	1	¾ × 48 × 48
Two-part block joints	12	
Woodworking adhesive		
Screws		

FINISH

Wood primer
Off-white enamel paint

CONSTRUCTION

The Limner's Table

designed by Floris van den Broecke and made by Mary Little
from the portrait of John and Abigail Montgomery (1836) by Joseph H. Davis
National Gallery of Art, Washington; gift of Edgar William and Bernice Chrysler Garbisch

Almost complete mystery surrounds Joseph H. Davis. All we know of him is a series of some 120 miniature watercolor portraits painted in a small area of New Hampshire and Maine in the 1830s. Even his name was unknown until a dusty portrait was uncovered in an attic in Dover, Maine, bearing the signature "Joseph H. Davis, Left Hand Painter." The evidence stopped there. Some now believe he is the legendary wandering Pine Hill Joe from Maine, but proof remains elusive.

Davis was a "limner," one of the itinerant painters who traveled across New England. Most were very versatile: they earned a living by putting paint on anything from barns and mirror frames to shop signs and furniture. Portrait painting was a sideline, and it rarely paid well. Pine Hill Joe earned only $1.50 per portrait.

The picture of John and Abigail Montgomery is a typical Joseph H. Davis job. A couple dressed in their best Sunday clothes sit facing each other placidly across the bizarrely grained table which figures prominently in many Davis interiors. The couple sit among the symbols of a worthy life style – the Bible and the dignified top hat. The shooting scene on the wall no doubt reflects Mr Montgomery's sporting interests. A small dog – a cat is a common variant in other Davis paintings – sits under the table on a wonderfully gaudy floor.

Designing the Limner's Table

Few of Davis's admirers would argue that he was an accomplished master. He clearly had problems painting hands and feet, as Mrs Montgomery's pudgy paws prove. The limner's imperfect grasp of perspective created an interesting geometrical challenge for furniture designer Floris van den Broecke. He wanted to retain the table's exuberant oddity while constructing a stable and functional piece of furniture.

The interpretation began with a decision to design a

small side table, suitable for a hall, rather than a full-sized dining table, where the shortage of stretchers could lead to instability.

The Montgomerys' little dog has turned his back on one of the table's major geometric problems – where does that leg meet the table top? It is a problem the designer must face. First glance suggests this is the rear leg on Abigail's right, but if so, why is the bottom of the leg as far forward as the Montgomerys' feet? Could it be a central leg fixed on the front, hiding a perfectly normal rear leg? The legs, as painted, are patently of unequal length.

The designer's solution to the geometrical puzzle was to make a table of normal height with legs of equal length, but to abandon the usual pattern of a rectangular top set on a rectangular base in favor of a pair of offset parallelograms. It was found that simple angles faithfully reproduced Davis's geometric oddity: the top was cut with acute angles of 45°, the base with 60° acute angles. These angles were established by taking a tracing of the table from a postcard reproduction of the painting, then transposing this into a plan view of the table top.

The curious geometry of the table is emphasized by the drawer design. The drawer is a strictly rectangular box opening in the normal manner – at right angles to the stretcher. Its oddity arises from the need to accommodate it within the parallelogram frame. The solution was to make the drawer's front panel twice as wide as the box behind.

The decoration of the table is its obvious appeal, but the legs are one of its minor delights. Such legs cannot be bought, they must be custom-made on a lathe. The Davis legs are an easy if unusual job for a professional wood turner. All the information the turner needs is contained in the profile shown in the working drawings. At the same time the turner was asked to turn a pair of wooden drawer knobs for the table. To avoid delays we put in the order to the turner at a very early stage.

The table's top, sides and drawer are cut from Medium Density Overlay (MDO), also known as Medium Density Fibreboard (MDF), a modern sheet material with much to recommend it for this type of job. As it is strong and grain-free, it is easy to cut with great precision in any direction to make clean sharp angles and smooth edges. It also remains remarkably flat. Although its looks are ordinary, it provides an admirable surface for paint.

The flamboyant paintwork on the Montgomerys' original table could have covered cheap pine, which is an acceptable alternative to the MDO used in this project. Particleboard (blockboard) is also suitable, though the edges would have to be covered.

Making the Limner's Table

Unusual tools are not needed to construct the table. Speed – and perhaps accuracy – can be improved by a power saw and a router. Inexpensive models of both tools are designed specifically for the amateur. Accurate cutting and drilling are made easier by a drill stand. A bevel, a protractor or a pair of compasses can be used to measure the angles on the parallelograms. A multi-needle contour former is useful when marking the curve of the leg bulge on stretchers and drawer rail.

Using a straight edge, pencil and protractor to fix the 60° and 120° angles, mark out the parallelogram top with sides of 24 and 39¼in. Saw out the top. When cutting with a saber saw (jigsaw), sawing straight lines which are not parallel to the edge of the board is easier if you clamp a piece of timber to the board parallel with the cutting line and use this to guide the saw.

Plane the edges of the top square and smooth.

Mark out and cut the stretchers from the same 1in MDO sheet – two 4 × 24in rectangles for the long sides, two 4 × 16½in for the short sides.

From the center of one long stretcher cut out the 3 × 16¼in drawer panel. To begin the cut, drill a hole to provide access for the saber saw's blade. Clean up the edges with a chisel.

The top bulge on each leg must now be flattened off in two places where it will house the ends of the stretchers. This involves cutting a pair of 1in-wide slots using a router. (A chisel is a slower alternative.) To avoid removing too much bulk from the leg, the maker routed out only part of the bulge, leaving the top ¾in untouched. She then shaped the stretcher to fit as shown in the drawings, rounding off the top and bottom of the stretcher to match the curve of the leg. The shape of the curve on the stretcher is established by pushing a multi-needle contour former into the groove in the leg and transfering this shape to the side of the stretcher to provide a cutting line for the saber saw.

The operation outlined above is tricky – it is much simpler to rout out a housing to take the complete stretcher, allowing the end of the stretcher to remain square. To do this, set the router to begin cutting precisely at the circumference of the leg top.

Whichever method you choose, the slot in the leg must be cut perfectly square, running straight down the center line of the leg. This guarantees that the stretchers will sit horizontally. For this reason it is essential to hold the leg at right angles to the router.

A simple three-sided wooden box as shown on p. 30 is quickly screwed and glued together to make the work faster and easier. Take care to check that the box sides are perfectly perpendicular and parallel. The leg must lie

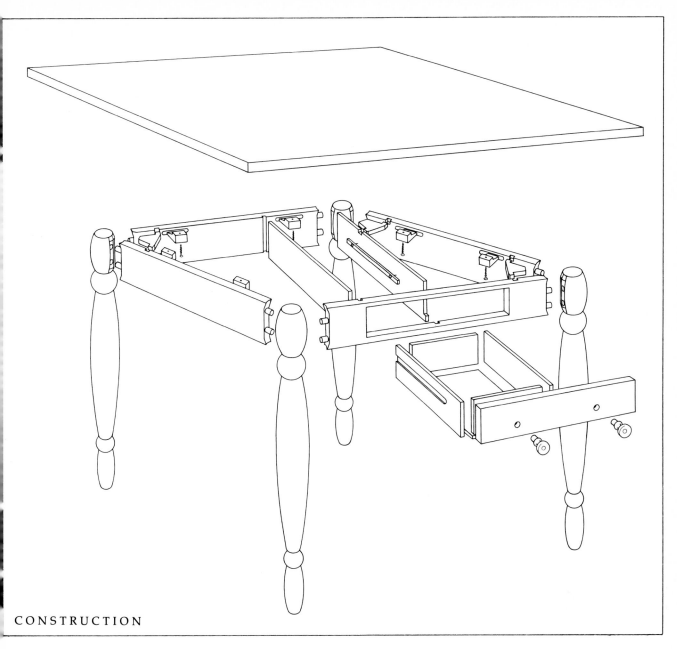

in the box with the central marks made at each end of the leg where it was held in the lathe at exactly the same distance from the bottom of the box and equidistant from the box sides. Hold the leg in the correct position by jamming improvized wooden wedges at the sides and blocks under the narrow sections. Keep the router (or chisel) parallel to the edges of the box and make the cut to the required depth.

Two grooves are made in each leg, and the success of the table construction depends on the two being at the correct angle to each other. In one pair of legs the angle between the two grooves is 45°, in the other pair 135°.

Having made the first groove, measure and mark the position for the second – at an angle of 45° or 135° to the first – on the end of the leg, using a bevel or protractor. Turn the leg until the new cutting point is directly under

the router, wedge the leg in position again and cut the second groove, identical to the first.

Holes are now drilled for the dowels that will hold the stretchers to the legs. With the leg wedged in the box, drill a pair of ¼in diameter holes ¾in deep in each groove. A drill stand, and adhesive tape wrapped round the drill bit ¾in from the tip, help accurate drilling. The dowel holes in each leg's two grooves should be staggered as in the drawing on p. 30 to avoid weakening the leg. Drill matching ¼in-diameter dowel holes in the ends of the stretchers. To avoid confusion, mark the legs A,B,C,D and identify the stretchers by similar markings.

The table's strength and stability are improved by fitting wooden wedges in the two acute angles of the frame. A third wedge will later be fitted between the drawer rail and the side of the table.

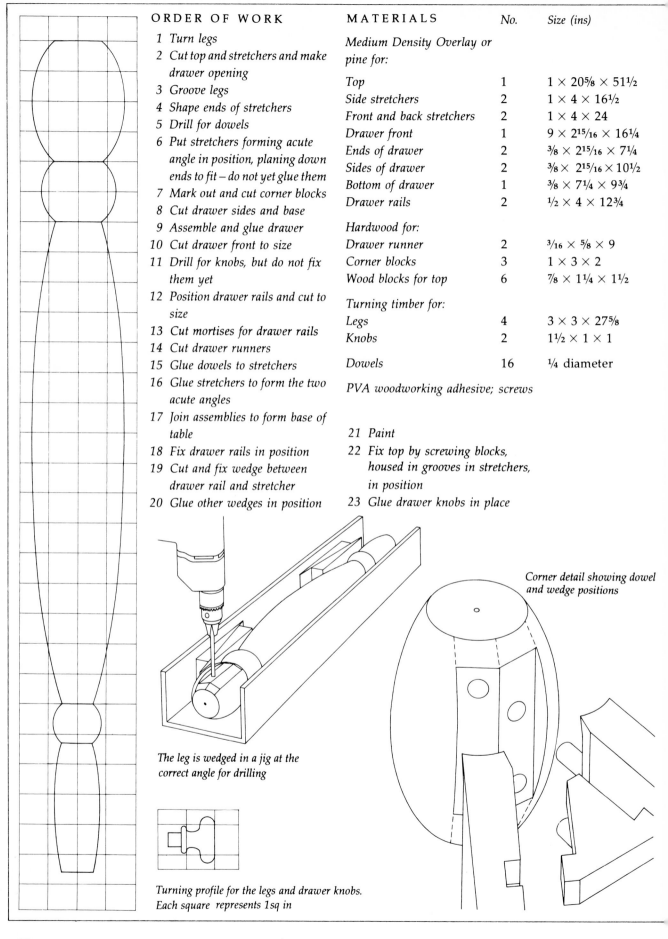

ORDER OF WORK

1 Turn legs
2 Cut top and stretchers and make drawer opening
3 Groove legs
4 Shape ends of stretchers
5 Drill for dowels
6 Put stretchers forming acute angle in position, planing down ends to fit – do not yet glue them
7 Mark out and cut corner blocks
8 Cut drawer sides and base
9 Assemble and glue drawer
10 Cut drawer front to size
11 Drill for knobs, but do not fix them yet
12 Position drawer rails and cut to size
13 Cut mortises for drawer rails
14 Cut drawer runners
15 Glue dowels to stretchers
16 Glue stretchers to form the two acute angles
17 Join assemblies to form base of table
18 Fix drawer rails in position
19 Cut and fix wedge between drawer rail and stretcher
20 Glue other wedges in position
21 Paint
22 Fix top by screwing blocks, housed in grooves in stretchers, in position
23 Glue drawer knobs in place

MATERIALS	No.	Size (ins)
Medium Density Overlay or pine for:		
Top	1	$1 \times 20^5/_8 \times 51^1/_2$
Side stretchers	2	$1 \times 4 \times 16^1/_2$
Front and back stretchers	2	$1 \times 4 \times 24$
Drawer front	1	$9 \times 2^{15}/_{16} \times 16^1/_4$
Ends of drawer	2	$3/_8 \times 2^{15}/_{16} \times 7^1/_4$
Sides of drawer	2	$3/_8 \times 2^{15}/_{16} \times 10^1/_2$
Bottom of drawer	1	$3/_8 \times 7^1/_4 \times 9^3/_4$
Drawer rails	2	$1/_2 \times 4 \times 12^3/_4$
Hardwood for:		
Drawer runner	2	$3/_{16} \times 5/_8 \times 9$
Corner blocks	3	$1 \times 3 \times 2$
Wood blocks for top	6	$7/_8 \times 1^1/_4 \times 1^1/_2$
Turning timber for:		
Legs	4	$3 \times 3 \times 27^5/_8$
Knobs	2	$1^1/_2 \times 1 \times 1$
Dowels	16	$1/_4$ diameter

PVA woodworking adhesive; screws

The leg is wedged in a jig at the correct angle for drilling

Corner detail showing dowel and wedge positions

Turning profile for the legs and drawer knobs. Each square represents 1sq in

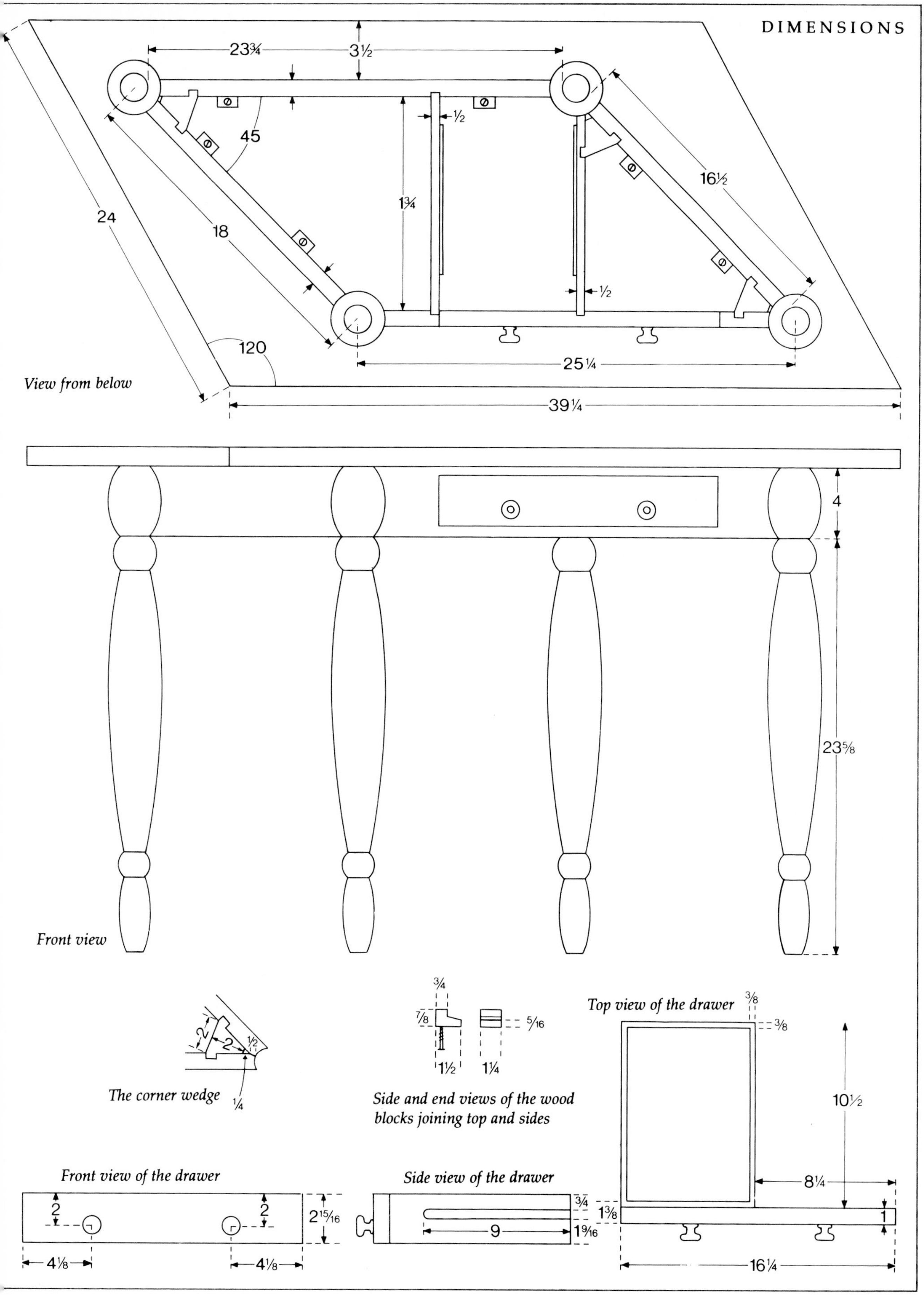
DIMENSIONS
23¾
3½
45
24
18
1¾
½
16½
½
120
25¼
View from below
39¼
4
23⅝
Front view
The corner wedge
2
2
½
¼
¾
⅞
5/16
1½
1¼
Side and end views of the wood blocks joining top and sides
Top view of the drawer
⅜
⅜
10½
8¼
1
16¼
Front view of the drawer
2
2
2 15/16
4⅛
4⅛
Side view of the drawer
¾
1⅜
9
1 9/16

A wing on each side of the wedge sits in a ½in deep and ½in wide groove chiseled into the stretcher 2in from the leg and cut at right angles to the stretcher (see diagram). Each wedge is cut individually by handsaw from a 3in piece of 1 × 2in timber to match the slots. The wedge will split if the grain runs towards the leg rather than from stretcher to stretcher.

Without gluing the table together, put the stretchers in position in the legs to form the two acute angles. The inside edges of the stretcher ends will have to be planed or ground down to fit. Hold the offcut in position in the angle, mark out the shape to be cut and cut it out using a handsaw and chisel.

The drawer
Mark out and cut the five panels for the drawer's sides and base. In the drawer's two side panels rout or chisel out a ⅝in wide groove ¼in deep and 9in long (see diagram). Take care to make the cut parallel to the panel edges. Cut 9in-long strips to match the grooves.

To assemble the drawer, simply butt the base and four sides of the box together and glue and pin in position. Clamp the assembly together until it is dry.

The drawer joints were reinforced with leaf-shaped wafers of wood known as 'biscuit' joints, which are quicker than traditional drawer construction but not universally available. Triangular glued blocks may also be used.

Cut the drawer's long front panel to size. Drill ½in deep holes for the drawer knobs in the position shown in the drawing. Do not glue the knobs in place until the panel is painted. Glue the front panel to the drawer.

With the drawer in the table establish the positions for the side rails. Mark and chisel (or rout) out a slot ½in deep in the rear and front stretchers to house the drawer's left-hand rail. At the front the other rail is butt-jointed to the stretcher at the top; at the bottom of the rail a ½in tenon is glued into a mortise in the stretcher. This secures the rail while allowing the drawer to close.

This outer rail is rounded at the rear end to fit around the leg. Press the multi-needle contour former against the leg's top bulge, transfer the shape to the side of the rail and cut to shape with the saber saw. Hollow out the end of the rail with a gouge until it fits snugly around the bulge. No dowels are needed to hold it in position.

To establish the position of the mahogany drawer runners, place them in their grooves, stick double-sided tape to them and push the drawer home. When the drawer is withdrawn the strips should adhere to the rails. In each runner drill and countersink a pair of holes for screws. Screw the runners in place after painting.

Assembly
Glue the dowels in the stretcher ends. Glue two stretchers into one leg to form one of the acute-angled corners. Repeat to make the other acute angle. Join the two

Watercolor of the Pender Family of New Hampshire (1833) by Joseph H. Davis. The Essex Institute, Salem, Ma.

32

assemblies to form the complete base. Glue the drawer rails in position. Cut out a third wedge to fit between the drawer rail and stretcher. Glue all three wedges in position. At this point the table can be painted.

When the table is painted, the top is attached to the base by six wooden blocks of the shape and size shown in the diagram. These were sawed to shape for the job, but manufactured equivalents can be bought. Two blocks are set in grooves in the side and back stretchers of the table base. These ½in-deep grooves are routed or chiseled out with the top of the groove ½in from the top of the stretchers. They are 2½in wide. With the table top placed on the base, mark the position of the blocks on the underside of the table top. Remove the top and screw the blocks loosely to its underside, leaving them free to swing into the grooves to grip the base and complete assembly of the table.

Painting the table

Painted furniture clearly interested Joseph H. Davis. Throughout his mysterious career he tried many variations on the themes of wood-graining and marbling. Davis's painting reflects New England fashion in the 1830s, when imitation wood-grain on furniture or walls was popular. The technique involves covering cheap wood to imitate the grain pattern of pricier timber such as mahogany, cedar or walnut. Marble was also imitated.

Floris van den Broecke's initial reaction to Davis's painting was approval of the artist's vigor and the color scheme built up of strong bands of light and dark paint. He wanted to retain the "camouflage" feel of the paintwork but to introduce a more painterly effect by losing the strong outlines around the bands of color. He decided to tone down the brassy yellow of the handles and paint them the same as the rest of the table. The two colors chosen were violet and burnt Siena.

Technically the job is easy – the paint is applied at speed using just one brush 1½in wide for the entire job. Confident brushstrokes improve the vigor of the paintwork, which must not look weak. Scraps of wood can be used to try out technique and color effects. The stages in the painting are shown by the three sample boards reproduced above right.

The first stage is to paint the white acrylic gesso base all over. Three applications will probably be needed to cover the entire surface. Rub down between applications with fine steel wool, but do not try to obliterate all traces of brushwork.

When the white base is satisfactory, the violet stripes are applied to the table top. Begin by painting the underside. The paint is prepared by mixing a squirt from the tube of violet in the acrylic medium. Test for correct color on waste wood.

The painting sequence: white acrylic gesso base (top); violet stripes (center); burnt Siena stripes (bottom)

The stripes are roughly 4in wide and are built up by making rapid brushstrokes approximately 4in long moving across the board from the back edge and from left to right towards the center of the stripe, forming a pattern of V-shapes. One coat was sufficient.

The burnt Siena stripes were painted on in precisely the same way, frequently overlapping the violet to create interesting color mixes.

The overall impression created by the two colors was too purple until a very thin yellow glaze was applied over the whole surface.

The drawer is painted both inside and out. The drawer's rails are also painted, but the runners are left paint-free. If the drawer front is a very tight fit in the frame before painting begins, plane it down a little to prevent it sticking when the layers of paint have increased its thickness.

When painting was complete, the drawer knobs were glued in place and the top was fixed on the base.

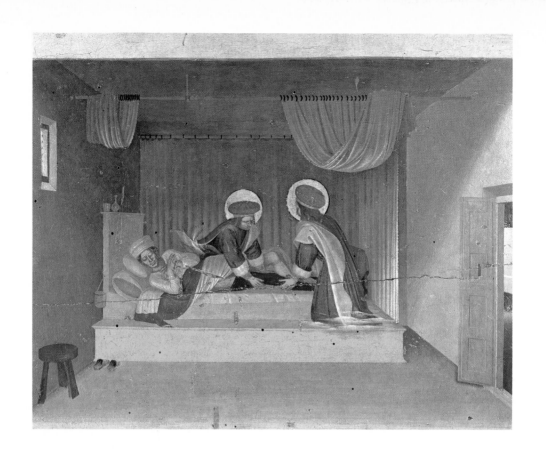

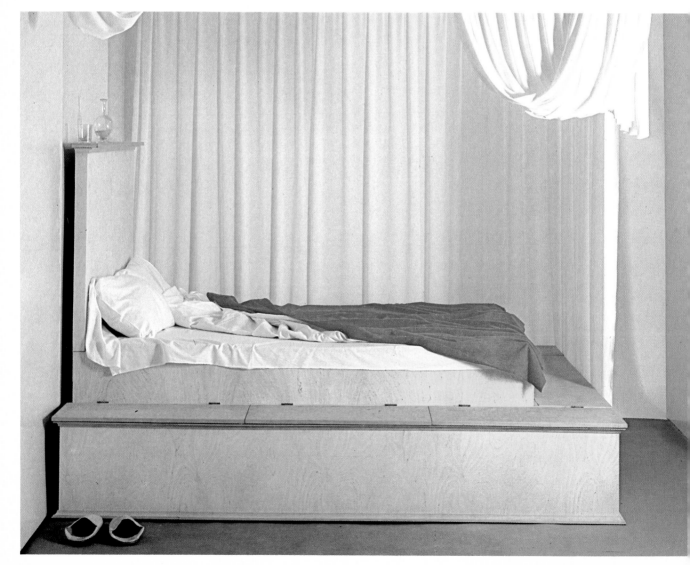

Deacon Justinian's Platform Bed
by Peter Baker
from *The Dream of the Deacon Justinian* (c. 1440) by Fra Angelico (c. 1400-55)
San Marco, Florence

F

ra Angelico was a Dominican friar with a reputation for saintly behavior. He was attached to the newly-founded convent of San Marco in the prosperous and peaceful city of Florence. Much of his work can still be seen in the monks' cells, cloisters and corridors of San Marco.

The Dream of the Deacon Justinian is a predella panel from Fra Angelico's San Marco altarpiece, painted about 1440 and showing eight scenes from the legend of the martyred saints Cosmas and Damian, patron saints of the powerful Florentine Medici family and specialists in medical miracles. It shows the surgical saints in the bedroom of the sick and sleeping Deacon performing one of their spectacular cures. They have removed the Deacon's gangrenous leg and replaced it with the sound leg of a freshly-dead Ethiopian, thereby anticipating transplant surgery by centuries.

During the operation Justinian sleeps soundly under his linen sheets and woolen blanket. His bed is a popular Florentine model of the early fifteenth century, surrounded by an indigo curtain of fine Florentine wool, drawn back dramatically to reveal the miracle.

The bed base is raised to keep it off damp floors. On three sides it is surrounded by chests with hinged lids. These chests – *cassoni* – dominated Italian furnishing throughout the Middle Ages. Large households might own fifty of them, and ten was a normal number for a family according to fifteenth-century inventories. Clothes and valuables would be stored inside the *cassoni*, many of which could be locked. The flat tops served as seats during the day and were therefore often topped by cushions. At night they provided a step up to the bed. The popularity of such a versatile item is easily understood. The entire unit forms an all-in-one bed-sitting room.

Many *cassoni* were highly decorated by the famous Florentine craftsmen with wood inlays or paint, but Fra Angelico's version is monastically plain, making it a very suitable subject for do-it-yourself construction.

Designing Deacon Justinian's bed

Peter Baker's Angelico-inspired bed is essentially a large central box surrounded by three similar boxes. They are clad in plywood, which reproduces the flatness of the surface in the painting. The tall bedhead and the chests on three sides of the bed are made independently and bolted to the main bed frame; they can be removed in seconds for transport or to adapt the bed to a new room layout. Although the bed is large, the framed plywood construction results in a surprisingly light and simple piece. It is also much cheaper than the solid timber which would have been used in the Renaissance originals.

The bed is designed to take a standard modern double mattress 5in thick. Once the principle of the box construction is grasped, the dimensions can easily be adapted to take mattresses of different sizes.

Readily available planed 2×2in and 1×2in softwood is used throughout. Take care when buying timber to select straight pieces. No nails or screws are used in the main construction, which is held together by drilling $\frac{1}{4}$in-diameter holes through the joints and filling them with glued $\frac{1}{4}$in hardwood dowels hammered home with a mallet. Protruding ends are chiseled flush. An electric drill is a great time saver in this job, and an electric saw saves effort when long sheets of plywood must be sawed. No special tools are needed.

Making the bed

The bed is built up from the base. The sequence of construction is best seen in the drawings on p. 39. To make the lower bed frame, cut two 57in and two 76in lengths of 2×2in softwood. With a tenon saw cut 1×2in lap joints at both ends of all four pieces. Like all the joints in the bed these are glued together with PVA wood-working adhesive and reinforced with $\frac{1}{4}$in dowels. Glue and clamp the frame together. At each joint drill a $\frac{1}{4}$in-diameter hole down through the top piece and $\frac{1}{2}$in into the lower one. (A piece of adhesive tape wrapped around the drill bit $1\frac{1}{2}$in from the tip will ensure the correct depth.) Glue the dowels and hammer them in. The protruding stumps of the dowels can be pared off with a chisel when the glue has dried.

The main frame of the bed rises from the base rectangle. Nine 2×2in posts, stepped back at the top to take the upper bed frame and the rail of the mattress surround, rise from the lower frame. The nine are not all the same length, as the four corner posts are butted onto the half-joints at the frame corners, while the rest are set in housings in the frame. Before fixing the posts in position, mark, and cut out with a tenon saw, a 1×6in end-lap joint on each one, and recess the top of the joint further by marking and sawing out a second $\frac{1}{2} \times 2$in lap in the same end (see drawing).

A more ornate version of Deacon Justinian's bed appears in The Birth of St. John the Baptist *by Ghirlandaio. S. Maria Novella, Florence*

Using a miter box or a 45° bevel, mark out and cut eight 6in lengths of 1 × 2in softwood, mitered at each end. These brace the corner posts. The four corner posts are 22½in long. To fix each corner post, place it in position, check that it stands vertically, glue and clamp the braces in position and drill horizontally and vertically through the brace and 1in into the post and lower frame. Hammer in glued dowels.

The five other posts are 23in long, with the same 1 × 6in and ½ × 2in double-lapped joints at one end. These sit in 1 × 2in housings marked and cut in the lower frame. Mark the position of the housings on the lower frame. Make 1in-deep saw cuts on the inside of a line marked on each side of the joint, and chisel out the waste wood. The posts are glued in position, checked for verticality and reinforced by a dowel hammered in obliquely from each side, through the post and into the frame.

A flat-topped tenth post 16in long is fitted in a similar housing at the head of the bed. The layout of the posts is shown in the drawing (p. 39).

The upper bed frame of 2 × 2in softwood is now attached. The frame's side and foot rails engage the five non-corner posts with half-lap joints. Where the rails cross these posts mark 1 × 2in housings and saw them out on the workbench. One inch inside each post position on the side rails cut out a 1in deep housing across the whole rail to take the cross rails which support the mattress. Mark and cut out a ½ × 2in housing in the under side of the head rail to house the upright post.

The corner detail is complicated by the fact that side and end members meet here. The drawing on p. 39 shows how three quarters of the side rail are cut away to fit round the post and under the end rail. The joint is not difficult to cut, as long as it is carefully marked out on the end and sides of the rail. Use a tenon saw to cut away the waste wood, leaving a 1 × 1in projection 2in long. A 1in lap joint is cut at each end of the end rail. Make sure you cut the projection in the appropriate corner to match the housings. Reinforce the corners by cutting, gluing and doweling a further eight mitered 1 × 2in braces.

The mattress sits in a well. A sheet of chipboard – perforated for ventilation – rests on the upper bed frame below a 6in-high surround which runs across the bottom and along both sides to the bedhead. Two 57in long cross rails of 2 × 2in softwood support the chipboard. At each end of these mark and saw out a 1 × 2in half-lap. Glue and dowel them in place.

The surround is carried by a 1 × 2in rail running along the sides and end. This is topped by a ¼ × 1¼in hardwood edging to give a neat finish. The side rails are 75in long, the end rail 56in. They are butt-jointed.

ORDER OF WORK

The bed

1 Saw the 4 lower frame members to length
2 Mark and cut lap joints at both ends of all four pieces
3 Glue and clamp the frame together
4 Drill ¼in diameter holes through the joints
5 Hammer glued dowels into the drilled holes
6 Chisel off protruding stumps of dowels
7 Cut the four corner posts to length
8 Mark and cut out the double lap joint on each post
9 Cut eight softwood braces with mitered ends
10 Glue the posts in position, reinforcing each one with a pair of doweled braces
11 Cut the five 23in posts to length
12 Mark and cut out the double lap joint on each post
13 Mark and cut out dadoes (housings) in the lower frame for the five posts
14 Glue the posts in their dadoes, reinforcing each joint with dowels hammered in obliquely at each side
15 Cut and fit a tenth post at the head of the bed frame
16 Cut the four upper frame members to length
17 Mark and cut half lap joints in the two long rails where they cross the five upright posts
18 Mark and cut lap joints in each long rail for cross bars
19 Mark and cut a half lap in the foot rail where it crosses the upright post
20 Mark and cut a dado in the head rail for the upright post
21 Mark and cut the end joints on all four rails where they meet the corner posts
22 Glue, brace and dowel the upper frame in position
23 Cut the mattress surround rails to length
24 Mark and cut lap joints where rails cross upright posts
25 Mark and cut lap joints where rails sit on corner posts
26 Glue and dowel the rails in position
27 Cut the three mitered pieces of edging to length
28 Glue and nail the edging in position
29 Cut three pieces of plywood to cover the mattress surround
30 Glue and nail the covering in position

The chests

1 Cut twenty-two 15in and twenty-two 12in pieces of 2 × 2in softwood
2 Mark and cut half-lap joints at each end of all pieces
3 Glue and dowel them together to make eleven frames
4 Saw notches in the frame corners
5 Saw the twelve 1 × 2in chest sides to length
6 Mark and cut a notch at each end of the two 91½in sides
7 Glue and dowel the sides to the frames to form three chests

continued on page 39

CONSTRUCTION

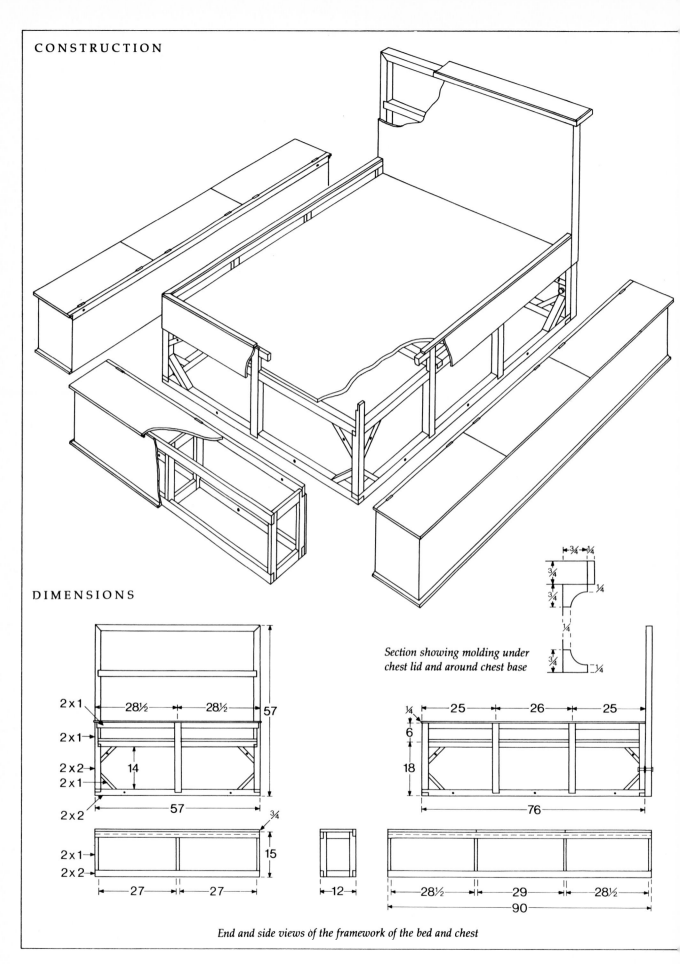

DIMENSIONS

Section showing molding under
chest lid and around chest base

2 x 1
2 x 1

28½   28½   57

14

2 x 2
2 x 1

57

2 x 2

¾

2 x 1
2 x 2

15

27   27

12

¼
6

18

25   26   25

76

28½   29   28½

90

End and side views of the framework of the bed and chest

ASSEMBLE

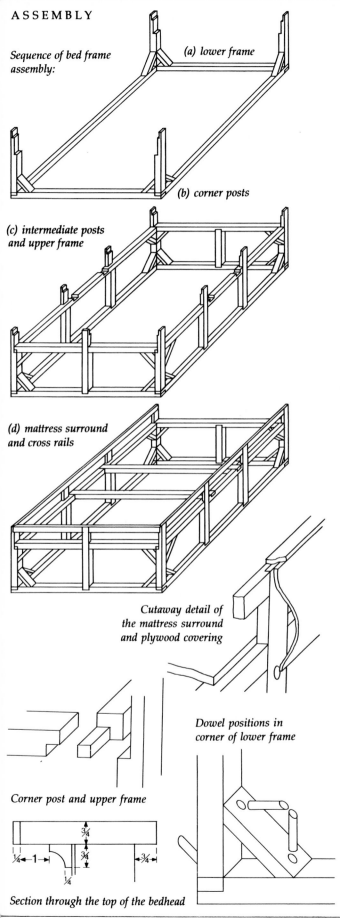

Sequence of bed frame assembly:

(a) lower frame

(b) corner posts

(c) intermediate posts and upper frame

(d) mattress surround and cross rails

Cutaway detail of the mattress surround and plywood covering

Dowel positions in corner of lower frame

Corner post and upper frame

Section through the top of the bedhead

continued from page 37

8 Mark and cut out the particleboard (blockboard) lids
9 Saw the two long lids into three sections
10 Mark and chisel out the hinge housings
11 Hinge the lids to the body
12 Cover the chests in plywood
13 Cut the moldings to fit under the projecting edge of the lids and around the base of the chests
14 Glue and nail the moldings in position

The bedhead

1 Cut the two upright posts to length, mitered at one end
2 Cut the top rail with mitered ends
3 Cut the two lower rails to length
4 Mark and cut housings in the uprights for lower rails
5 Glue and dowel the bedhead together
6 Clad the front and sides of the bedhead in plywood, mitering meeting edges
7 Cut the particleboard (blockboard) top shelf to length
8 Screw it in position
9 Cut and fix the molding under the shelf

Assembly and Finishing

1 Glue plywood spacers to the bedhead uprights
2 Clamp the bedhead and chests in position
3 Drill bolt holes and attach bolts
4 Apply three coats of dilute matt polyurethane varnish

MATERIALS

THE BED

	No.	Size (ins)
Pine for:		
Lower frame	2	2 × 2 × 76
Lower frame	2	2 × 2 × 57
Corner posts	4	2 × 2 × 22
Posts	5	2 × 2 × 23
Post	1	2 × 2 × 16
Upper frame	2	2 × 2 × 76
Upper frame	2	2 × 2 × 55
Cross rails	2	2 × 2 × 57
Surround frame	2	1 × 2 × 75
Surround frame	1	1 × 2 × 56
Braces	16	1 × 2 × 6
Edging	2	¼ × 1¼ × 76¼
Edging	1	¼ × 10 × 57½
Plywood for:		
Surround	2	¼ × 10 × 76¼
Surround	1	¼ × 10 × 57½

Woodworking adhesive
¾ finishing nails (panel pins)
¼ hardwood dowels

THE CHESTS

Pine for:

Frame sides	22	1 × 2 × 12
Frame sides	22	1 × 2 × 15
Outer frame	4	1 × 2 × 57
Outer frame	6	1 × 2 × 90
Outer frame	2	1 × 2 × 91½
Lid edging	2	¼ × ¾ × 92
Lid edging	4	¼ × ¾ × 12¼
Lid edging	1	¼ × ¾ × 57
Scotia molding	4	¾ × 91½
Scotia molding	8	¾ × 12
Scotia molding	2	¾ × 57

Particleboard (blockboard) for:

Lid	2	¾ × 12¼ × 91½
Lid	1	¾ × 12¼ × 57

Plywood for:

Covering	2	³⁄₁₆ × 15 × 90⅜
Covering	1	³⁄₁₆ × 15 × 57⅜
Covering	6	³⁄₁₆ × 15 × 12⅜
Covering	2	³⁄₁₆ × 12 × 90⅜
Covering	1	³⁄₁₆ × 12 × 57⅜

2in cast iron hinges	15	

1in finishing nails (panel pins)
Woodworking adhesive
¼ hardwood dowels
Screws

THE BEDHEAD

Pine for:

Frame	3	2 × 2 × 57
Cross rails	2	2 × 2 × 58
Scotia molding	1	¾ × 57⅞
Scotia molding	2	¾ × 2⅞

Plywood for:

Covering	1	³⁄₁₆ × 43 × 57⅜
Covering	1	³⁄₁₆ × 43 × 2
Spacers	2	³⁄₁₆ × 2 × 2

Particleboard (blockboard) for:

Shelf	1	¾ × 4½ × 60½

5in bolts	2	
4in bolts	14	

Screws

FINISH

Matt polyurethane varnish
Denatured alcohol (white spirit)

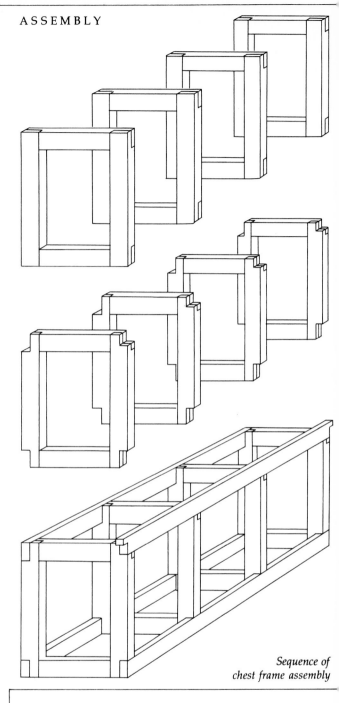

*Sequence of
chest frame assembly*

Where these 1 × 2in rails cross the side posts and the central post at the bed end, mark and cut out ½ × 2in laps, again with the tenon saw and chisel. Cut ½ × 1in end-laps where the side rails sit on the corner posts at the foot of the bed, and ½ × 2in laps at the head corners. Glue and dowel these in position.

Cut the edging to length, with 45° miters at the foot ends. Glue and nail in position, using ¾in finishing nails (panel pins) at 9in intervals.

When the frame is complete, the thin (³⁄₁₆in) plywood covering for the sides and foot is cut carefully to shape. To keep the cutting lines straight, clamp a piece of wood alongside the cutting line and use this as a saw guide. The corners of the plywood are mitered using a block plane, and the sheets glued and nailed in place. They are 10in deep and project 2in below the tops of the surrounding chests.

Making the chests

The sequence of construction for the chests is shown in the drawings on p. 40. Begin by making eleven identical lap-jointed frames of 1 × 2in softwood – four for each side chest, three for the end chest. On each frame the horizontal members are 12in long, the verticals 15in. Mark and saw out ½ × 2in end-laps on all four pieces of the frame. Glue and clamp the frame together and reinforce each joint with a ¼in dowel.

Saw out 1 × 2in notches in three corners of each frame, and a 1 × 1¼in notch on the fourth corner. These take the four long 1 × 2in frame members. Four 57in-long pieces are needed for the end chest. Each side chest requires three 90in pieces and a fourth 91½in long. This fourth piece is the top bed-side of the frame. While the other three pieces lie flush with the frame, the fourth projects ¾in above the cross frames and ¾in at each end. A notch is cut out of the ends where the edging will later be attached. The top of the piece runs flush with the ¾in particleboard (blockboard) lid, and the hinges are attached to it. Glue and dowel the frame members in place.

Cut out a ¾in blockboard lid for each chest – 12¼ × 91½in for the side chests, 12¼ × 57in for the end chest. The lids on the side chests are too cumbersome to open in one piece. Saw them into three sections, corresponding with the frames inside the chests. Each lid section is held by a pair of 2in cast-iron hinges. Mark and chisel out the hinge housings in the lid edge and frame; screw them in position. Three similar hinges hold the lid on the end chest.

The chests are covered in ³⁄₁₆in plywood on their exposed sides in the same way as the bed frame, the meeting edges being chamfered with a block plane. If you are using ³⁄₁₆in plywood the panels will have to be ³⁄₈in longer than the sides they are covering to allow for the miters. A 12in-high back panel was also fitted.

The bed as constructed was left with the chests open to the floor. It makes cleaner storage if plywood or composition board bases are inserted. These can be dropped in loose. Notches are cut at the corners to fit around the upright frame members and the boards rest on top of the horizontal frame bases.

To finish off the chests, glue and pin a ¼ × ¾in molding along the outside edges of the lids. Glue and pin a ¾in scotia molding under the projecting front lip of the lids of all three chests and under the side lips of the two side chests. Miter the molding at the corners of the side chests. A similar molding – mitered at the corners – is glued and nailed along the lower edges of the chests.

Making the bedhead

Cut the bedhead's two 57in uprights of 2 × 2in pine to length, with a 45° miter at the top end. Mark and cut matching miters on both ends of the 57in top rail. Two 58in rails of 2 × 2in timber are let into ½in-deep housings in the vertical posts. Saw and chisel out these ½ × 2in housings 20in and 41in from the mitered end of the uprights. Glue and dowel the bedhead together.

The front and outside edges of the bedhead are now given a covering of ³⁄₁₆in plywood. The front plywood panel is 43in deep and ³⁄₈in wider than the bedhead. The side panels are 43in deep and ³⁄₁₆in wider than the posts. Meeting edges are mitered with a block plane. The panels are glued and nailed in place. For a neat finish the nailheads can be punched below the surface and covered with wood filler.

The Deacon Justinian's bed has a useful shelf on top of the bedhead where he keeps his flask and glass of water for the night. This feature is reproduced by fixing a 4½in × 60½in piece of ¾in particleboard to the top rail with three screws driven up through clearance holes in the top rail. A molding of the same pattern as that running under the chest lids is glued into place under the shelf on three sides.

Assembling the bed

The bedhead is held to the main frame at each side by a 5in bolt. Before drilling the boltholes, glue a 2 × 2in plywood panel to each upright centered 9in above floor level. This will act as a spacer to ensure the bedhead stands upright. Clamp the bedhead in position against the bed frame and drill clearance holes for the bolts through the posts, the spacers and the frame's corner posts. Bolt the bedhead in position.

The chests are also held to the frame by bolts. Clamp the chests in position, check the fit, and drill holes through the chests and the frame members. The bolt positions are indicated on the drawing (p. 38). Join the chests to the frame with 4in bolts.

Finishing the bed

The bed could be waxed, but this is hard labor over such a large surface. Paint is a possibility, but it would of course hide the wood surface, which the designer wanted to leave on display. He also wanted to avoid a shiny surface. He chose tough matt polyurethane varnish diluted with denatured alcohol (white spirit). Three coats were applied.

The Café Table

by Howard Raybould
from *The Card Players* (1892) by Paul Cézanne (1839-1906)
Courtauld Institute Galleries, London

Cézanne brought solidity back to painting. The impressionist haze clears, and a world of solid objects emerges. *The Card Players* belongs to this monumentally weighty world. In 1892, working in his home town of Aix-en-Provence, Cézanne produced a series of five paintings on the "Card Players" theme. There were fears that the number would be cut to four when in 1961 art thieves stole one of the five from an exhibition in Aix. The French government solemnly marked the nation's loss by issuing a large, full-color postage stamp showing the stolen painting. Cézanne's original was recovered shortly afterwards, when the government paid the thieves' ransom.

The version we have used is one of the last and simplest of the five. The two seated men, dressed in loose peasant clothes, face each other over a simple café table. The sitters probably worked on the Cézanne family estate at Aix-en-Provence – the Jas de Bouffan, which the artist inherited after the death in 1886 of his father, a wealthy Aix banker.

The painting, typical of Cézanne's work, represents a laborious attempt to paint objects strong enough to resist the attacks of time. The shapes are built from deliberate, squarish brush strokes. The café table is anonymous, with no sign of decoration. The cloth seems to be hewn from the same dense material as the table's legs. This strong sculptural quality led Cézanne's contemporary Jules Renard to call him the "carpenter of color," and it makes the table an ideal subject for carving.

Designing the café table
Howard Raybould first had to decide which wood to use. He rejected the traditional even-grained woods used by carvers – hard pear and box wood, which will hold the finest detail, or the softer lime favored by the great German wood carvers of the sixteenth century. They would have been suitable for delicate *trompe l'oeil* effects in the Grinling Gibbons manner, but that kind of

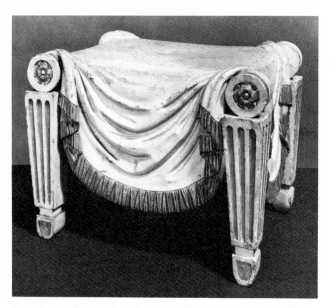

A stool carved in beech and painted white in imitation of marble, c. 1800. The design was inspired by a contemporary drawing by C.H. Tatham showing a classical Roman marble seat. Victoria and Albert Museum, London

Making the table

The table is made in two parts. The simple base – four legs, joined by stretchers – is made first. The carved top is then shaped separately to fit over it. The two are joined by six wooden blocks linking the top and the stretchers.

Making the base

The base is made of pine. Plane the four 2 × 2in legs smooth and cut them to length. Mark and cut the mortises for the stretchers by drilling them out to a depth of ¾in and chiseling them smooth. Cut the four stretchers to length. Mark and saw the tenons on each end. Assemble the table base without glue and make sure that all the members are at right angles to each other. The verticality of the legs on each side can be checked by measuring the two diagonals (bottom left to top right, bottom right to top left) – when they are equal, the table is square.

Glue and clamp a stretcher between each pair of legs and lay them flat on the workbench until the glue has set firm. Glue the two remaining stretchers in position and clamp the whole job, again making sure the structure is square before the glue sets.

The joints can be reinforced by drilling a pair of ¼in-diameter holes through each mortise and tenon, plugging them with ¼in-diameter glued hardwood dowels. Chisel protruding ends of the dowels flush with the surfaces.

Making the top

The cloth is not carved out of a single block of wood. Instead, a number of 1½in-thick planks are glued together to make a box-shaped piece for the carver to work. PVA adhesive was used throughout, as it allows a little flexibility and can withstand knocks.

In order to find out how much he would have to build up the "cloth" at the corners, the carver made a small scale model of the top in plasticine and mounted it on a wooden base. During the modeling stage he referred back constantly to the painting and experimented for hours with real cloths to see how they hang and to work out the obscure architecture of the folds in the painting. His resolution of the problems is shown in the photographs on p. 45.

When these basic decisions have been taken, the top is constructed by joining two 1½in planks with glue and three 2in dowels, ½in in diameter, set in ½in-diameter holes drilled 1⅛in into each plank (see p. 68 for note on joining planks with dowels).

There is some danger when pieces of wood are glued together in this way that cracks will open when the parts

virtuosity would have gone against the strong, simple presence of Cézanne's table. Eventually the designer chose ash.

Ash is a tough wood, often used for the handles of tools, and carving it is slow, hard work. The shape emerges only slowly, and in the finished table the gouge marks – like the brush strokes of Cézanne's painting – remain, with a life of their own. They tell you clearly that this cloth has been chipped out of something solid and resistant. The folds of the cloth are strong enough to take the knocks a café table might expect. Raybould's table is in some ways closer to sculpture than to furniture, yet the table will serve as a surface to put things on. It looks at its best when the carved cloth carries real fruit, bottles, playing cards or crockery.

A beginner would find lime wood easier to work than ash. Pine is another possibility: it is easy to carve roughly to shape but it has an unfortunate tendency to tear. Neither wood will give the substantial feel of ash.

Wood carving is a technique few amateur furniture makers use. However, the rugged top of the Cézanne table calls for no delicate manipulation of the carver's tools. It provides a perfect introduction to wood carving.

Cézanne's innovative use of perspective – defying the traditional rules to show several faces of an object – creates problems for the designer trying to read the painting. Raybould considered reproducing the odd perspective by making one end of the table narrower than the other. When the difficulty and impracticality of this notion were added to the risk of creating an unappealing object he decided to make the top square.

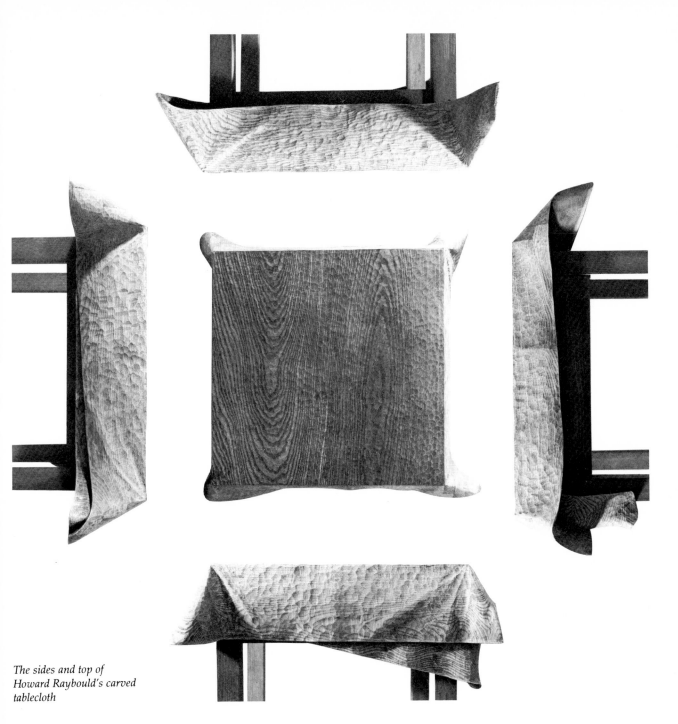

*The sides and top of
Howard Raybould's carved
tablecloth*

expand or contract at different rates. While cracks in fine cabinet making would look like mistakes, they are acceptable in a carved piece such as this.

When the top is made, the four sides are added, using the same 1½in-thick planks. These are simply glued onto the top without dowels, the overlap of one butting up against the end of the next at the corners (see drawing). Each side of the table is marked (A,B,C,D) on both the model and the table to facilitate identification and assembly.

Consulting the model to calculate how many inches each corner extends from the sides, the corners are built out by gluing on short overlapping blocks of 1½in-thick ash (see drawing). No dowels are used, as they would show after carving. At the corners, each overlap is sawed down – a plane could also be used – to ensure a smooth surface for the next piece to be glued to.

The carver preferred this technique to mitered corners which would be weaker and liable to open up, revealing a gap which bears no relation to the folds in the cloth. The chosen method is also much simpler, as all surfaces meet at right angles. Moreover, complex joints would look ugly – and could be weakened – when the wood has been carved away around them.

DIMENSIONS

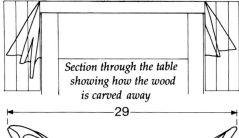

*Section through the table
showing how the wood
is carved away*

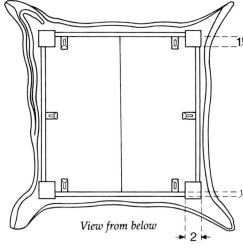

— 29 —

1¼

½

View from below

2

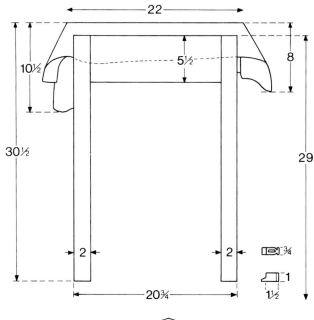

— 22 —

10½

5½

8

30½

29

2

2

¾

1

1½

20¾

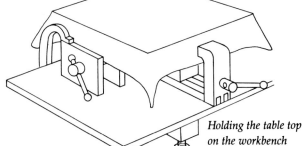

*Holding the table top
on the workbench*

ORDER OF WORK

The base

1 Plane the four legs smooth and cut them to length
2 Mark and cut mortises for the stretchers
3 Cut the four stretchers to length
4 Mark and cut tenons at both ends of each stretcher
5 Glue and clamp two legs to one stretcher, the other two legs to a second stretcher
6 Glue and clamp the other two stretchers in place
7 Fix glued dowels through each mortise and tenon joint, and pare away protruding ends

The top

1 Cut the top's two panels to length
2 Glue and dowel them together
3 Cut the four sides to length
4 Glue them to the top
5 Mark the table sides for identification
6 Build out the four corners by gluing on short overlapping blocks
7 Saw the corners roughly to shape
8 Carve the sides precisely to shape
9 Gouge the top surface lightly to match the texture of the sides
10 Sand lightly

Sequence:

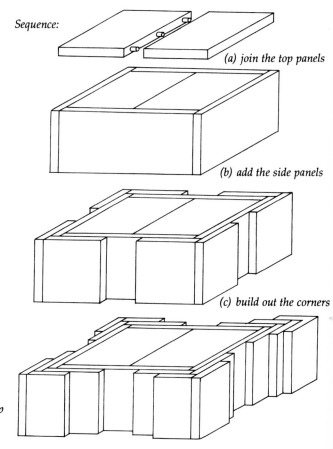

(a) join the top panels

(b) add the side panels

(c) build out the corners

CONSTRUCTION

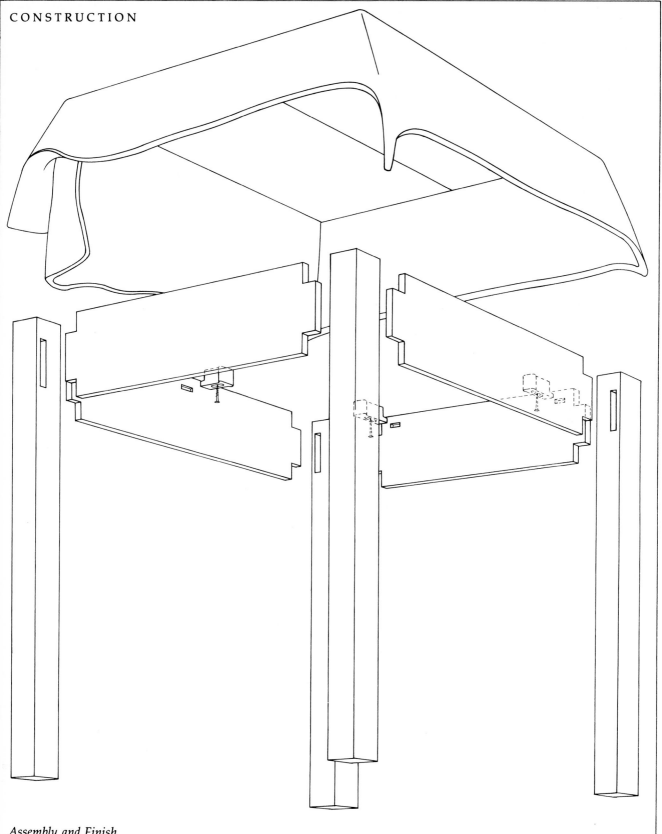

Assembly and Finish

1 *Place top on base and mark positions of attaching blocks*

2 *Chisel grooves for blocks on inside face of stretchers*

3 *Cut the wooden blocks to shape (manufactured blocks can be bought)*

4 *Screw the six blocks to the underside of the table top*

5 *Swing the blocks into the grooves to hold the table top*

6 *Apply a coat of wax dissolved in denatured alcohol (white spirit) and colored with yellow ochre and burnt umber*

MATERIALS	No.	Size (ins)
Pine for:		
Legs	4	2 × 2 × 29
Stretchers	4	½ × 5½ × 18¼
Ash for:		
Top	2	1½ × 11 × 22
Sides (1st layer)	2	1½ × 11 × 22
Sides (1st layer)	2	1½ × 11 × 25
Sides from	1	1½ × 11 × 200
Fixing blocks	6	¾ × 1 × 2
Woodworking adhesive		
½ dia dowels	3	2

FINISH

Wax; Denatured alcohol (white spirit); Yellow ochre powder paint; Burnt umber powder paint

Tools

The work so far has been done using ordinary woodworking tools. To carve the folds in the cloth and to hold the work still during carving requires special carving tools and equipment.

The carving was done with gouges. These come in various widths and degrees of curvature. Curvature is indicated by a number: the blade of a number 1 is flat, a number 6 substantially curved and a number 10 almost V-shaped. To carve the Cézanne table the carver used a 1in number 3, a 1in number 6, a ⅝in number 7 and a ⅞in number 10. These are all straight-bladed gouges. Special bent-bladed tools for cutting into tight corners were not needed for this job. Tools must be kept sharp for clean, efficient and safe cutting. A round-section stone is needed to smooth the inside of the curve of the gouge.

The gouges are hit with a round-headed wooden mallet.

The workpiece could be held firmly on the bench or table top with carving screws, fitted through holes drilled in the bench and screwed into the piece. They are unobtrusive and allow the work to be turned round easily. Clamps are a workable alternative, but they can be slightly awkward to use, restricting access to the work. The carver wanted to remove the top from the bench to try it on the base at regular intervals. He therefore improvised a simple holding system. He used two vises, both fixed to the top of the working surface – one by a bolt through the bench, one by a large C-clamp (see drawing). In this way two sides of the box could be held firm while work proceeded on the other two.

Carving the tablecloth

The wood carver removes wood until he gets down to the surface which he visualizes lying within the workpiece. He cuts away waste wood quite roughly at first, delicacy increasing as he approaches the final form. In the case of the tablecloth a handsaw was used to smooth the "steps" at each corner, creating a smooth line on which to work with the gouges. This saved a lot of labor with gouges. The sawing must be done carefully – there is comparatively little wood left at the point where the top meets the sides of the cloth.

Two life-size piglets by Nick Johnson show how a pattern of wood blocks is used by the carver

Kurumabiki, an early carving (1914-18) by Insho Domoto showing a trio of characters from a traditional kabuki *entertainment. The marks left by the carver's tools are used to full effect. Domoto Museum, Kyoto*

At first, constant reference was made to the plasticine model and the painting. As the work progressed, the table took on its own identity, and it became more important to make it look right in itself.

Everyone makes mistakes – the mark of the expert is that he knows how to get out of them without starting all over again. At one point the carver found that he had taken too much off one corner. The solution was simple – he glued on a new piece to fill it out, waited for the glue to set and began carving again. The addition of blocks does not impair the look of the cloth; on the contrary, it reflects Cézanne's block-like approach.

A pencil was in constant use during the carving. Contour lines are drawn on the wood to show where a fold is to go, and used as a guide for gouging. Areas which are to be left standing proud after carving are shaded in. It is unwise to draw on areas to be carved away, as the marks are soon obliterated and useless.

Cutting away the underside of the cloth is important. This technique of undercutting is a traditional device of the wood carver. It gives a crisper edge to the piece without reducing its strength by carving too thin. In the case of the Cézanne table the carver also wanted the cloth to feel right to the touch when fingers are run along the bottom edge of the carving. The inside face of the cloth therefore roughly follows the profile of the outside.

The carving left a regular ripple of gouge marks on all the surfaces. These have been kept, but the sharpness of the cuts was softened by sanding down the whole job. During the carving the "cloth" was often turned upside down on the workbench. To avoid scratches, work on the top surface is therefore left until the sides are complete. Finally the flat top is lightly gouged all over and sanded, to match the texture of the sides. This shallow gouging does not impair the performance of the table.

Finishing the table

The final finish is a coat of wax, dissolved in denatured alcohol (white spirit) and colored with traces of yellow ochre and burnt umber powder paint. This is rubbed into the surface. You can experiment with various colors on pieces of the ash. If the color seems too dense it can be lightened by rubbing the surface down with denatured alcohol. A wood stain is more difficult to control on this kind of work – it soaks into the wood, reveals rough edges and cannot be removed.

The outline of the table is sharpened by rubbing away the color along the edges. This should be done with sandpaper rather than steel wool, as slivers of steel can stick in the wood.

The finished top is placed on the base and the position of the six mounting blocks marked under the top and on the inside faces of the stretchers. At these points grooves are chiseled out. The hand-made wooden blocks (see drawing) are held to the underside of the table top by a single screw. They swing into the grooves to provide a firm but temporary fixing. Patent plastic blocks are an adequate – but less harmonious – alternative.

The medieval craftsman's young assistant clears wood shavings from the floor, while his master uses tools today's woodworker would still recognize. The workbench is decorated with linen-fold carving. The Craftsman *by Bourdichon*

49

The Study Furniture
by John Makepeace
from *St. Jerome in his Study* by Antonello da Messina (*c.* 1430-79)
National Gallery, London

J erome appears in countless paintings, poring over books in an enviable study, working on his great Latin translation of the Bible, and watched by his loyal lion. Legend tells us that Jerome won the injured lion's heart by drawing a thorn from its paw. The story of the biblical scholar and the grateful lion became a favorite subject for artists, giving rise to some anatomically odd animals appearing in paintings.

In Antonello's *St. Jerome*, the dignified saint sits in the center of a vast building, dressed in cardinal's robes and surrounded by books. A ghostly domestic cat sits on the draught-free raised platform, while Jerome's big cat prowls in the background.

It is likely that Antonello learned the secrets of oil painting by examining the Flemish paintings in the collection of Alfonso of Aragon, King of Naples. Naples was within easy reach of Messina, Sicily, where Antonello was born and stayed for most of his life. He lived briefly but influentially in Venice from 1475-6; his innovatory oil painting technique was much admired by the Venetian artists, who were still using tempera at the time.

Jerome's chair, with its rounded back, is a popular medieval model, a direct descendant of the barrels which ancient Greeks would regularly convert into seats. The saint's chest is the standard storage piece of the time. The desk and platform remain unique, and it was this feature which attracted John Makepeace.

Designing the study furniture
John Makepeace was anxious to retain the prominent features of the structure in the painting and to preserve the important relationships between the elements. It seemed to him that the essential elements were the three arches and the staircase leading up to the work area. The arches seemed interesting and useful, offering practical possibilities as storage space and visual appeal when light shines through them or artificial lights are mounted inside. The low rectangular slots, on the other hand,

51

presented no such possibilities and might just be a nuisance. They were therefore lost in the design.

The desk and base are made almost entirely of Medium Density Overlay (MDO) – Medium Density Fibreboard in U.K. – a relatively new sheet material which offers significant structural advantages over other boards. Its strength is absolutely even in all directions, sawed edges look exactly like the faces, and the sheets provide an excellent ground for paint.

The desk and base are painted. Although they are impeccably functional and neatly finished, they remain structurally simple. The combination of the chosen method of construction and the MDO makes it possible to produce sizable objects which have a strong individual character without the need for high skills.

Making the desk

Apart from the low footrest, which is leather-clad timber, the entire structure is made from MDO. Construction is extremely simple, as MDO can be butt-jointed, glued and nailed together.

The basic construction sequence is to cut out the two side panels and then to glue and nail the other elements between them in a simple box construction. The shelf positions can be altered to accommodate books and objects of different sizes. The back of the desk is left open to give access to the rear shelves.

Everything follows from the shape and dimensions of the side panels. Mark and cut out the two identical side panels. The curve is drawn in freehand. Any saw will cut through MDO, but a bandsaw or saber saw (jigsaw) is the best tool for cutting curves. Even so, a completely regular curve is hard to achieve, and the curves were therefore cut to their final shape with a hand router. Because of the inherent strength of MDO, the narrow section at the top of the curve remains strong.

Two pieces of MDO are used to form the top. These are fixed between the two side panels, not on top. Read off the angle where the two pieces meet on the side panel, divide the angle by two and cut the meeting edges of the two pieces to this angle. If one of the pieces were given a right-angled edge there would be an unsightly ridge at the joint.

A reinforcing rail is centered under the joint. Cut it to length and, with a saw or plane, angle its top face to match the angle on the top of the side.

The sloping element of the top comes right to the front of the desk. A piece is cut to butt under it at the front. The bottom edge of this piece follows the line of the side. It can either be sawed at the required angle or cut square and planed to fit. A rail is also fitted at the back.

Before fitting the top, pencil in the positions of the shelf and dividers on the inside faces of both side panels.

Glue and nail the rails, the top and the front panel in position, using casein glue and 1in finishing nails (panel pins) at 2-3in intervals. Clamp until the glue sets.

Cut the shelf, base and dividers to length. Cut the 1 × 2in pine footrest to length and round off its top edge with a plane. Glue and nail all the pieces in position, using strap clamps (sash cramps) from side to side to pull the job together until the glue sets. Nail heads can be punched below the surface and filled.

Making the base
The base is made entirely of ⅝in MDO, with a thin skin of ⅛in plywood fitted inside the arches. The top is clad in leather tiles.

Mark and cut out the two side walls. Each arch in the wall is a semicircle with a 7in radius, centered 5⅛in above floor level. As there are six identical arches to cut, it is worth making a jig. A piece of ¼in plywood is cut to the shape of the arch and used as a guide for the saw.

On the inside face of each arch rout out a ⅛ × ¼in rabbet to house the plywood.

Cut out the fins which run between the sides and act as formers for the plywood.

Glue and nail the formers between the sides, in the positions shown in the drawing (p. 54), lining up with the routed edge in the arches.

The next stage is to fit the staircase. This must be done before the top goes on, otherwise access from the inside – necessary to nail the stairs – becomes impossible.

Mark and cut out the section of the side wall which forms the right-hand side of the stairs. Its left side follows the line of the panel behind the stairs. Cut out the base panel of the stairs. Its outside edge is cut at an angle to match the slope of the side panel.

Mark and cut out the back panel of the stairs. The top and bottom edges are sawed parallel and at an angle. As the panel is fitted parallel to the sloping edge of the side wall, the cutting angles can be read off the top right and bottom right corners of the side wall.

Cut the brace which fits behind the sloping panel and acts as a former for the plywood. The right edge is cut at the same angle as the front edge of the base panel.

Mark and cut out the two pieces – tread and support – which make up the step. These meet at 45°, this angle being convenient and unobtrusive. The edges are beveled to form a sharp point where they meet. Each edge is therefore cut at 22½°. The inside edges are also sawed, or planed, at an angle to meet the stairs' sloping back panel. A third piece is cut to fit under the top.

Mark and cut out the rectangular end walls. Glue and nail all the elements of the stairs in position. Because strength is vital in the staircase, both faces of the absorbent MDO are glued, whereas glue on only one

ORDER OF WORK

The Desk

1 Mark and cut out two side panels
2 Mark and cut out two top panels
3 Mark and cut out top, front and back rails
4 Mark positions of shelf and dividers on side panels
5 Glue and nail top rails, top and front panels to sides
6 Mark and cut out base, shelf, dividers and footrest
7 Glue and nail them in position
8 Glue leather on footrest

The Base

1 Mark and cut out two side walls
2 Rout out rabbets in arches for plywood
3 Cut formers to length
4 Glue and nail formers between the sides
5 Mark and cut out side wall of stairs
6 Mark and cut out base panel and back panel of stairs
7 Mark and cut out bracing panel
8 Mark and cut out stair tread and two risers
9 Glue and nail staircase in position
10 Cut out and attach two end walls
11 Cut and attach base panel
12 Glue and nail plywood in arches
13 Cut and attach top panel
14 Paint. Glue leather tiles on top and steps

The Chair

1 Cut out the strips of ash for the three curves
2 Bend, glue and clamp strips around former
3 Round top edge of top curve with a spokeshave
4 Cut curves to length
5 Mark and cut tenon on center curve
6 Mark and cut mortises for uprights
7 Cut out plywood loose tongues
8 Cut short uprights to length
9 Mark and cut tenons at each end of the uprights
10 Hollow out inside face of uprights set on the curve
11 Glue and clamp curved rails and uprights together
12 Cut out two full-length uprights
13 Mark and cut mortises at each end
14 Glue and clamp uprights to chair
15 Chamfer inside corners of short uprights
16 Scoop out bottom curve
17 Apply polyurethane
18 Cut out plywood seat frame
19 Drill five clearance holes for screws
20 Tack webbing to frame
21 Fit three layers of upholstery
22 Cut out leather top and tack it in groove under frame
23 Screw seat to chair
24 Cut out and attach leather for seat base

MATERIALS

	No.	Size (ins)
Desk		
Medium Density Overlay For:		
Side panels	2	$1/2 \times 31^{1}/_2 \times 34^{1}/_4$
Top panel	1	$1/2 \times 21^{5}/_8 \times 28^{1}/_2$
Top panel	1	$1/2 \times 13 \times 28^{1}/_2$
Top and front rails	3	$1/2 \times 2 \times 28^{1}/_2$
Base panel and shelf	2	$1/2 \times 19^{1}/_2 \times 28^{1}/_2$
Lower divider	1	$1/2 \times 16 \times 28^{1}/_2$
Upper divider	1	$1/2 \times 14 \times 28^{1}/_2$
Hardwood for footrail	1	$1/2 \times 2 \times 28^{1}/_2$
Leather for footrail	1	$5 \times 28^{1}/_2$
Base		
Medium Density Overlay For:		
Side wall	1	$5/8 \times 15^{7}/_8 \times 78^{11}/_{16}$
Side wall	1	$5/8 \times 15^{7}/_8 \times 64^{1}/_{16}$
Formers	6	$5/8 \times 2^{7}/_8 \times 46$
Formers	8	$5/8 \times 3^{1}/_2 \times 46$
Side wall	1	$5/8 \times 15^{7}/_8 \times 32^{1}/_2$
Stair base	1	$5/8 \times 11^{3}/_4 \times 13^{1}/_8$
Stair back panel	1	$5/8 \times 13^{1}/_8 \times 19^{1}/_2$
Brace	1	$5/8 \times 2 \times 13^{1}/_8$
Tread	1	$5/8 \times 5^{3}/_4 \times 13^{1}/_8$
Riser	1	$5/8 \times 4^{1}/_2 \times 13^{1}/_8$
Riser	1	$5/8 \times 3^{5}/_8 \times 13^{1}/_8$
End wall	1	$5/8 \times 15^{7}/_8 \times 32^{1}/_4$
End wall	1	$5/8 \times 15^{7}/_8 \times 46$
Base panel	1	$5/8 \times 32^{1}/_4 \times 26$
Top panel	1	$5/8 \times 47^{1}/_4 \times 78^{3}/_4$
Plywood for cladding	3	$1/8 \times 32^{1}/_2 \times 46^{1}/_2$
Leather for:		
Tiles	54	8×8
Treads	2	$5^{3}/_4 \times 13^{1}/_8$

Casein glue; PVA leather adhesive; Finishing nails (panel pins); Acrylic paint

	No.	Size (ins)
Chair		
Ash for:		
Curved rails	24	$1/_{10} \times 2 \times 47$
Lower uprights	6	$7/8 \times 1^{9}/_{16} \times 13^{1}/_8$
Upper uprights	6	$7/8 \times 1^{9}/_{16} \times 10^{3}/_4$
Front uprights	2	$7/8 \times 2 \times 27^{1}/_2$
Plywood for:		
Loose tongues	4	$5/_{16} \times 1 \times 1^{7}/_{16}$
Seat frame	1	$1^{1}/_2 \times 16^{1}/_2 \times 17$

Webbing; Upholstery; Leather; Tacks; Screws; Casein glue; Leather dye; Polyurethane varnish

The joint between the long upright and top rail. The loose tongue is shown by the dotted lines

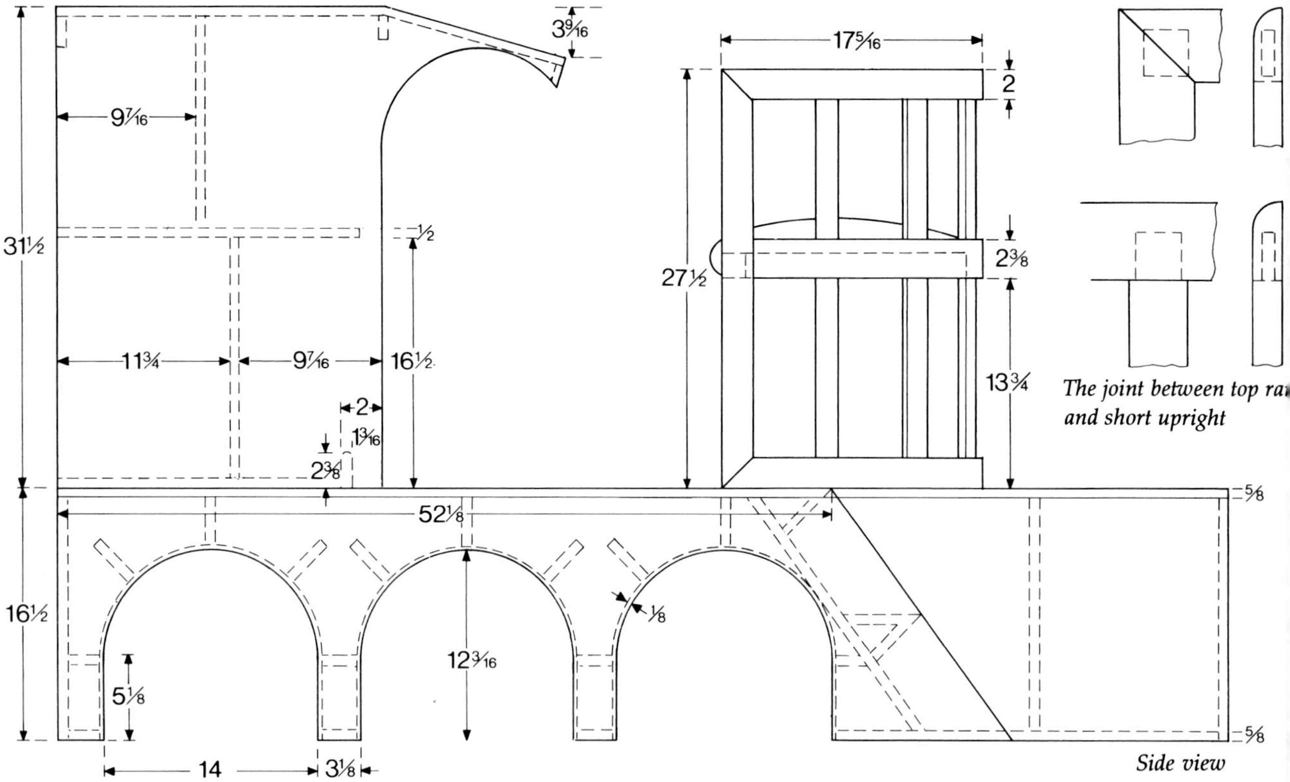

$3\frac{9}{16}$

$9\frac{7}{16}$

$31\frac{1}{2}$

$\frac{1}{2}$

$11\frac{3}{4}$ $9\frac{7}{16}$ $16\frac{1}{2}$

2

$1\frac{3}{16}$

$2\frac{3}{8}$

$17\frac{5}{16}$

2

$27\frac{1}{2}$

$2\frac{3}{8}$

$13\frac{3}{4}$

The joint between top rail and short upright

$52\frac{1}{8}$

$\frac{5}{8}$

$16\frac{1}{2}$

$12\frac{3}{16}$

$\frac{1}{8}$

$5\frac{1}{8}$

$\frac{5}{8}$

14 $3\frac{1}{8}$

Side view

$21\frac{5}{8}$ $12\frac{9}{16}$ $12\frac{9}{16}$

2

$4\frac{3}{4}$

$29\frac{1}{2}$

$19\frac{1}{4}$

$33\frac{1}{2}$

$4\frac{15}{16}$

$1\frac{9}{16}$

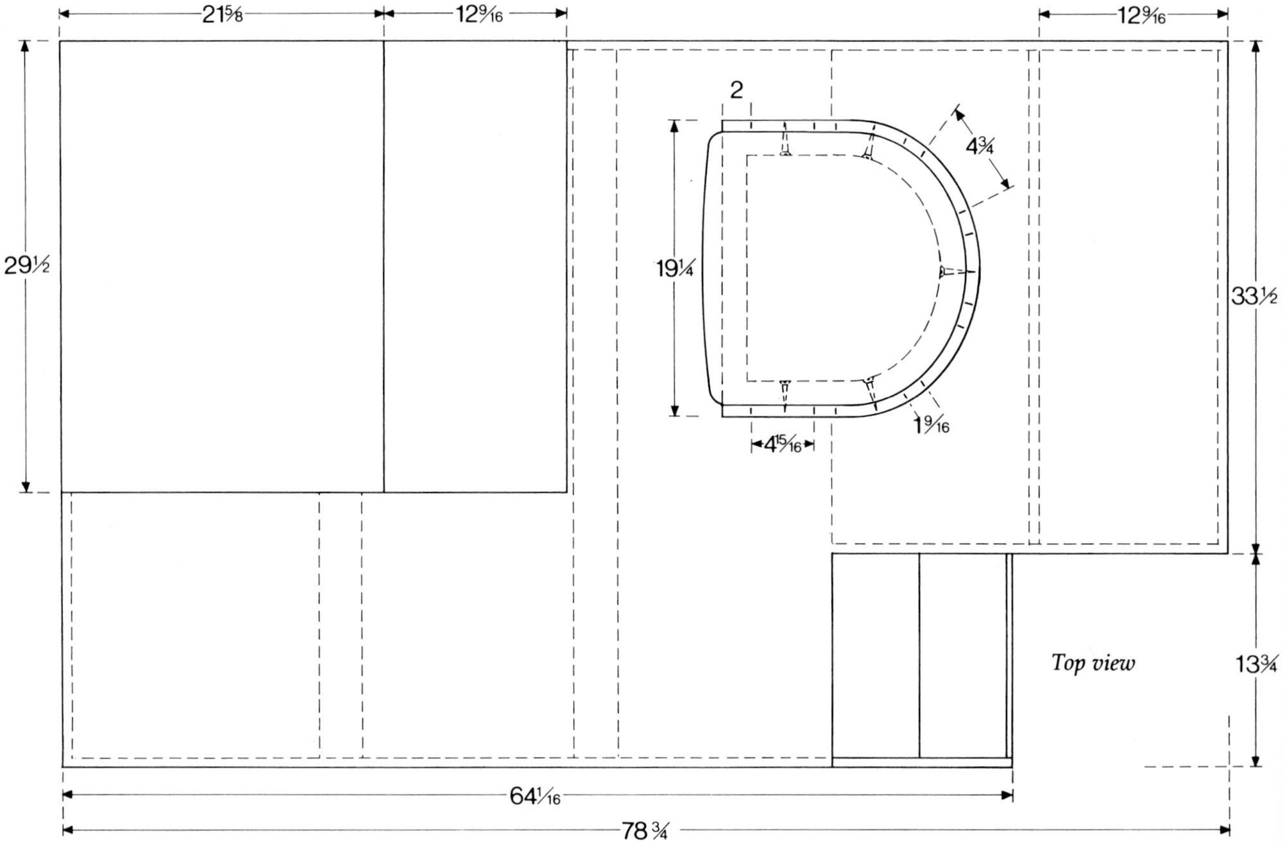

Top view $13\frac{3}{4}$

$64\frac{1}{16}$

$78\frac{3}{4}$

54

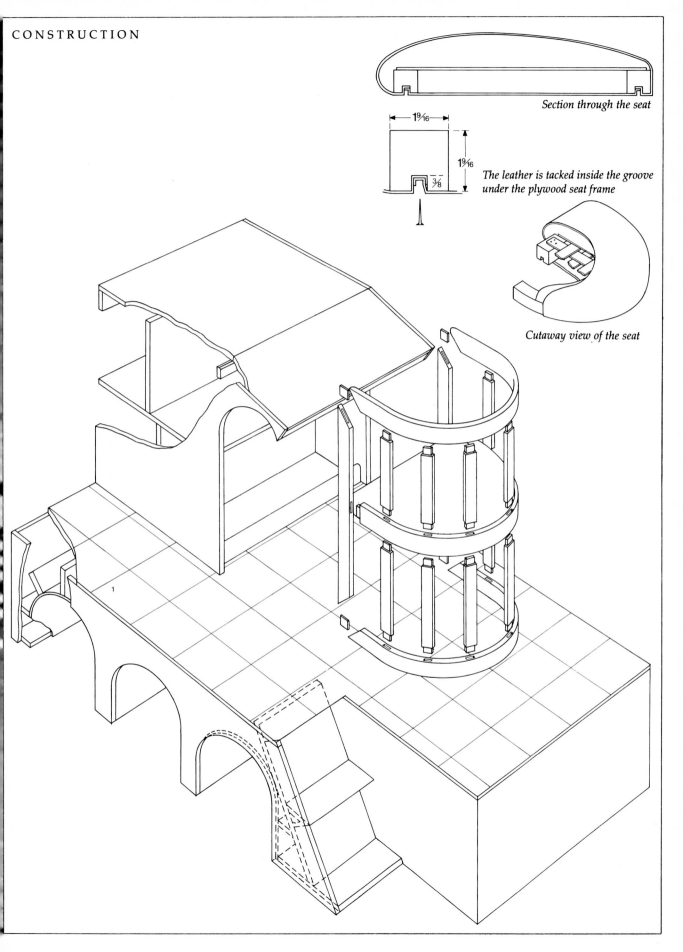

Section through the seat

19⁄16

19⁄16

3⁄8

The leather is tacked inside the groove
under the plywood seat frame

Cutaway view of the seat

1

face is adequate on the rest of the structure. The two pieces forming the step must be clamped together while the glue sets. A clamp fixed at such an angle can easily slip off. This problem can be overcome by placing a piece of abrasive paper over the clamping block to increase friction between the surfaces.

Glue and nail the end walls in place. Clamp the structure until the glue sets.

Cut out the rectangular base panel which encloses the space between the stairs and the back wall. Glue and nail the panel in place.

The structure is now rigid enough for the plywood skin to be applied. The visible grain of the plywood runs from front to back of the arches. Cut out the pieces, glue and nail them to the fins and inside the arch rabbets.

Finally cut the top panel out of a single sheet of MDO. This sits on top of the walls, to which it is glued and nailed. Where it forms the top of the staircase the edge is planed away to meet the brace below.

Finishing the desk and base

MDO is an admirable surface for paint, and John Makepeace decided to finish both desk and base with acrylic paint. He experimented with pale tones, covering every surface including the top of the platform. He then decided that leather tiles would be a more practical and pleasing surface for the floor. Eight-inch squares of dark brown coach hide were glued to the top using PVA leather adhesive. This adhesive retains a certain elasticity and does not attack the leather. The edges of the tiles are beveled, leaving a narrow V-shaped groove between tiles which catches the light. The leather is not treated in any way. The same leather is glued on the stair treads and the desk footrest.

The use of dark brown tiles dictated a darkening of the painted surfaces. The pale surface was retained as a ground for the darker top coat, which was applied with a sponge to create a dappled effect.

Making the chair

The chair is made from ash. A high degree of skill is needed to match John Makepeace's refined design. The piece could be simplified by using chunkier, less finished frame elements and a wooden panel seat.

The line of the curved rails is a freehand ellipse, a constantly changing shape. John Makepeace felt that the chair in the painting was not a simple semicircle, and he did not want to reduce its appeal by resorting to a plain semicircle. He also felt it would look too mechanical if an ordinary ellipse was used. Once the chair was made it became apparent that the form was admirably suited for groups of people to use, as a dining chair for instance.

The first stage in construction is to form three curved rails of laminated ash strips. The twelve short uprights of solid ash are joined to the rails by mortise and tenon joints, and the two front uprights attached by loose tongues. The upholstered seat is made separately and attached to the frame after this has been polished.

The curved rails are built up by bending thin pieces of ash in layers around a former, with casein glue between the layers. To bend to the necessary curve, the maximum thickness of the laminates is $\frac{1}{10}$in. Laminating veneers can be bought from specialist suppliers, but as the sections used in the chair are shallow – only $2\frac{3}{8}$in for the central curve, 2in for the top and bottom curves – they can be sliced from $2\frac{3}{8}$ and 2in thick planks of ash with a circular saw fitted with a guide.

Several types of former are available. The simplest approach is to build up a strong hoop by gluing together three layers of good quality stiff plywood, 1in thick. The laminates are then bent around the hoop and held in position with C-clamps until the glue sets. They are all glued together in a single operation. Leave them for at least 24 hours before removing them from the former.

There is a tendency for laminates to spring outward slightly when they are released from the former; the hoop is therefore cut $\frac{1}{8}$in narrower at the front than the desired final shape. When the seat is pushed into position it will force the frame to the correct shape if it has not already rectified itself.

The top inside edge of the top curve is rounded with a spokeshave, leaving a relatively sharp edge on the outside. The ends of the top and bottom rail are sawed at an angle of 45°. A shouldered tenon is cut on the ends of the center rail.

The mortises for the six short rails are now marked and cut in the underside of the top rail, the upper and lower face of the center rail and the top face of the bottom rail. The problem of cutting square mortises in the center of the curve is eased by making up a card or plywood pattern of a section of the curve, marking the mortise shape on this and laying it on the rail to mark out the mortises.

The front uprights are joined to the three curved rails by loose tongues of plywood, one third the thickness of the rails they connect. Plywood is chosen in preference to solid timber as it is strong in every direction and presents no short-grain problems. The mortises for the tongues are marked and cut in the rail ends at this stage.

Cut the twelve solid ash rails to length. They are approximately $\frac{1}{16}$in over-thickness and are shaped back later. Mark and cut tenons $1\frac{3}{16}$in long with $\frac{1}{8}$in shoulders, at each end of all twelve. The tenons are marked in the conventional way and cut with a circular saw.

Hollow out the inside face of the rails which will be set on the curves, to follow the curve of the horizontal rails,

St. Jerome is often depicted in a well-furnished study, at work on his great translation of the Bible, with his faithful lion looking on. This version of St. Jerome in his Study *is by Hendrik van Steenwyck (1624). Courtauld Institute, London*

using a moulding plane. A scraper is a less effective substitute for the moulding plane.

The chair can now be glued together. To avoid putting too much weight of clamp on the piece at any one time the gluing is carried out in two stages. First the curved rails and short uprights are glued and clamped together in a single operation. To do this, lay the chair frame on its face and clamp straight through from top to bottom rail. It is important to keep the piece out of twist during gluing.

Cut the solid front uprights to length. Saw the two ends at 45° to meet the top and bottom rails. Mark and cut the mortises for the loose tongues. When the first gluing is dry, remove the clamps and glue the two full-length uprights to the curves using the plywood loose tongues. Little pressure is required to hold them in position, so they can be clamped across onto the front half-upright until the glue sets.

Slightly chamfer the inside corners of the half-length uprights between the top and middle rails. The chamfer reduces toward the top, so that at the point where the upright meets the rail the corners are almost square.

A chair of this form sitting on an uneven floor surface could become rather unstable. To overcome the problem

the lower edge of the bottom rail is scooped out to a depth of about ⅛in between four points, in effect creating four minute "legs".

Finishing the seat
After careful sanding, the wood is stained using a leather dye. A base coat of acid catalysed resin (polyurethane) is put on to seal the grain. Two more coats of resin are applied, cutting back carefully between coats.

Making the seat
The seat is made separately, and fitted only when the leather upholstery is in position. The upholstery is built on a frame of 1½in thick plywood with the center cut out. Cut out a ⅜ × ⅜in groove in the underside of the plywood – the edges of the leather top and base will be tacked in this.

Tack the webbing to the top surface of the plywood. Because the seat is horizontal, the webbing is designed to throw the sitter's weight toward the back of the seat. The webbing is stretched tightly across the front and at the two sides, but more loosely where the sitter's bottom will be.

The webbing is topped with three layers of upholstery of different grades. The lowest is a dense foam, the middle layer softer foam and the top a crimped terylene. The upholstery is packed round the front of the seat panel, curling up underneath to create a sense of softness when you curl your legs under the seat. Careful upholstery creates the rounded effect of the seat.

The leather top is stretched over the upholstery, curled under the plywood panel and tacked in the groove.

The seat is now screwed inside the chair frame, using five screws – one near the front at each side, one at the back, and an intermediate screw on each side. The screws are driven through clearance holes in the plywood frame, through the leather and into the center rail.

The fixings are hidden by cutting a piece of the same leather to fit across the base. This too is fixed by tacks in the groove. With four thicknesses of leather in the groove, no fixings can be seen.

It would be unfortunate to spoil an elegant piece by inept upholstery. Inexperienced upholsterers may prefer to sidestep the difficulty by fitting a plain wooden seat. Allowance must be made for such a seat to move with changes in humidity. A thick slab of timber could be sculpted to a comfortable shape and grooved around the edge. A tongue would then be fixed in a corresponding groove in the chair's center rail. The seat then slides into position. It would probably be unnecessary to glue the seat in place.

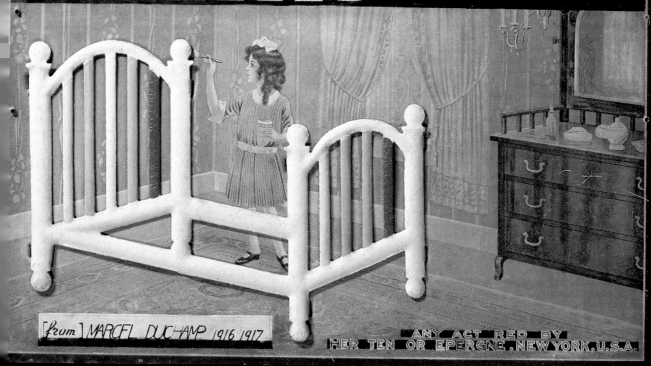

The Ready-Made Bed

by Patrick Daw

from *Apolinère Enameled* (1916-17) by Marcel Duchamp (1887-1968)

Philadelphia Museum of Art; The Louise and Walter Arensburg Collection

M arcel Duchamp bewildered people. He confused the critics by exhibiting a bicycle wheel mounted uselessly on a stool; he outraged the earnest by exhibiting a urinal – he called it *Fountain*; and he caused titters and snorts by drawing a moustache on a reproduction of the Mona Lisa and adding a rude title.

Eccentric French poet Guillaume Apollinaire, the misspelled hero of Duchamp's *Apolinère Enameled*, also had trouble with the Mona Lisa. When the painting vanished from the Louvre in 1911 suspicion fell, quite wrongly, on Apollinaire, and he was arrested. But there remains little reason why he should be enameled.

Apolinère Enameled is one of Duchamp's Ready-Mades, for which he took an everyday object, deprived it of its name and its normal context, and put it in an art gallery. He also suggested taking the opposite route, taking paintings off art gallery walls and placing them in the world outside – "use a Rembrandt as an ironing board" was one of his curious proposals. The idea was not taken up.

Apolinère Enameled began as a painted tin advertising sign for Sapolin Enamel paints. Duchamp altered the lettering and penciled in a pale reflection of the young decorator in the corner of the mirror.

As Duchamp wanted to abolish the distinction between art and the useful, it is fitting to create a real bed from this bizarre tin image, in which the dictates of perspective are flouted and one of the bed rails is partially missing.

Designing the ready-made bed

In the interests of making a usable bed, the gap between rail and bedpost was closed. This means that someone can sleep peacefully in the bed without propping up one of the corners on bricks. The picture's perspective is confused, making the dimensions hard to calculate. The presence of the child and the bed's bright color scheme argued in favor of a child-sized bed. If one assumes that the child in the picture is relatively normal, the bed's dimensions might be as small as 36in × 4ft 6in . A foam supplier could cut a mattress to this size, but for maximum economy and a broader choice of mattress types the practical bed designer takes standard mattress sizes into account. Children are increasingly using full-sized beds, and the designer decided to follow this trend. He settled on a single bed size, built to take a 36in × 6ft 3in mattress. If you want a shorter bed, simply reduce the length of the rails in the drawing.

Making the bed

The project involves some fairly advanced joinery, but the most difficult part – making the metal frame mountings –can be entrusted to an engineering workshop.

The designer's strategy was to construct two separate bed ends and then to join them together by fitting the two long side rails. The rails are cut to length from normal square-section timber and then, to reproduce the rounded impression of the original advertisement, the corners are all rounded off. The designer wanted a strong but collapsible bed, and this influenced his choice of mountings between the side rails and the corner posts. The mattress rests on slats set in a rabbet on the inside face of the side rails.

The bedhead

The four corner posts are turned to shape on a lathe. They are made in three separate parts – the main shaft with its ball-shaped foot, the disc, and the top ball. The ball is fixed to the shaft by a 1in diameter dowel, 4in long, glued in 1½in deep sockets drilled in the ball and shaft, and passing through a 1in diameter hole bored through the center of the disc. The dowel could be turned as part of the ball.

The finished shaft diameter is 4½in. It could be turned from a single piece of 5 × 5in timber, but this is expensive to buy. To cut costs the designer began with a much cheaper plank of 4 x 5in softwood and glued a piece of 1 × 5in softwood to it to build up the 5 × 5in section. Such a glued block presents no problem to a turner as long as there are no glued joints in the very center of the block. Unsightly joins will be hidden under a coat of paint. The turning can be entrusted to a professional turner if you have no lathe. All the turner needs is a profile (as on p. 63). Money may be saved by supplying the turning timber yourself. Discuss precise requirements with the turner before buying the timber.

The bedhead's top (curved) and bottom rails are joined to the posts by mortise and tenon joints. To cut the mortises in the posts, first draw a line down the entire post at any point on its circumference. Center a 1in diameter drill bit on this line 2½in from the top of the shaft and drill a 2in deep socket. Square off the corners

The imagination of the children's book illustrator turns to furnishing in Maurice Sendak's Where the Wild Things Are. *Max's chunky wood bed is transformed in the night into a design calling for the combined skills of the cabinet maker and the forester*

of the socket using a chisel. On the same line, drill an identical 2in deep hole centered 11½in from the bottom. Drill a 1in diameter hole above and below it and clean out with a chisel to form a 1 × 3in mortise, 2in deep.

The curved top rail

The curved top rail is too hefty to steam-bend from a straight plank without complex manufacturing machinery. It is cut out of a solid plank of 2 × 9in softwood as a curve of rectangular section; then the corners are rounded off. To mark the arc on the plank the designer tied one end of a piece of string to a chair leg and tied a pencil to the other end. He calculated that to reproduce the arc in the picture he would need to draw an arc with a maximum rise of 6⅛in between the two uprights. He also calculated that the chosen mattress width of 36in required a distance between posts of 29¼in. He drew a line 29¼in long on the 2 × 9in plank, leaving at least 2in of spare timber at each end. He placed the plank on the ground and moved the chair until with the stretched string he could draw an arc going through both ends of the line and reaching a point 6⅛in above the line at the center. He then moved the chair 2in further away from the plank and drew a second line to mark the bottom of the rail. Each end of the rail extends horizontally for 2in (see diagram) to allow for the tenons. Saw the rail out of the plank with a bandsaw or saber saw (jigsaw).

The ends of the rail were rounded on Patrick Daw's piece to wrap snugly around the upright. However, many people will find it easier to square off the face of the posts where they meet the rails, thereby avoiding the need to cut curves. If you choose curves, mark them out before cutting the tenons. Begin by making a cardboard template of the post. This can be done by taking a tracing from the top of the post or by using a pair of compasses to draw a 4½in diameter circle on the cardboard. Cut out the cardboard profile, lay it on the top of the rail and transfer the arc to the rail at each end, top and bottom. The two arcs must be 29¼in apart at their nearest points, centered on the rail, and far enough from the ends of the rail to allow for the 2in deep tenon to be sawed and chiseled out.

Draw a line across the top and bottom of the rail at each end joining the points where each arc hits the sides of the rail. Mark and saw out a 1in-square shouldered tenon 2in long measured from these lines. Use a gouge

to chop the tenon back to the line of the arc. The gouge can easily chip away the bottom of the rail ends, where the grain is weak. Any gaps can be filled later and will be hidden by the paint.

At this stage the main body of the stretcher is still rectangular in section. Use a spokeshave to round the corners off. This is a long job. The designer spent an entire afternoon whittling away until he achieved a

ORDER OF WORK

1 The four corner posts – shaft, disc and ball – are turned to shape on a lathe. (This job can be given to a professional wood turner)
2 Dowel the shaft, disc and ball of each post together
3 Mark and cut the mortises in the posts
4 Mark and cut out the top curved rail
5 Mark and cut out a tenon at each end of the rail
6 Round off the rail
7 Cut the bottom rail to length
8 Mark and cut a tenon at each end of the rail
9 Mark and drill dadoes (housings) for the five upright bars
10 Saw the five bars 3in overlength, and shape the top ends to fit around the curved rail
11 Cut the bars precisely to length
12 Round off the corners of the rail
13 Glue and assemble the bedhead
14 Drive glued dowels through top rail into the uprights
15 The bedhead is constructed in the same way but with different dimensions
16 Cut the two side rails to length
17 Round off the ends to match the posts
18 Round off the sides of the rails
19 Cut out a 1 × 1in rabbet along the top inside edge of the side rails
20 Drill the countersunk bolt holes through the corner posts and into the rail ends
21 Drill the entry holes for the metal blocks in the inside face of the side rails
22 Coat the block in epoxy resin adhesive and push it into position. The bolt should be in position while the adhesive sets
23 Fit the wooden plugs

Finish

1 Sand the whole bed
2 Paint on a coat of primer
3 Fill any surface irregularities and sand smooth
4 Paint on a coat of acrylic primer/undercoat
5 Paint on two coats of brilliant white flat enamel (eggshell) paint, sanding lightly between coats
6 Paint the bars with gloss enamel paint

Comics and cartoons are interesting sources of furniture designs. Here Little Nemo wakes up in his monumental bed after another adventure in Slumberland, from Winsor McCay's famous weekly comic strip Little Nemo in Slumberland, which began in 1905

MATERIALS   *No.*   *Size (ins)*

The Bedhead

Pine for:

	No.	Size (ins)
Corner posts	2	4 × 5 × 43
Corner posts	2	1 × 5 × 43
Discs	2	1 × 6½
Balls	2	4 × 4 × 5
Balls	2	1 × 4 × 5
Top rail	1	2 × 9 × 33¼
Bottom rail	1	3 × 4 × 33¼
Upright bars	5	38 × 1¾ dia

Hardwood dowels for:

Corner posts	2	1 dia × 4
Upright bars	5	¾ dia × 3¾

The Bedend

Pine for:

Corner posts	2	4 × 5 × 33¼
Corner posts	2	1 × 5 × 33¼
Discs	2	1 × 6½
Balls	2	4 × 4 × 5
Balls	2	1 × 4 × 5
Top rail	1	2 × 9 × 33¼
Bottom rail	1	3 × 4 × 33¼
Upright bars	5	28 × 1¾ dia

Hardwood dowels for:

Corner posts	2	4 × 1 dia
Upright bars	5	3¾ × ¾ dia

Rail assembly
Pine for:

Rails	2	3 × 4 × 80
Plugs	4	1½ × 1 dia

Beech for:

Slats	14	1 × 1½

Threaded steel bolts	4	8 × ½ dia
Drilled and tapped steel blocks	4	1 dia
Woodworking adhesive		
Epoxy resin adhesive		
Webbing		
Tacks		

DIMENSIONS

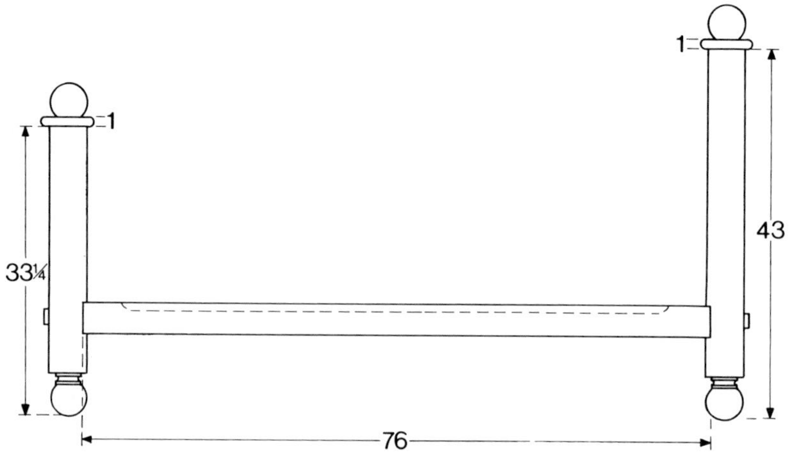

Side and top views of the bed

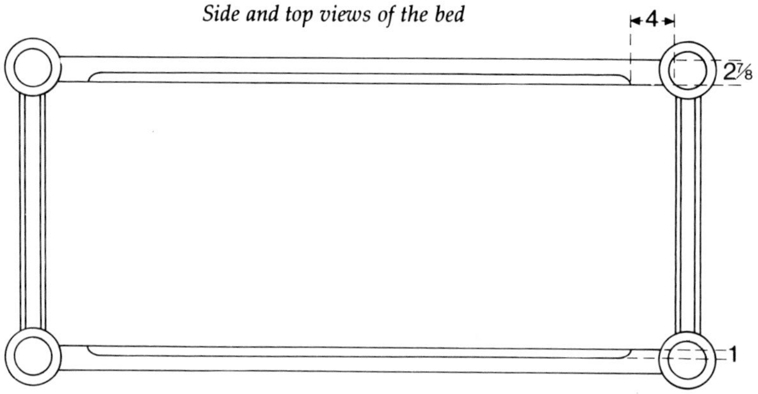

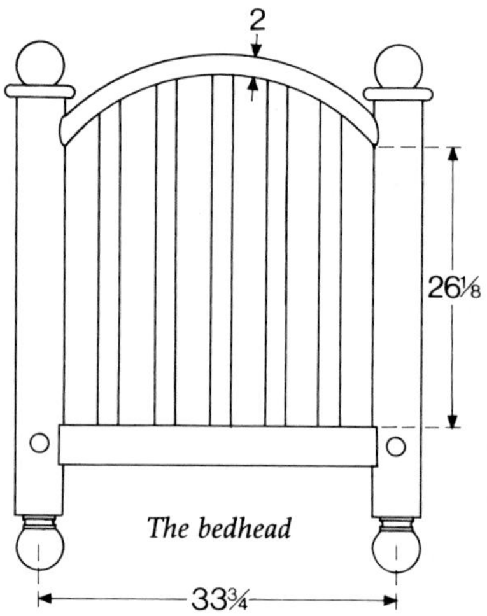

The bedhead

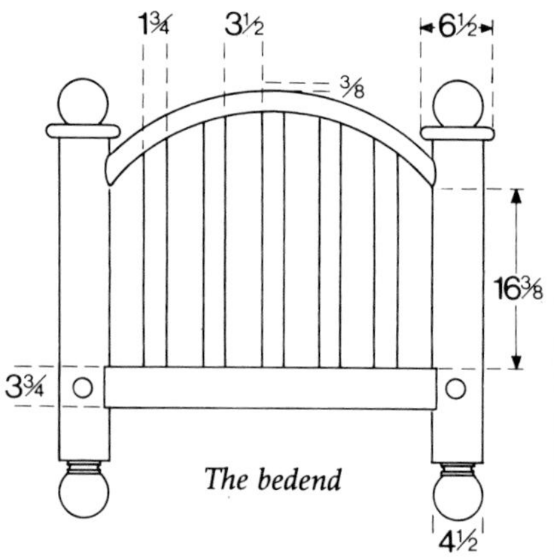

The bedend

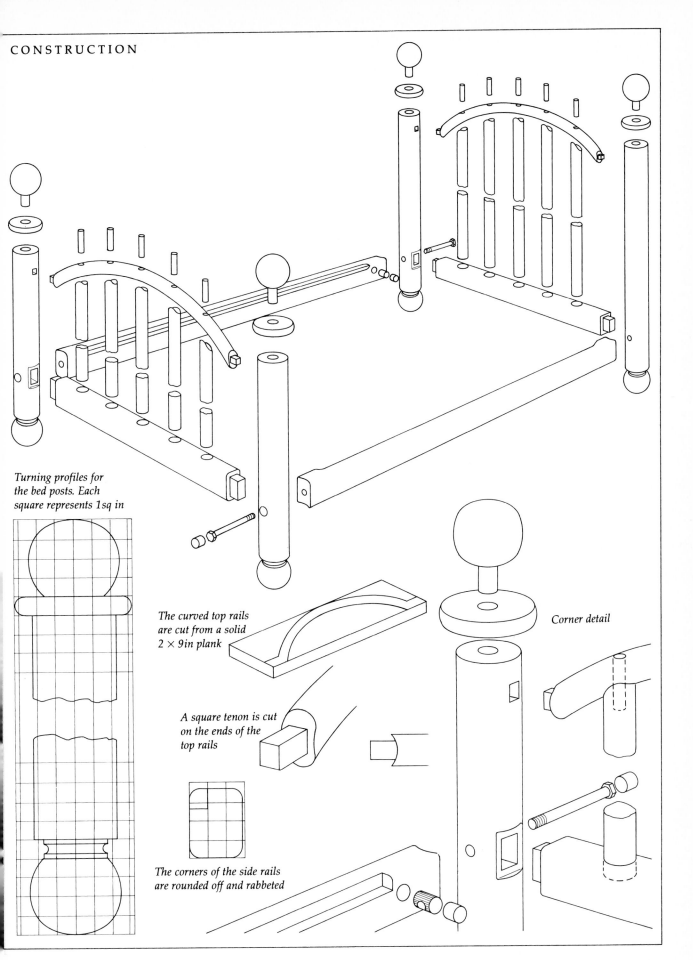

Turning profiles for
the bed posts. Each
square represents 1sq in

The curved top rails
are cut from a solid
2 × 9in plank

Corner detail

A square tenon is cut
on the ends of the
top rails

The corners of the side rails
are rounded off and rabbeted

satisfactory shape. He found it a pleasant afternoon.

The bottom rail is cut from a 33¼in length of 3 × 4in softwood. Either square off the posts where the rail enters them or round off the rail ends using the template as before, cutting a 2in deep mortise, 1 × 3in, at each end. Before rounding off the edges of the rail, draw a center line along the rail's top surface. The housings for the five upright bars will be cut along this line. Mark the position for the central bar and mark two points 5¼in apart on each side of this central mark. Place the rail in a vise and drill 1in deep housings 1¾in diameter. Use a hole borer for this job rather than a flat bit, as large-diameter flat bits tend to rip the wood. A hole-boring attachment will fit a standard electric drill. Round off the rail.

Make a paper template of the lower rail with the five mortise positions marked on it. Use this template to mark the positions on the curving top rail where the five bars will meet it. Because the whole structure will later be painted, all the surfaces can be very clearly marked.

Saw the bars at least 3in too long and shape their tops to fit. To fix the shape, place the bar against the rail to get a rough idea of the finished profile and cut it roughly to shape with a saw. Fine finishing is a laborious job for a shaping tool, cutting and matching rail and bar until they fit properly. Work with the rail laid flat on the workbench.

When the five bars are shaped satisfactorily, cut them to length. Calculating the lengths accurately is complicated and uncertain. To avoid error, lay the rail and bars on the bench, place the bars in position on the top rail, put the lower rail in place, mark the point where it cuts all the bars and saw them to length, allowing for a 1in tenon at the bottom.

At this point the bedhead can be glued together. When the bars are in position, drill ¾in diameter holes down through the top rail and 1½in into the top of each bar. Hammer glued ¾in diameter dowels into the holes to secure the bars. Pare off protruding ends with a chisel.

The bed end
The bed end is made in identical fashion, but with slightly different dimensions (see measured drawings).

The bed rails
The two side rails are cut from 3 × 4in timber. A 1 × 1in rabbet is cut along the top inside corner of the rails. The slats supporting the mattress will rest on these. Cutting the rabbet is a job for a router or a circular saw. The rabbet begins and ends 4in from the ends of the rail.

The rail ends can be shaped in exactly the same way as those of the lower rail on the bedhead, with tenons glued in matching mortises in the bedpost. The face of

the bedpost could be flattened to avoid the need to cut a curve on the rails. This is probably the simplest approach, but the ends of the rails could equally be curved to fit around the post using the cardboard template as before. The designer chose to reinforce the joint in the way described below, employing a method which makes the tenons redundant but demands the intervention of an engineer. Mortise and tenon joints could be reinforced by a bolt driven through the bedpost to engage a nut (with washer) set in the bed rail, in a way similar to that described below.

Joining posts and rails (optional method)
Standard mountings can be bought to hold the side rails to the posts, but the designer decided on a custom job. He rejected the glued mortise and tenon as he thought the bed should be easy to dismantle. He chose 8in long ½in diameter threaded bolts driven through holes in the posts into a tapped metal block. The block is set 4in into the rails and held in place by epoxy resin adhesive. It is a cylinder of 1in diameter mild steel drilled and tapped to ½in. Its outside surface is fluted in the same plane as the bolt. The task of making these mountings was entrusted to a local engineer.

Drilling the bolt holes is difficult, as accuracy is crucial. If the holes stray off center, the bolt and block will not link up. The designer began by drilling a 1in diameter hole 1in into the posts 11½in from their base. To make sure he was drilling horizontally he held the leg upright in a vise and built up a pile of blocks alongside it until he could rest his brace and bit on the pile and drill in at the correct angle.

Having drilled the 1in diameter holes, he counterbored ½in diameter holes right through the posts. It is important to drill the larger diameter holes first when using a brace and bit, as the bit has nothing to grip otherwise.

Place the side rails against the bedposts, propped up at the correct height. Use the same pile of blocks as before to guide the drill as you drill a hole 5in into the rail end.

To fit the metal block, drill a 1in diameter hole on the inside face of the rail 4in from the end and 3in deep. Coat the block in epoxy resin adhesive, push it all the way in and install the bolt before the glue sets. In this way you can be sure it will fit properly when the glue dries.

The head of each bolt is recessed into the posts, and covered with a wooden plug. This is a 1in diameter dowel, 1½in long, rounded off at one end and pushed – not glued – over the bolt.

Finishing the bed
The bed must be painted to remain faithful to its model,

as *Apolinère Enameled* began as a paint advertisement. Having sanded the surface smooth, paint on a coat of primer. This will show up the flaws in the wood surface; fill these with plastic filler and sand smooth. After a further coat of acrylic primer/undercoat, finish with two coats of brilliant flat white enamel. The designer rejected gloss paint because he wanted to suggest that the child had come across a rather plain white bed and had decided to brighten it up with her glossy Sapolin enamels. Enamel paint was, of course, used to paint the bars.

Putting a mattress on a solid base is an unhealthy practice leading to damp beds – air must be allowed to circulate under the mattress. Fourteen 1in × 1½in slats were joined by tacks to a strip of webbing at each side at 5 in centers. They are laid in the rabbet and the mattress is placed on top. When selecting a mattress, check that it is suitable for use with a slatted base.

A painting which became a child's bed: in 1914 English architect Edwin Lutyens designed a pair of four-poster beds for his eldest daughters based on the bed in Carpaccio's The Dream of St. Ursula. Accademia, Venice

Simon's Trestle Table
by Patrick Daw
from *Christ in the House of Simon* by Dirk Bouts (*c.* 1415-1475)
Berlin Gallery

D irk Bouts's painting illustrates the story of Christ in the house of Simon the Pharisee, as told in St. Luke's Gospel, chapter 7, verses 36-50. Simon is shown craning over the table, expressing strong disapproval as a known sinner kneels at the feet of Jesus, washes them with her tears, dries them with her hair and anoints them with precious ointment. Jesus answers with a parable, saying that her sins are forgiven for she has loved much. Saint Peter looks on while John has a word with the donor (the sponsor of the painting), who is a frequent figure in fifteenth-century paintings. In this case the donor is a Dominican monk, shown kneeling on the right in humble garb.

Bouts was born in Haarlem, Holland, about 1415, where he grew up as Theoderik Romboutsz. He was a sober and wealthy man, twice the husband of rich women and official painter in the thriving university town of Louvain. He was a devout Christian, and he specialized in religious subjects.

Bouts's painting reflects the sober simplicity characteristic of Modern Devotion, the reforming religious movement to which the artist and other followers of Thomas à Kempis belonged.

The meal provided by Simon is painted with almost photographic clarity. Yet the whole painting looks odd. The diners seem curiously cramped in the miniature room which is more reminiscent of Alice in Wonderland than the New Testament. The painting has a sloping perspective as if the whole meal could slide forward and out of the frame.

Designing Simon's table
The crisp white tablecloth hides the top part of the table completely. This leaves today's furniture designer free to invent a suitable form. Patrick Daw chose a drawing board construction, with the top sitting on two I-shaped trestles. He felt oak would be the natural choice for the table top. Oak was a popular choice in the Middle Ages, when furniture needed to be strong enough to withstand

rough treatment and frequent moving. To keep costs down he used old oak floorboards. The boards were sanded clean and the ragged holes where nails had been withdrawn were drilled through and plugged with dowels of the same oak. If oak is unavailable, softwood boards are an adequate alternative.

Trestle tables were widely used in the Middle Ages, when large parties assembled for meals in medieval manors. When the feasting was over, the heavy top boards would be lifted off and leaned against a wall. An average medieval noble would own several residences, and the entire household would be moved from one to another several times a year. The collapsible trestle table had obvious advantages for the mobile noble.

Making the table

The top is made of eight $1 \times 3\frac{1}{2}$in oak boards. Plane the edges of the boards until they butt snugly together. Wider boards would mean less planing.

The boards are doweled and glued together. The hardwood dowels are $\frac{1}{4}$in diameter and 2in long. They are glued into $1\frac{1}{8}$in deep holes drilled into the edges of each board, 12in from each end and in the center. To locate the points where dowel holes should be drilled, stack the boards neatly in a pile. Using a combination square and pencil, draw three lines, one across the center of the top board and two 12in from the ends. Carry these lines down the sides of the pile. Drill the dowel holes on these marked lines. Note that the outside edges of the outer boards are not drilled.

The dowel holes must be drilled at the correct angle, and it is depressingly easy for an unguided drill to stray off line. A doweling jig will help to keep the drill straight.

The Last Supper is served on a very solid table. Woodcut by Dürer

Coat the dowels in woodworking adhesive and push them into their holes. Glue the board edges and assemble the table top. Hold the boards together with strap clamps (sash cramps) until the glue is set. When clamps are removed, there are almost inevitably ridges where the boards meet. These can be planed flat. The ends can then be sawed and planed to even length.

The designer used an electric router to cut a tongue along the ends of the boards, $\frac{3}{8}$in wide and projecting $\frac{1}{2}$in. With the same tool he cut a matching central groove in the edge of the two 1×3in end rails. A handsaw and chisel can do the same job more laboriously. The end rails are pushed into position without glue and marked where they project above and below the boards. They are then removed, planed to the exact thickness of the boards and finally glued and clamped in position.

Gently chamfer all four edges of the table top on both sides with a plane. Battens screwed underneath the top add strength to the structure and provide a positive location for the trestles. Drill and chisel out slots in the battens as wide as the shank of the screws. These will allow subsequent expansion and contraction of the top boards. Each slot runs along the bottom of a wider recess, $\frac{1}{4}$in deep, which is drilled and cleaned out first. These recesses stop the $\frac{1}{4}$in dome heads of the screws from projecting above the battens and scratching the trestles. Bore pilot holes for the screws in the underside of the table top and screw the battens in place.

Making the trestles
The first stage in construction is to make an I-shaped upright for each trestle. Begin by marking and cutting out the ends of the two $2 \times 2 \times 24\frac{1}{2}$in rails which make the top and base of each I. This job can be done on a bandsaw or with a saber saw (jigsaw) or coping saw. A half-round file followed by sandpaper can be used to smooth the shaped ends.

Mark and cut a $\frac{3}{4} \times 4\frac{3}{4}$in mortise through the center of all four rails with an electric mortiser or, in the traditional way, drill out most of the waste wood and clean out the corners with a chisel. A stand helps keep the drill at right angles to the work.

Cut the two $2 \times 5\frac{1}{2}$in uprights 28in long, and mark and cut matching tenons at each end of the uprights, with shoulders all round to improve stability. Careful marking is important, but cutting the tenon is a simple job involving eight straight saw cuts. The I sections are then coated in adhesive and clamped together until the adhesive is completely dry.

In making designs from furniture in paintings – or indeed from scratch – one crucial measurement usually

The Flemish artist Robert Campin (1378/9-1444) was among the first and most influential painters of furnished interiors. A rustic variation on the table design seen here in The Annunciation appears in Bruegel's Peasant Dance (c. 1565). Central panel of the Merode Altarpiece; Metropolitan Museum of Art, New York, The Cloisters Collection, Purchase

sets the scale. For example, the height of a chair (15-18in) or a table (25-30in) is only narrowly variable. The other dimensions of the piece will follow from them if the proportions are fixed. In this case the table height was decided first. The proportions of the table in the painting then gave the length of the top and the distance between the trestles. This was fixed at 47½in.

The distance between stay and I section, measured from a tracing of the painting, provided the information needed to draw up the triangle formed by the I, the stay and the floor. This in turn gave the measurement along the floor from the inside of the stay to the inside of the I – 10in.

Set the bottom of the stay 10in from the base of the I and as near the floor as possible mark off on its side a line parallel to the floor. Cut along this line so the stay will sit flat on the floor. A line marked where the leaning stay crosses the upright gives the base line of the shouldered tenon which joins the two pieces at the apex of the triangle.

Use an adjustable bevel to mark the side of the stay where it meets the I. A tenon is marked and cut out with a ¼in shoulder all around (see drawing). A corresponding mortise is drilled in each I section. Take care not to cut right through. The joint can be reinforced with dowels (see drawing on p. 71). The strut is not glued in

place at this stage, as the short horizontal stretcher has to be installed first.

The position of the small stretcher is worked out by drawing on a scaled tracing or photocopy of the painting, continuing the line of the angled strut under the tablecloth to a point where it meets the upright and then measuring how far up the trestle the stretcher is.

Assemble the I sections and leaning struts without glue. Place a rule between them where the stretcher would be and mark with a pencil where the stretcher will enter. These marks give guidelines for drilling the mortises. Keeping the rule at right angles to the upright, measure the precise length of the stretcher across the gap, both top and bottom. Dismantle the sloping arm and place it on the workbench, propped up with a block of wood under one end so that you can drill down vertically into it to cut the ¾ × 1½in mortise, 1in deep. The piece could be held at the correct angle in a vise. Cut a similar mortise in each upright. Mark out and cut the stretcher, allowing for the 1in tenon at each end. At this point the trestles are glued and clamped together.

Finishing the table
The surface is sanded down by hand, working down from a coarse grade of sandpaper to fine. It is then polished with beeswax.

69

DIMENSIONS

Views of the trestle (a) from end and (b) from side.
The dotted lines represent tenons

MATERIALS

	No.	Size (ins)
Table top		
Oak for:		
Top boards	8	1 × 3½ × 59¼
End rails	2	1 × 3 × 25½
Battens	2	¾ × 2 × 19¾
Battens	4	¾ × 2 × 9
¼ dia dowels	21	2
The trestles		
Oak for:		
Uprights	2	2 × 5½ × 28
Horizontal rails	4	2 × 2 × 24½
Leaning stays	2	1½ × 2 × 31
Stretchers	2	1½ × 1½ × 7½
¼ dia dowels	4	2

Dome head screws
Woodworking adhesive

The table top from below and from the end

ORDER OF WORK

The table top

1 Cut the seven top boards to length and plane the edges
2 Drill the dowel locating holes in the board edges
3 Glue, assemble and clamp the top
4 Plane the joints between boards flat
5 Cut a tongue at each end of the top panel
6 Cut a matching groove in the inside edge of the end rails
7 Glue and clamp the end rails in position
8 Chamfer the top's edges with a plane
9 Make screw slots in the battens locating the trestles
10 Screw the battens to the underside of the top

The trestles

1 Mark and cut to shape the trestles' horizontal top and base rails
2 Mark and cut mortises in the rails for the uprights

3 Mark and cut matching shouldered tenons on the uprights
4 Glue and clamp uprights and rails together
5 Mark and cut the angle on the base of the leaning stays so they rest flat on the floor
6 Mark the stays where they cross the uprights at an angle
7 Mark and cut the shouldered tenon on the leaning stays
8 Cut a corresponding mortise in the I sections
9 Assemble the I sections and leaning stays without glue, and mark out the mortise positions for the short stretchers
10 Drill mortises in the uprights and leaning stays
11 Cut the horizontal stretchers to length, with a tenon at each end
12 Glue and clamp the trestles together

Finish

Sand the table and apply a coat of beeswax

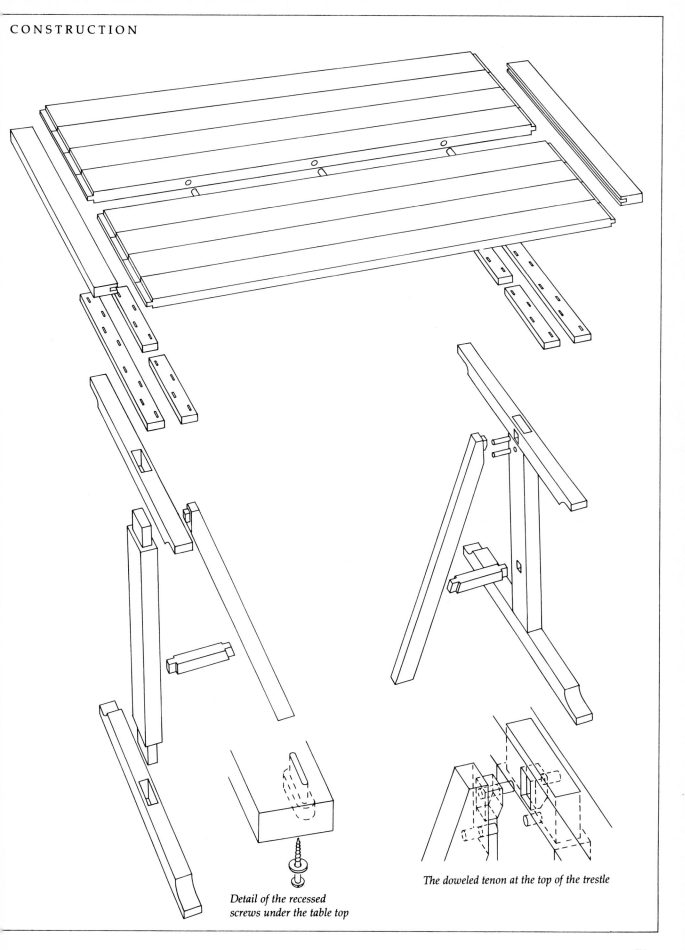

Detail of the recessed
screws under the table top

The doweled tenon at the top of the trestle

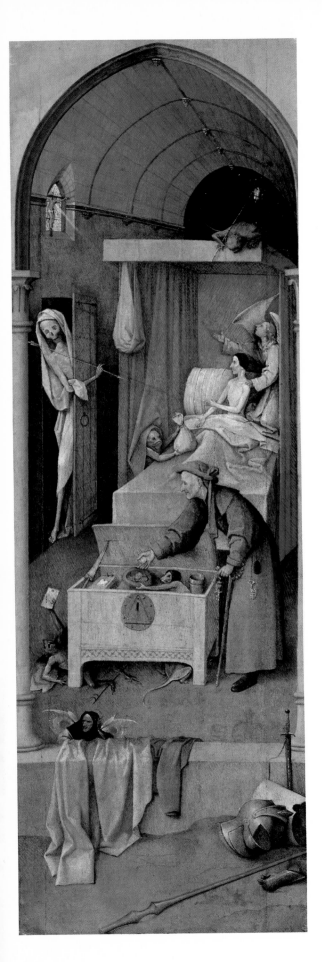

The Miser's Chest
by Nicholas Partridge from *Death and the Miser*
by Hieronymus Bosch (*c.* 1450-1516)
National Gallery of Art, Washington;
Samuel H. Kress Collection

Bosch lived, worked and died in 's Hertogenbosch, dominated by the dread of damnation. As a fifteenth-century Christian, he held grim views about life on earth. He believed the devil and his demonic aides ran the world, and few humans would be saved.

Bosch is best known for his monstrous visions of Hell in all its eternal unpleasantness. In our painting a dying miser hovers on the edge of the abyss, and Jesus appears to have lost again. The picture shows the skeletal figure of Death entering the moribund miser's room, a lethal arrow in his hand. A devil carrying hellfire crawls overhead, and an ugly demon appears from under the curtain to offer a bag of money. An angel fights back, turning the miser's attention to the tiny figure of Christ shining in the window.

The chest, with its complement of demons, stands as a symbol of avarice at the foot of the bed – the favorite position for chests throughout the Middle Ages. The cloth draped over the foreground could be a reference to the story of St. Martin, the kind knight who gave half his coat to a cold beggar and who represents Generosity.

A secure chest was an important item of furniture in the Middle Ages. Chests were built to last, and many have in fact survived centuries of use. There were two basic types. The first was made for traveling, with a flat bottom and a domed top that would throw off the rain when the seigneurial household undertook one of its frequent moves from manor to manor. This dome unfortunately made such chests unsuitable for use as tables or seats. The second type was designed for domestic use, with a flat lid and feet to raise the base off damp floors.

Designing the miser's chest
A security-conscious medieval miser might have owned a chest made entirely of iron, a few of which survive. The best wooden chests were made of oak at the time, but

73

poplar and pine were also common. Nicholas Partridge chose beech, which matches the flat color of the chest in the painting.

He bought 1in-thick kiln-dried beech planks and planed them smooth and square. Ready-planed timber would be equally suitable. One of the planks he selected had a dark streak matching the scar made by the blade propping up the lid in the painting. For the legs he used a slightly darker $2\frac{1}{4} \times 2\frac{1}{4}$in beech, which he planed down to the desired dimension.

Doweled joints were reserved for rustic chests in the Middle Ages. The better chests employed mortise and tenon joints. The designer therefore based his construction on the mortise and tenon. Tenons in the side panels are housed in mortises cut in the four legs, and tenons in the top boards are set in mortises in the lid's end rails. With the exception of the carved lower boards, the joints on all the boards are identical, and time can be saved by cutting them all at the same time with a power saw.

Accurate marking and cutting of the mortises and tenons is the key to satisfactory construction. The boards themselves are not joined to each other at all.

The dimensions we give are those of the chest the designer made. The length of the boards can be altered – to create a longer chest, for example – without in any way affecting the dimensions of the joints or the method of construction.

Making the chest

Mark and cut all the boards precisely to length, allowing for the tenons at both ends. Check that the ends are perfectly square.

There are double shoulders and double tenons at the end of all the boards except the 4in-wide carved boards along the bottom of the chest; these have only a single tenon. All the tenons are $\frac{3}{8}$in wide and shouldered all round as shown in the drawing.

To make the tenons, begin by marking and cutting the shoulder running all around the boards at each end. The designer used a cutting gauge to mark the cutting lines.

Note that the two boards on the top of the chest are 1in wider than the others, but the tenons on all boards (top, front, sides and back) are identical. To accommodate this difference, the central gap between the tenons on the top planks is 1in wider than on the rest.

Cutting can be done with a handsaw, but a circular saw will save hours. Once the saw is set, the same cut can be repeated on every board without altering the position of the saw blade. A fence on the saw table will keep the boards at right angles to the blade as you push them through. The typical low fence on a bench saw will be insufficient when the boards are stood on end to cut the

tenon. It can be built up by attaching a vertical board to the fence to act as a guide.

When the shoulder is cut, use the same method to mark and saw out the block shape from which the double tenon will be formed, and make the two saw cuts which define the inside faces of the tenons. Clean out the waste wood between the two tenons with a chisel.

Cut the four legs to length and plane them to the $1\frac{3}{4} \times 2\frac{1}{4}$in section. Mark out the mortise positions using a cutting gauge and try square. Note that these mortises are not cut down the center of the legs but are positioned so that the boards will be inset $\frac{1}{8}$in from the outer faces of the legs. If the boards are set flush with the front face of the legs, problems can occur later when the wood starts to move with changes in the environment. Because of the $\frac{1}{8}$in shoulder, differential movement will not cause ugly gaps to open.

Cutting such complex mortises by hand is a long and laborious process. Machine tools once again speed the work up considerably. The designer used a mortising attachment on a power drill. A standard wood bit on the drill, or a brace and bit, can be used to chop out the meat of the mortise, with a chisel to tidy up the edges.

First chop out the two deeper parts of the mortises, making sure the drill enters the leg at right angles. Now cut the shallow central parts of the mortises. These could be routed out to save time or cut out with a chisel.

Assemble the legs and panels without glue to check the fit, and make any necessary adjustments.

Now make the lid. First mark out and cut the mortises in the two end rails, and check them for fit. Any slight ridges where the boards meet are planed away. When the fit is satisfactory, glue the tenons and assemble the lid. Hold the work together with a pair of strap clamps (sash cramps) until the glue sets.

The carving
The lower edge of the bottom boards on all four sides is shaped as in the painting. Cut it to the shape in the drawing, using a bandsaw or coping saw. Plane the cut edge smooth.

A 13th-century English chest with chip carved decoration

The carving, which is well within the reach of the beginner, is done before the chest is assembled. The V-shaped horizontal grooves are cut with a pointed scraper, a simple and useful home-made tool (see drawing). To form the tool's cutting edge the tip of an old hacksaw blade is ground down to a V shape. The blade is clamped between two blocks of wood and can be set to cut at any depth and at any distance from the edge of the wood.

Cut the horizontal grooves and draw the pattern between them with a pencil. The carving is done with a ¾in chisel. First chop vertically down the lines and then cut in at an angle from either side.

Assembling the chest

Before assembling the chest, plane a slight chamfer on all four edges of every board. This chamfer reproduces the lines on the painting where boards meet; moreover, it prevents the slight gaps which may open between boards becoming unsightly. Chamfer the top edges of the legs in a similar way.

Using the scraper, score the decorative groove on the lower boards ½in above the top of the chamfer where they meet the carved boards.

The chest can now be glued together. Clamp it tightly until the glue sets, using waste wood to prevent the clamps damaging the surface.

The two ¾in-thick base boards are loose-laid on ¾ × ¾in battens at each side of the chest. The boards do not fit tightly against each other, to allow for future expansion. One board is 8¾in wide, the other 5½in. Before fitting the battens, drill two countersunk clearance holes through them to take the screws which fix them to the chest sides, and bore corresponding pilot holes in the side boards. Glue and screw the battens in position. Cut notches in the outer corners of the two boards so they will fit around the legs, and drop the boards onto the battens.

The shelf in Nicholas Partridge's piece is an optional extra. It is cut from a 1in × 4¼in × 14½in beech board, with a 1 × 1⅜in notch sawn out of each corner to allow the shelf to fit around the legs. The two shallow depressions were cut out with a router. An alternative approach is to glue strips of ⅜ × ⅜in molding onto a flat shelf ½in thick.

The shelf sits on 3in-long battens at each end. These are fitted to the side by two countersunk screws driven through clearance holes in the battens into the chest. The shelf is located by a ¼in-diameter dowel 1in long glued in the underside of the shelf at each end. Drill a ¼in-diameter hole ½in deep in the base of the shelf in the position shown in the drawing (p. 76). Glue the

The chest occupies its normal medieval position at the foot of the bed in Jan van Eyck's Birth of St. John the Baptist *(c. 1415) from "The Milan Hours". The stools are similar to Bruegel's (p. 98). Museo Civico di Torino*

dowels in position. File out depressions in the edge of the battens to house the dowels.

The lid is propped up by a ½ × ½in piece of beech 18in long. At one end it is planed and sanded down, tapering to ¼in square at the tip. A shallow indentation is countersunk in the top to take the tip.

Hinging the top

A pair of 2½in cast-iron hinges attaches the lid to the chest. The hinges are ⅛in thick. Housings ⅛ × 2½in are therefore chiseled into the top edge of the chest and the inside face of the lid. The hinges are held by ¾in screws.

The lockplate

The designer turned the lockplate into a purely decorative feature. He cut a triangle out of a sheet of lead and pressed a disc of the same sheet lead over this until the outline of the triangle became visible. Lead is soft and easy to work, but care must be taken not to scratch or cut it. The plate is fixed to the chest by ¾in tacks. The nails shown on the painting are reproduced by punching the impression of a nail head into the lead.

Finishing the chest

The finish is simple. The chest is sanded smooth and given a single application of beeswax.

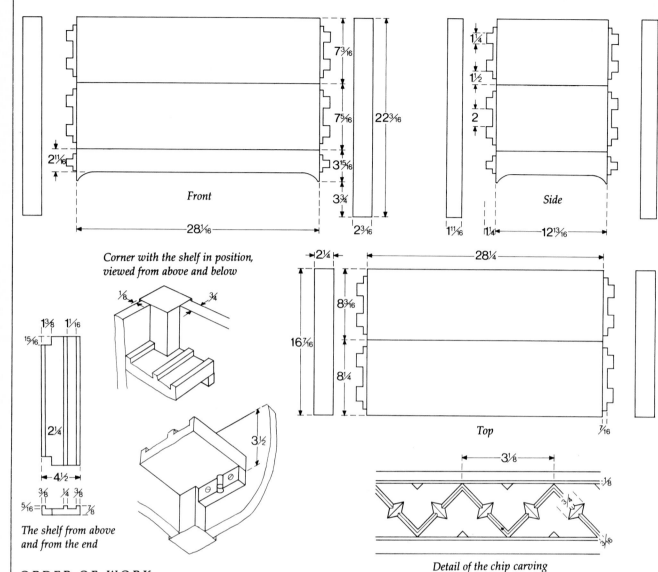

Corner with the shelf in position,
viewed from above and below

Front

Side

Top

The shelf from above
and from the end

Detail of the chip carving

ORDER OF WORK

1 Cut all the boards to length
2 Mark out and cut the tenons on all boards
3 Plane the four legs and cut them to length
4 Mark and cut the mortises in the legs
5 Assemble the legs and sides without glue to check the fit
6 Mark and cut mortises in the lid's two end rails
7 Assemble the lid without glue, and plane away ridges where boards meet
8 Glue and assemble the lid
9 Cut the lower edge of the bottom boards to shape
10 Cut the horizontal grooves with a pointed scraper
11 Pencil in the pattern between the grooves
12 Chisel out the pattern.
13 Chamfer all the long edges of every board and the top of the legs
14 Score a horizontal groove in the lower boards

15 Glue and clamp the chest together
16 Fix two battens inside the chest to support the base
17 Notch the base boards to fit around the legs
18 Drop the base boards onto the battens
19 Cut the shelf to size and shape
20 Fit the dowels in the shelf base
21 Fit the shelf's two supporting battens
22 File depressions in the battens to locate the dowels
23 Drop the shelf into position
24 Cut and shape the shelf prop
25 Bore a shallow indentation in the underside of the lid
26 Attach the hinges
27 Cut out the triangle and disc of sheet lead
28 Press them together
29 Fix the lockplate to the front of the chest
30 Sand the entire piece and apply a coat of beeswax

MATERIALS

	No.	Size (ins)
Beech for:		
Front and back panels	4	1 × 7½ × 30
Carved panels	2	1 × 4 × 30
Side panels	4	1 × 7½ × 14¾
Carved panels	2	1 × 4 × 14¾
Top panels	2	1 × 8½ × 30¼
End rails	2	1 × 2¼ × 16⁷/₁₆
Legs	4	1¼ × 2¼ × 22³/₁₆
Battens	2	¾ × ¾ × 12¾
Base panel	1	¾ × 8¾ × 30⅝
Base panel	1	¾ × 5½ × 30⅝
Shelf	1	1 × 4¼ × 14½

	No.	Size (ins)
Battens	2	½ × ½ × 3
Prop	1	½ × ½ × 18
Hardwood dowels	2	1 × ¼ dia
2½ in cast iron hinges	2	
Sheet lead triangle	1	7⅛ × 7⅛
Sheet lead	1	8¾ dia

¾in tacks; Screws; PVA woodworking adhesive

FINISH

Beeswax

CONSTRUCTION

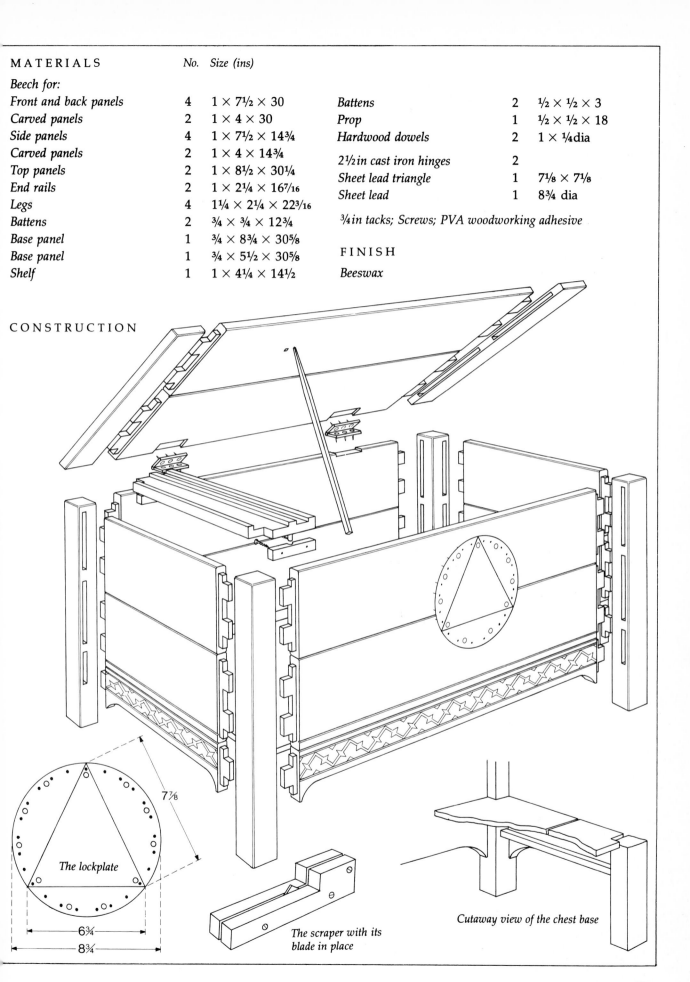

7⅞

The lockplate

6¾

8¾

The scraper with its blade in place

Cutaway view of the chest base

The Humanoid Table

by Patrick Daw

from *Difficult Crossing* (1926) by René Magritte (1889-1967)

Private Collection

Magritte's table is a surreal contribution to the old and odd tradition of humanoid furniture, which historians have traced back to ancient Egypt. It reached strange extremes in eighteenth-century France, where the notorious Marquis de Sade wrote of an unsavory dinner in the dreadful Minski's castle, at which the guests sat on seats formed by live slaves. Less sadistic Frenchmen meanwhile delighted in human shapes on the legs of their Empire furniture.

The idea appeals strongly to the surrealist imagination. Chairs – like people – have legs, arms, backs and seats: the surrealists revelled in confusing the two. Kurt Seligmann, for example, made a grotesque *Ultrameuble* (p. 80) that used the stockinged legs of store mannequins to support its seat. Salvador Dali created his famous sofa in the shape of Mae West's lips, upholstered aptly in Schiaparelli's shocking pink (p. 9), and constructed a flippant *Venus de Milo of Drawers*.

Furniture features throughout Magritte's work. There are white chairs in flames and cupboards no larger than combs. He cast a bronze version of Madame Récamier's daybed complete with reclining coffin and drew a table with a burning candle acting as a highly destabilizing leg (p. 81).

Designing the humanoid table

The problem of deciding the table's dimensions was complicated by the predictable absence of sensible reference points in Magritte's surreal painting. Patrick Daw based his calculations on the table's "human" leg, which soon became known as the "leg-leg." This, he thought, must be more or less life size. A child's leg would give a table height of some 28 inches, a suitable height for a useful dinner table. The painting's bizarre perspective makes almost any length justifiable, but after mounting sheets of various sizes 28in from the floor, the designer decided that a top 36 × 47in would be both functional and faithful.

"Human" legs support the seat of Kurt Seligmann's surreal Ultrameuble, *made about 1938. Seligmann used the disembodied legs of mannequins, dressed in white stockings.* Ultrameuble *is now lost*

The stability of the legs is a problem. They are slender, and fixed very close to the corners of the table. He wanted to avoid expensive custom-made metal fittings. He overcame the difficulty by mortising the three 1¾ in diameter wooden legs in a plywood top; the socket holes are hidden under the stainless steel sheet which forms the table top.

The designer considered a variety of materials for the table top. The piece could be given the uniform look of Magritte's painting by making the table in wood and finally covering every surface in paint. Matte white and aluminium paint were considered. However, he wanted a cold unyielding surface true to the feel of Magritte's painting. Wood could never achieve this. Anodized aluminium – etched in acid and dyed – would reproduce the texture, but the material's poor resistance to scratches argued against it. He thought of plain aluminum – sandblasted or buffed with a power drill and flapwheel – but once again the liability to dents and scratches led him to reject it. Plate glass was ruled out as over-expensive. He settled on a sheet of tough, cold stainless steel glued to a plywood base.

Carving the leg-leg

In spite of its eccentricity, the table is simple to make. No unusual tools are required, and there are no difficult joints – the entire piece is held together by glue and screws.

To begin with the toughest part, first carve the leg-leg. The leg is carved from a 26¼ in-long plank of 6 × 8in pine. This can be built up by gluing smaller blocks together. The method of carving recalls the technique of ancient Egyptian and Greek sculptors. They would draw the outlines of the figure on the front and sides of a rectangular block of marble and chip away until the figure emerged. The Magritte leg's front and side profiles are given on p. 82 – they could of course be replaced by shapes taken from photographs of a favorite leg or indeed from a living model.

Draw the profiles on the front and sides of the plank. A grid of 1in squares can simplify plotting the lines.

Rough carving can be done with a saber saw (jigsaw) or bowsaw. Keeping the saw at right angles to the plank, carve the profiles out across all four sides of the plank. This creates a leg of rectangular section, closer to cubism than the surreal. The next step is to round off the four square corners, which can be done with an assortment of rasps, grinders or gouges and mallets. Go slowly, taking care not to pare away too much wood. Toes and knee must be judged by eye, although frequent pencil marks help. As the Magritte leg is not photographically precise, unskilled carving need not spoil the piece. This makes the leg-leg an excellent beginner's piece.

Final finish is provided by abrasive tools, going down from rough to smooth, from rasp to fine sandpaper.

Making the table

The table top is a sheet of 16-gauge stainless steel glued to a plywood base. Local availability dictated the choice of 16-gauge; a thinner 20- or 22-gauge would be lighter and easier to handle.

It is crucial to choose plywood with care, avoiding warped sheets, as the board must provide an absolutely flat surface for the steel. Start by cutting the plywood sheet to the size of the finished table minus ¼ in on each side.

Cut out the three 6 × 6in plates of ¾ in thick plywood into which the three "normal" legs will be set, and the larger 9 × 9in plate for the leg-leg. Glue and screw them to the corners of the plywood sheet, making sure the leg-leg will be in the right corner when the table is upright. Use three screws in each 6 × 6in plate, driving one into each corner except the outside one. The leg-leg's plate has four screws. Clamp the plates in place until the glue sets.

Use a hole borer to drill 1¾ in-diameter holes – ¼ in

A burning candle provides an unnervingly unstable leg for the table in Magritte's drawing. Galerie Isy Brachot, Brussels – Paris

less in diameter than the legs – through both layers of plywood in the three corners for the normal legs. Keep the holes very close to the edge, about ⅛in in.

The three normal legs are cut to length and shouldered at the top to fit into their sockets. To do this, mark a line around the leg 1½in from the top. Place the leg in a bench hook and saw a ⅛in deep groove into the line with a tenon saw, turning the leg as you cut. Hold the leg in a vise and chisel down to the groove. Smooth off with sandpaper.

When the legs fit snugly in their sockets, check that they stand at right angles to the table top and glue them in position.

To reinforce the fixing of the three cylindrical legs, Patrick Daw drilled a 3in-deep horizontal pilot hole through the center of the leg, drilling between the two layers of plywood from the outside corner. The holes were counterbored ½in and a 3in number 10 wood-screw was driven into each hole.

The leg-leg is fixed in position by three countersunk wood-screws driven through the top of the table down into the leg. Before driving the screws, drill pilot holes for the screws in the leg and clearance holes in the top.

A 2in-wide strip of ¾in plywood is glued on the underside of the table, flush with the edges, to fill the gaps between the plates. Clamp the strips in position until dry.

A strip of ¼ × 1½in battening is glued and nailed around the table edge, using ¾in finishing nails (panel pins) at 4in intervals. The corners are mitered. This edging covers the screw holes in the corners and the joints between the two layers of plywood.

The stainless steel top is now glued onto the plywood. Stainless steel is normally sold with a shiny surface. Abrade the underside using coarse sandpaper to provide

a grip for the adhesive, and clean away all traces of dust. Make sure the surface of the plywood is completely free from dust and grit and that the table legs are not protruding above the surface. If they are, plane them flat. Apply contact adhesive to both surfaces. Leave for 20 minutes (consult the manufacturer's instructions for precise timing). Lay the top very carefully in place. It is absolutely vital to get the position right the first time, as repositioning is all but impossible. It may be wise to try a few dry runs without adhesive first. Guide blocks can be tacked to the table side before the gluing.

The stainless steel sheet was cut approximately ⅟₃₂in larger than the plywood sheet all round to allow for slight errors in laying. When the steel is in place, file down any overlapping edges.

Finishing the table

To create an interesting matt finish on the shiny surface, finish it with a flapwheel attached to an electric drill, running the wheel in one direction only. Wear goggles and a face mask during this operation to prevent metal dust getting in eyes or lungs.

Finally paint the wooden parts of the table, using an acrylic primer/undercoat topped with two coats of aluminum paint.

French Empire furniture could be as anatomically odd as anything invented by the surrealists. This semicircular mahogany console table by Jacob Frères of Paris stands in the study at the Chateau de Fontainebleau

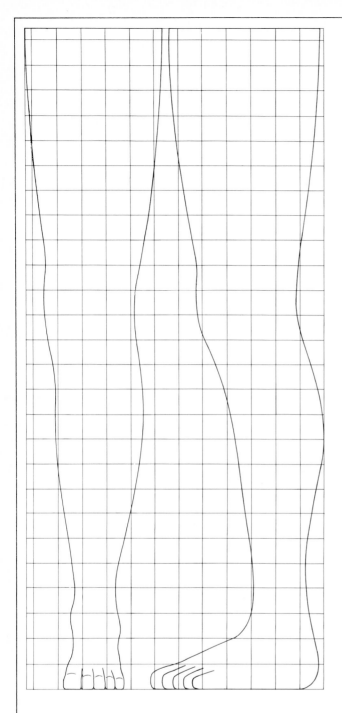

ORDER OF WORK

1 Draw the front and side profiles of the "leg-leg" on the block to be carved
2 Saw out the profiles on all four sides
3 Carve the leg to shape
4 Mark and cut out the plywood top
5 Cut out the four plywood corner plates
6 Glue and screw the corner plates in position
7 Drill sockets through top and corner plates for the 3 normal legs
8 Mark and cut shoulders on the top 1½in of the 3 legs
9 Glue the 3 normal legs in their sockets
10 Drill and counterbore holes through the legs in the joint between the 2 layers of plywood
11 Drive a screw into each hole to reinforce the leg
12 Drill clearance holes through the top for the 3 screws holding the leg-leg
13 Drive screws through the top into pilot holes in the top of the leg
14 Cut ¾ × 2in strips to fit between the corner plates
15 Glue these strips in place and clamp until dry
16 Cut 4 strips of ¼ × 1½in edging with mitered corners to fit around the table top
17 Glue and nail this edging in position
18 Abrade the under surface of the stainless steel top
19 Clean the plywood top
20 Glue the stainless steel in position
21 File down any overlapping edges
22 Abrade the steel surface with a flap wheel
23 Paint the wooden parts of the table with acrylic undercoat
24 Paint on two coats of aluminum paint

Front and side profiles of the leg-leg.
Each square represents 1sq in

DIMENSIONS

The table from below and from the side

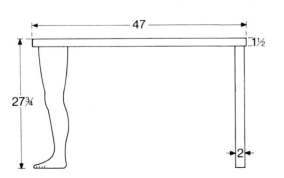

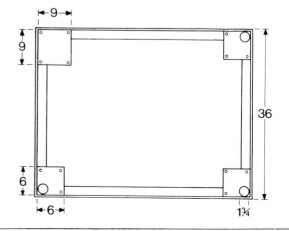

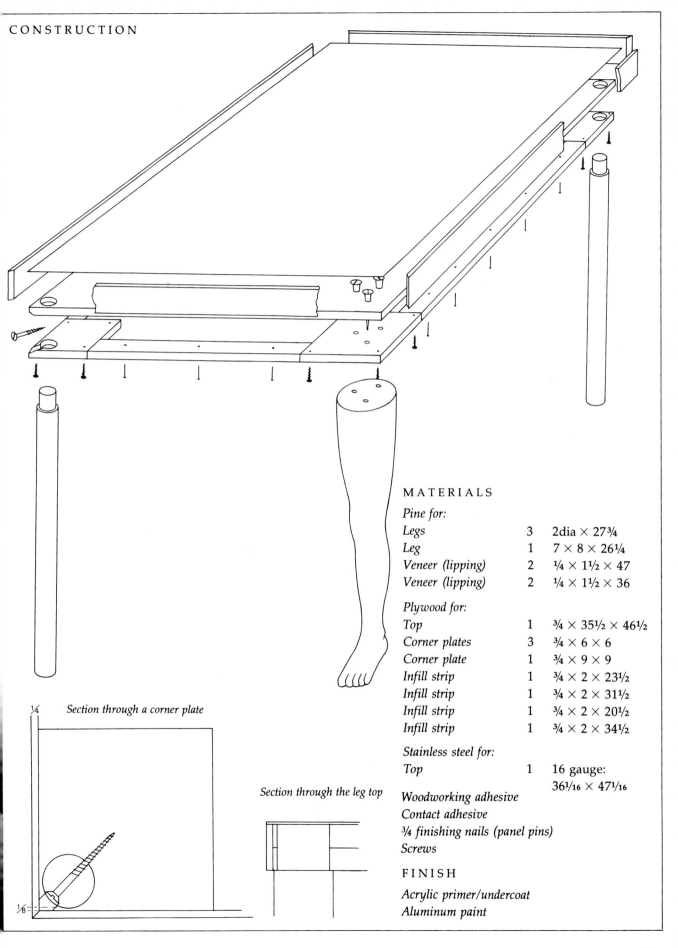

Section through a corner plate

Section through the leg top

MATERIALS

Pine for:

Legs	3	2dia × 27¾
Leg	1	7 × 8 × 26¼
Veneer (lipping)	2	¼ × 1½ × 47
Veneer (lipping)	2	¼ × 1½ × 36

Plywood for:

Top	1	¾ × 35½ × 46½
Corner plates	3	¾ × 6 × 6
Corner plate	1	¾ × 9 × 9
Infill strip	1	¾ × 2 × 23½
Infill strip	1	¾ × 2 × 31½
Infill strip	1	¾ × 2 × 20½
Infill strip	1	¾ × 2 × 34½

Stainless steel for:

Top	1	16 gauge: 36¹⁄₁₆ × 47¹⁄₁₆

Woodworking adhesive
Contact adhesive
¾ finishing nails (panel pins)
Screws

FINISH

Acrylic primer/undercoat
Aluminum paint

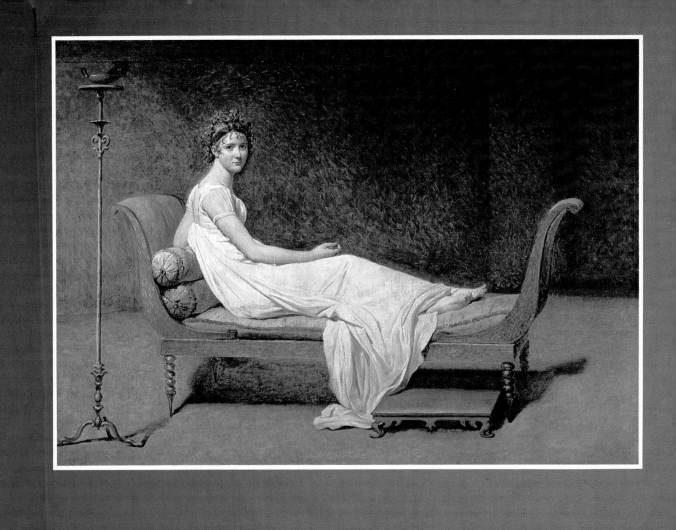

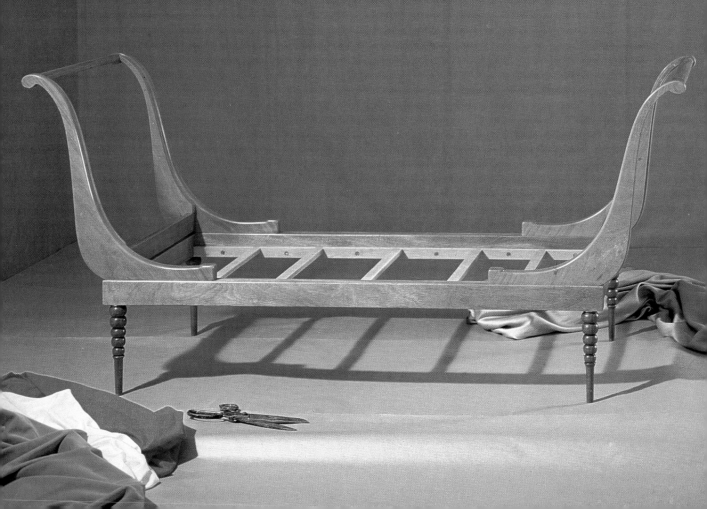

Madame Récamier's Bed

by Tim Rickard

from *Madame Récamier* (1802) by Jacques Louis David (1748-1825)

The Louvre, Paris

Madame Récamier was a main attraction in post-revolutionary Paris. She was a leader of fashion who led a life dotted with political and amorous dramas. She was loathed by Napoleon and loved by the artists and aristocrats of France. Even a plaster image of the enticing Récamier could rouse a Frenchman's passion; her cousin Brillat-Savarin, gourmet author of *Gastronomy as a Fine Art,* owned such a bust and found himself obliged to box an over-excited dinner guest's ears for kissing "that lovely bosom."

Paris was the center of European furniture making at the end of the eighteenth century. Admiration for classical Rome was rising; Napoleon's new Empire was on the horizon. Napoleon and Josephine were enthusiastic promoters of the classical revival in furnishing, but the center of the classical cult in fashionable Paris was Madame Récamier's bedroom.

Her famous bedroom furniture was designed in 1798 by Louis Martin Berthault and made by Jacob Frères, the most prestigious firm of the age. The centerpiece was a boat-shaped mahogany bed adorned with gilded swans. Its fame soon spread through Europe, until a glimpse of the bed became an essential part of any fashion-conscious tourist's trip to Paris.

The day bed, or *méridienne,* in David's painting did not belong to Madame Récamier, though she had a strikingly similar one made by Jacob Frères. The simple piece in the painting was the artist's own, part of the studio furniture made for him by the ubiquitous Jacob brothers. Furniture design was David's second talent; he designed furniture for Napoleon and had a large influence on the French Empire style.

The painting is unfinished. David abandoned it in self-righteous pique when Madame Récamier, twenty-three years old at the time, failed to turn up for regular sittings and commissioned a portrait from a rival artist.

The picture shows a barefoot Juliette Récamier reclining like a figure from an Etruscan vase. She is dressed in one of the simple, flowing, white dresses she made fashionable.

Simplicity is the keynote of the piece. The background is plain, the colors muted, and Madame wears no jewellery. Outside David's studio she is known to have favored pearls. She never wore diamonds, unlike the dazzling heroine of Anita Loos's *Gentlemen Prefer Blondes*, who reports that one of her wealthy admirers found she reminded him of "a girl called Madame Récamier who all the intelectual (sic) gentlemen use (sic) to tell all of their plans to, even when there was a French revolution going on all around them." If not academically exact, it gives a fair idea of the impact of Juliette Récamier on her time.

Designing Madame Récamier's bed
The design of the day bed is simple, but care and skill are demanded if the elegance of the original is to be matched.

Tim Rickard decided to make the piece from mahogany, the wood favored by Madame Récamier and the Jacob brothers before a Napoleonic decree of 1806 banned its import. As in Madame Récamier's original, the two ends are of equal height. Dimensions were based on those of the average modern woman, and were confirmed by reference to eighteenth-century precedents. The depth allows two people to sit comfortably side by side, or one person to lie down à la Récamier.

The legs taper as in the painting – and on Madame Récamier's own *méridienne* – but for practical reasons they are made less stiletto-like at the tip. Their strength was the most worrying feature for the designer. He considered setting a chock inside each corner and fixing the leg to this, but the positioning of the legs in the outside corner is one of the most distinctive features of the original, a feature he was anxious to retain. The problem was overcome simply and elegantly.

Making the day bed

The two dozen pieces which make up the piece were mainly cut, shaped, joined and finished with hand tools. A saber saw (jigsaw) was used to cut the curved uprights roughly to shape. The legs must be turned on a lathe, and a drill press was used to bore the holes in the frame which take them. Both these jobs can be given to a wood turner if you have no lathe.

The day bed is made of mahogany, but other hardwoods, for example beech, would be suitable. Strength and availability are the main criteria. Each of the four curved ends is cut from a single plank 2in thick and about 33in long and 14in wide. The line of the grain must be chosen with care. The curve of the "neck" at the

top will be too fragile unless the grain of the wood runs along its length. This means that the squarish projection at the base of the curve will have the grain of the wood crossing it diagonally. This part will have to be very carefully worked if it is not to split off during planing.

The four frame rails were cut from 2×3in mahogany and the legs turned from 2×2in pieces. The rails running between each pair of end uprights are also mahogany. The formers inside the curve of the uprights, which will be hidden by the upholstery, are beech. The battens and slats supporting the cushion are of oak.

First cut the frame's side and end rails to length and plane them square. A chamfer is planed along every edge and on the ends of the side rails. The designer felt sharp corners would be wrong – this is a delicate piece requiring soft edges. A chisel and block plane can be used to chamfer the end grain.

The frame members are joined by double mortises and tenons. The designer thought one large single tenon would involve the removal of too much wood in the mortise, seriously weakening the corners. Mark and cut the 1¼in long tenons in the end rails of the frame using a tenon saw and chisel. The double mortises in the side rails are marked out and cut to match. The designer cut these entirely with a mortise chisel – time could be saved by drilling out most of the material and cleaning the edges with a chisel. Check that they fit.

Cut the four curved uprights. The precise curves are shown on the drawing on p. 89. To transfer the shape to the workpiece, draw up the one-inch grid full scale on a piece of thin plywood or heavy card. Plot the outline of the end upright on this grid and make a template by cutting out the shape carefully with a saber saw or knife. Use this template to mark all four ends on the mahogany plank. The grain should follow the line shown in the drawing as closely as possible.

First cut the straight lines along the base and outer sides of the tenons with a tenon saw. Next cut the rough shape of the curves with a saber saw or bandsaw. It is difficult to cut a clean line with the saber saw through a 2in plank, so leave a safe margin outside the cutting line of about ¼in. Leave a substantial square block projecting at the lower end and around the top scroll to prevent damage at these delicate points when they are held against a bench stop during planing. Do not attempt to shape the knobs on the lower end of the curve at this stage – keep the cutting line outside. The final shaping of the curves and knobs will be done with a spokeshave and chisel, using the template to check progress.

Plane the outer and inner faces of the four uprights smooth. They are thinner in section at the top than the base, reducing from 1⅜in at the base to 1⅛in at the top.

Through paintings such as The Lictors bringing Brutus the Bodies of his Sons *David led the French Empire revival in simple classically-based furniture. Louvre, Paris*

To simplify upholstery, the wood is removed only from the outer face of each end piece; the pieces must therefore be labeled clearly for position (left and right, front and back) at this stage. When they are planed smooth and to the right thickness, the curves can be shaped precisely. Use a spokeshave to shape the main sweep of the end piece, cutting down to the profile, which has been redrawn on the planed outer and inner surfaces. The tight curves at the top, and the small square section projecting at the bottom, are cut with a chisel. All the exposed edges are chamfered.

With a tenon saw and chisel cut out the double tenons on the base of the uprights. Following a useful rule of thumb, the width of the tenons is one third that of the wood.

Having checked which end piece sits on which corner of the frame, mark and cut the mortises. Once again the designer used only a mortise chisel to cut these, but they could be drilled and chiseled out, or made with a mortiser on a drill press.

Mark out and cut the two smaller mortises on the inside face of all four end pieces to take the cross rails which span the space between them at the top and just above the bottom rail.

Assemble ends and frame without glue and cut the cross rails to length. This is done by measuring the actual span between the ends on the assembled piece rather than by relying on drawings. Allow ½in at each end for the tenons. At this stage the upper and lower cross rails are rectangular in section. Cut the ½in long tenons on their ends. Check that they fit.

The bottom cross rail remains rectangular and needs only to have its edges chamfered to create a smooth line for the upholstery material.

The top cross rail must be planed to an oval section, precisely following the curve of the scrolled top of the upright and cut slightly smaller. The shape can be penciled on the rail ends. Plane off the corners first and continue planing off all around until you have a regular oval.

ORDER OF WORK

1 Cut the frame's side and end rails to length
2 Plane them square
3 Chamfer the edges of all four rails and the ends of the two side rails
4 Mark and cut double tenons on the end rails
5 Mark and cut matching double mortises in the side rails
6 Make a template for the curved uprights
7 Mark and cut the four curved uprights roughly to shape
8 Plane the outer and inner faces of the uprights
9 Shape the curves precisely with spokeshave and chisel
10 Cut out the tenons
11 Mark out and cut the mortises for the cross rails in the uprights
11 Mark and cut the mortises for the uprights in the side rails
12 Mark out and cut the mortises for the cross rails in the uprights
13 Assemble without glue; measure and cut the cross rails
14 Cut the tenon at each end of the cross rails
15 Chamfer the edges of the lower cross rail
16 Plane the upper cross rail oval
17 With the frame assembled and clamped together, drill the sockets for the legs. (The legs themselves are turned on a lathe. The pattern was given to a wood turner)
18 Sand all pieces
19 Glue and clamp the frame and legs together
20 Glue and clamp the curved uprights and cross rails to the frame
21 Cut out the four curved formers
22 Screw the formers inside the curved uprights
23 Brush on a coat of sanding sealer and sand the piece smooth
24 Cut lap joints in the two battens supporting the slats
25 Screw the battens inside the side rails
26 Cut the slats to length and drop them in position
27 Finish with a mixture of beeswax and Carnauba wax

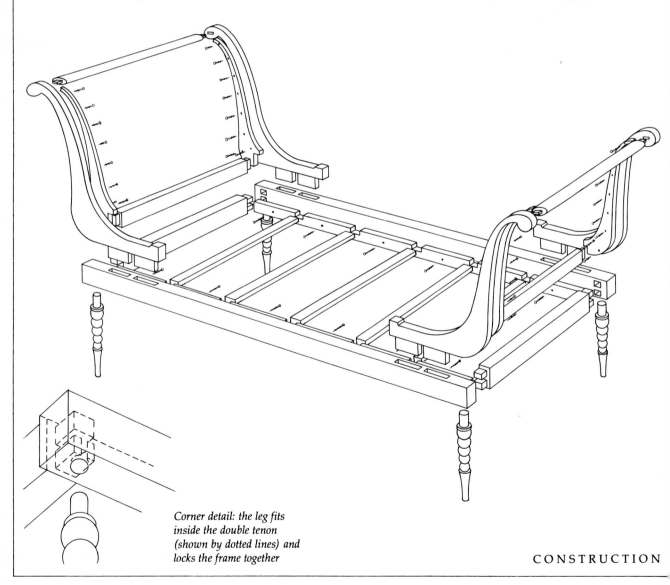

Corner detail: the leg fits inside the double tenon (shown by dotted lines) and locks the frame together

DIMENSIONS

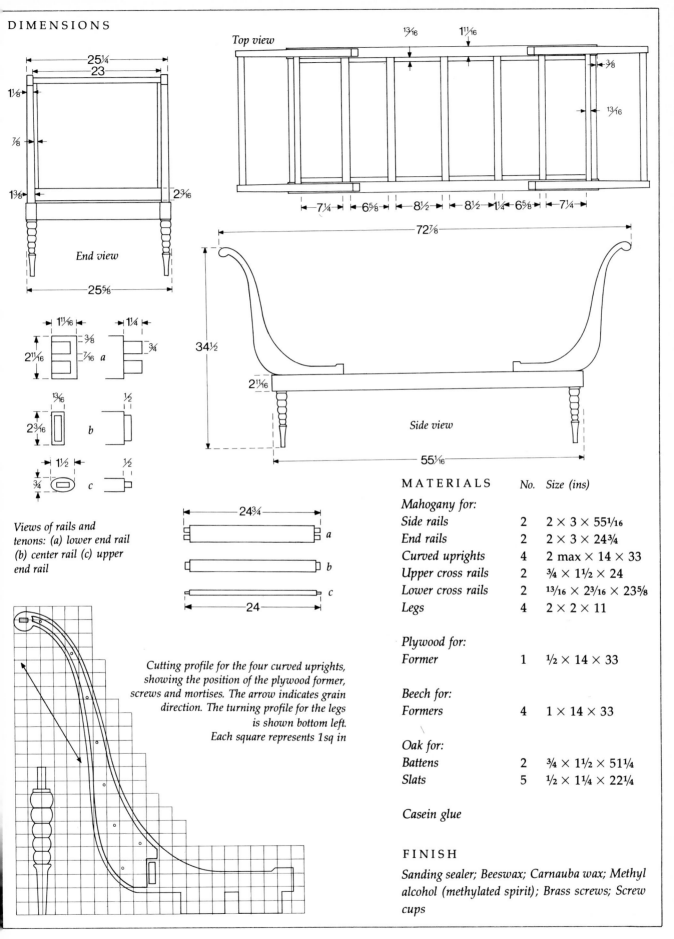

Top view

25¼
23
1⅛
⅞
1⅜
2³⁄₁₆

End view

25⅝

13⁄₁₆   1¹¹⁄₁₆
⅜
13⁄₁₆

7¼   6⅝   8½   8½   1¼   6⅝   7¼

72⅞

34½

2¹¹⁄₁₆

Side view

55¹⁄₁₆

1¹¹⁄₁₆   1¼
⅜   ¾
2¹¹⁄₁₆   *a*
7⁄₁₆

13⁄₁₆   ½
2³⁄₁₆   *b*

1½   ½
¾   *c*

Views of rails and
tenons: (a) lower end rail
(b) center rail (c) upper
end rail

24¾   *a*
b
24   *c*

Cutting profile for the four curved uprights,
showing the position of the plywood former,
screws and mortises. The arrow indicates grain
direction. The turning profile for the legs
is shown bottom left.
Each square represents 1sq in

MATERIALS	No.	Size (ins)
Mahogany for:		
Side rails	2	2 × 3 × 55¹⁄₁₆
End rails	2	2 × 3 × 24¾
Curved uprights	4	2 max × 14 × 33
Upper cross rails	2	¾ × 1½ × 24
Lower cross rails	2	13⁄₁₆ × 2³⁄₁₆ × 23⅝
Legs	4	2 × 2 × 11
Plywood for:		
Former	1	½ × 14 × 33
Beech for:		
Formers	4	1 × 14 × 33
Oak for:		
Battens	2	¾ × 1½ × 51¼
Slats	5	½ × 1¼ × 22¼

Casein glue

FINISH

Sanding sealer; Beeswax; Carnauba wax; Methyl
alcohol (methylated spirit); Brass screws; Screw
cups

The legs

The legs are turned on a lathe, and a professional wood turner will have to be employed if you have no lathe. The turner can also save you time by polishing the legs on the lathe, taking care not to allow polish to stray onto the parts to be glued. A turning pattern is given on page 89. This pattern was chosen after several options had been considered: one had a larger and therefore stronger lip around the top, but this would have projected unappealingly beyond the edge of the frame; another was too slim for security.

The 1½in long, ¾in diameter peg at the top of the leg fits into a socket drilled through the frame members using a Forstner bit and stand drill to give a very clean edge. The hole is made with the corner joint assembled (but unglued) and clamped in position. It should be just deep enough to lock in the upper tenon, having gone right through the center of the lower one (see diagram on p. 88). When the leg is in place the peg locks the corner joint as well as anchoring the leg, an elegant solution to the problem.

Assembling the day bed

At this point all the pieces are sanded with garnet paper, working down through coarse and medium grades to fine. The bed can now be assembled.

Assembly is in two stages. First the frame and legs are glued up and clamped. This must be done in one operation, as the leg is an integral part of the corner joint. Secondly the end pieces and rails are glued in place – again in a single operation.

Cut the four formers which fit inside the four curved end pieces and will take the upholstery tacks when the ends are padded and covered. They also provide valuable reinforcement for the curved ends. The formers were cut from 1in beech, but as they will be hidden under the upholstery any available timber could be used. They are cut with a saber saw and are shaped to follow a line ¼in inside the end pieces. No template was used to mark out the formers – each was fitted individually to its end. At the top the former is shaped to run hard up against the oval rail; at the base a notch is cut out of it to fit around the lower rail. The shape can be refined by spokeshave.

Like many others, Prince Augustus of Prussia fell in love with Mme Récamier, and begged her to abandon her husband for him. The scrupulous Juliette refused, but gave him this flattering portrait by David's pupil, Gérard, which she preferred to the portrait by David. Musée Carnavalet, Paris

The framework of a day bed by Jacob Frères of Paris, the makers of Mme Récamier's famous bedroom furniture. Jacob Frères also made David's studio furniture, including the day bed in his portrait of Mme Récamier

Fix the formers in place using eight 1½in brass screws driven through countersunk clearance holes into pilot holes in the inside face of the end pieces. Take care not to drill the holes right through.

A coat of sanding sealer is now brushed over the entire piece. This fills the grain and provides a good surface for the finish. The sealer is sanded down until it feels perfectly smooth to the touch.

Two oak battens, ¾ × 1½in, run along the length of the side rails, with their bottom edge flush with that of the frame. Each is fixed with six 1¼in screws driven through countersunk clearance holes in the battens into pilot holes in the frame and fitted with brass cups. Before fixing, five ½in × 1¼in lap-joints are cut in the top of each rail with a tenon saw and chisel. These take the ½in × 1¼in oak slats which run across the bed. The cross slats are strategically placed to support the weight of a sitter. Exact spacing is shown in the drawing (p. 89). The slats are cut to length and dropped into the housings. No glue is used.

Finishing the day bed

It is almost certain that the original was French polished, but the designer preferred to finish Madame Récamier's bed by waxing it with a mixture of beeswax and carnauba wax. Carnauba wax gives the beeswax a hard finish. Methyl alcohol (methylated spirit) was added to improve the flow of the wax during application.

Upholstery

The method of upholstery remains optional. The designer envisages a sheet of ⅜in plywood laid on top of the oak slats and topped with a stuffed mattress. Although the two sausage-shaped cushions are a relatively simple job, traditional upholstery remains a difficult task for the inexperienced amateur, and it would be unfortunate to spoil a fine piece of work with anything less. The entire job can be entrusted to a professional upholsterer. A less expensive and simpler option would be to lay a thin, flexible sheet of plywood over the formers and to cover this with foam and fabric.

The Acrobat's Cat's Chair

by Mark Dunhill

From *Acrobat and Partner* (1948) by Fernand Léger (1881-1955)

Tate Gallery, London

Léger loved the circus. Acrobats, clowns, jugglers and bareback riders whirl expressionlessly through his work. As a child he was thrilled when the circus came to town, and during his stay in the United States from 1940-5 he was amazed by the forty acrobats in Barnum's spectacular three-ring circus in Madison Square Garden.

Léger saw the circus as a circular symbol of life, and acrobats and trapeze artists wheeling and soaring through the air seemed to him the very essence of freedom. At the time he painted *Acrobat and Partner* in 1948 he was writing and illustrating *Cirque*, a book devoted to the circus. In it he invited his readers to "go to the circus. Nothing is rounder than the circus . . . You leave your rectangles and geometrical windows behind and enter the land of circles in action."

Contrast – the clash between movement and stillness, circles and lines – is at the heart of Léger's paintings. In *Acrobat and Partner*, according to the artist, the revolving acrobat and the concentric discs around him represent movement. The straight lines of the chair, together with the ladder and the acrobat's partner, make up the contrasting static element in the picture. The colored areas of the chair are separated by Léger's characteristic strong black lines, which break up the colors like the lead in a stained glass window.

Designing the acrobat's cat's chair

Cats home in on warm, soft seats, and it is therefore reasonable to assume the rounded contours under the gray cat represent a cushioned surface. Mark Dunhill, the sculptor who designed our reconstruction, decided to reproduce the supposedly upholstered shapes in wood. He made the chair entirely from wood and painted the pattern of the fabric on the surface.

Like the Carpaccio chair made by the same designer (p. 132), the Léger chair is constructed by gluing pieces

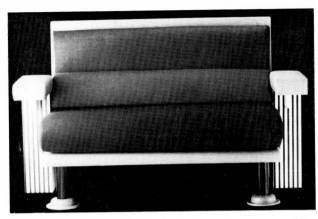

There are echoes of Léger's "tubist" shapes in Michele de Lucchi's Lido *couch (1982)*

of wood together and then cutting, rasping or grinding them down to size. If care is taken with filling and finishing, a near-perfect surface for paint can be created.

The stability of the rear legs was at first worrying. The designer's inventive resolution of the problem was to turn the segment of the circle passing behind the chair in the painting into a curving stretcher linking the legs. The front rail in the painting is not set absolutely horizontally. The designer decided to reproduce this feature.

Making the chair

The first stage in construction is to assemble a pair of plywood leg units, each with a front leg, a back leg and upright, and a linking rail along the top of the legs. The seat and back panel are made as separate units and attached to the legs. Finally the square-section rail which joins the two front legs, and the curved panel which joins the back legs, are fitted, and the chair is then finished and painted.

The legs
The two leg units are made from ¾in plywood. This simplifies construction by taking advantage of plywood's lack of weakness along the grain. Mark out the shapes needed to construct the leg units. Each unit requires a single piece comprising back leg/upright/front-to-back rail, plus two back leg pieces, two full-length front leg pieces and one short front leg piece (the full length of the leg minus the depth of the horizontal rail).

Cut the pieces out. Glue and clamp them together to make the two leg units. Notice that the two leg units are assembled differently – although for the back legs a piece is fixed on each side of the upright, the longer front leg pieces are both glued *outside* the shorter upright, to make the chair wider at the front than at the back. The front leg joint can be strengthened with screws or dowels.

The seat and back
The back and seat are made by rounding off the edges of shallow boxes built up on plywood boards. Cut pieces of ½in plywood to the shape of the seat and back. To make the seat, glue a frame of 1 × 1¾in softwood around the underneath of the seat and a similar frame of 2 × 3in softwood around the top. The frame members are simply butt-jointed together, but as the seat is wider across the front than the back, no two pieces meet quite at right angles. Mark the cutting lines by holding one piece of the frame against its edge of the seat and scribing on it the line made by the adjacent pieces when they are placed on top. When the pieces are glued in position, clamp until dry. Within the 2 × 3in frame glue an inner frame of 1 × 1in softwood. Once again the members are butt-jointed. Finally cut a piece of 1in softwood to fit just within the 2 × 3in frame and rest on the inner 1 × 1in frame. Glue this in place.

When the seat has been built up in this way the edges are rounded off all around, both on top and bottom, to give it a "cushion" shape. A plane, rasp, mechanical grinder or any other abrading tool will do the job. Hollow out the middle of the "cushion" slightly, to mark where the cat has been sitting.

The back is made like the seat. The front frame is set in 1¾in from the edge of the plywood panel, but in all other ways the "upholstered" panel is made up just as the seat was. The lines on the finished piece indicating mitered joints are misleading – they are painted on the plywood panel. The "box" has a 1 × 1in outer frame, a ½ × ½in inner frame and a ½in panel set on the inner frame. Its edges are rounded off in the same way as the seat, and a slight hollow is ground into the center of the panel.

The frame behind the back panel runs around the panel edges, but its bottom member is cut 1½in short, to leave a ¾in slot on each side to take the uprights. The vertical sides of the back frame are ¾ × ¾in softwood, the horizontals ¾ × 1¾in.

Assembling the chair
The leg units lean inwards. The back uprights are fixed against the inside edges of the back panel's rear frame. Clamp the back panel temporarily in position while the seat is fitted.

Place the seat unit on the leg rails and slide it back until it touches the back uprights. Mark where the back legs touch the underside of the seat and cut away the bottom frame of the seat to this width. Put it in position again and mark where the back uprights touch the seat. Cut notches through the whole thickness of the seat at these points. The depth of the notch determines how far the seat will slide back round the uprights. It must be cut at an angle if the seat is to fit snugly round the upright.

The chair can now be assembled. Screws hold the seat to the horizontal rails. Drill a pair of countersunk clearance holes through the underside of each seat rail and drive 3in screws through them into the inner frame of the seat. Fill the screw holes with plastic filler for a neat finish.

The back is held in place on each side by three screws driven into pilot holes in the frame sides through countersunk clearance holes drilled in the inside face of the uprights.

The front rail is a piece of planed 2 × 2in softwood, meeting the legs at 45° and notched to fit around the back of the front legs. It is not set horizontally. Cut the rail a few inches over length and place it in position at what appears to be the correct angle and tilted so that one corner touches the legs. At each side mark the point where the rail touches the inside face of the leg. Place a try square against the inside of the leg and over the rail: mark the point where it touches the top corner of the rail. Repeat to mark a similar point on the bottom corner of the rail. Join up these three points with a line.

Hold the rail in a vise and saw along the line linking the three points. Make a second sawcut along the diagonal to remove the notch. Fit the rail in place and mark the line where the legs cross its ends. Cut it to length. Fix it to the legs with glue and a single screw at each end driven through a countersunk clearance hole in the rail into pilot holes in the back of the legs. Fill the screw holes and sand smooth.

The curved back rail is cut from ½in plywood using a saber saw (jigsaw). It may help to mock it up in cardboard first to see how it looks. When it is cut, mark the curves it makes where it crosses the back legs. Chisel out ½in-deep housings for it, so that it will fit flush with the legs. Glue it in position and clamp until dry.

Finishing the chair
The finish should be as smooth as possible. Since the surface will be entirely hidden by paint, uneven surfaces and open joints can be filled with plastic wood filler and sanded smooth. The designer applied a coat of sanding sealer to fill out the grain and provide a surface for the paint. The sealer is sanded with fine grade sandpaper before the paint goes on.

Four colors of paint are used – red, maroon (for the curved rear rail), black and white. The pattern is applied with gloss paint over a coat of primer/undercoat. Masking tape can be used to obtain clean edges along the straight lines, but most of the outlines must be painted freehand. To be Léger-like, keep the colors separate. Talking about his work, Léger said he wanted isolated colors, a very red red and a very blue blue.

Léger's three women relax on a sumptuous couch with striped legs. Their meal is set out on a simple red table. Interesting variations on the women's furniture appear in several drawings of the same subject. Three Women *(1921). Oil on canvas 72¼ × 99in. Collection, The Museum of Modern Art, New York; Mrs Simon Guggenheim Fund*

ORDER OF WORK

The legs

1 Mark and cut out the plywood elements of the leg units
2 Glue and clamp them together to form the two leg units
3 Plane and sand them smooth

The seat

1 Mark and cut the plywood panel to the shape of the seat
2 Glue a frame of 1 × 1in softwood under the plywood
3 Glue a frame of 2 × 3in softwood on top of the plywood
4 Glue an inner frame of 1 × 1in softwood inside the 2 × 3in frame
5 Glue a panel of 1in softwood on top of this inner frame
6 Round off the edges of the seat to the cushion shape
7 Repeat steps 1 - 6 to make the back, but with the front frame set in 1¾in from the edge. The dimensions of the "box" elements are also different

Assembly

1 Clamp the back panel temporarily to the legs
2 With the seat temporarily in place, mark where the back legs meet the seat
3 Cut away the seat's lower frame to allow it to fit around the legs
4 Mark where the back uprights touch the seat
5 Cut notches in the seat at these points
6 Screw the seat to the horizontal seat rails
7 Screw the back to the rear uprights
8 Cut the front stretcher a little over length
9 Mark and cut notches at each end of the stretcher where it fits around the legs
10 Cut the stretcher to length
11 Glue and screw the stretcher to the legs
12 Cut the plywood back panel
13 Mark and chisel out a ½in deep dado (housing) for the panel in the back legs
14 Glue the panel in place

Finish

1 Sand all surfaces smooth
2 Apply a coat of sanding sealer, and resand
3 Paint the chair with primer/undercoat
4 Pencil in the pattern
5 Paint the pattern with gloss paint

MATERIAL	No.	Size (ins)
Plywood for:		
Leg units	2	¾ × 22½ × 40½
Back legs	4	¾ × 2 × 17
Front legs	4	¾ × 2 × 15½
Front legs	2	¾ × 2 × 13½
Back panel	1	¾ × 15 × 26
Seat base	1	½ × 18 × 20
Back rail	1	½ × 8 × 20
Softwood for:		
Back box frame	2	1 × 1 × 22½
Back box frame	1	1 × 1 × 8¾
Back box frame	1	1 × 1 × 9½
Inner box frame	2	½ × ½ × 20½

(continued on facing page)

The assembled left leg unit

The front rail

CONSTRUCTION

96

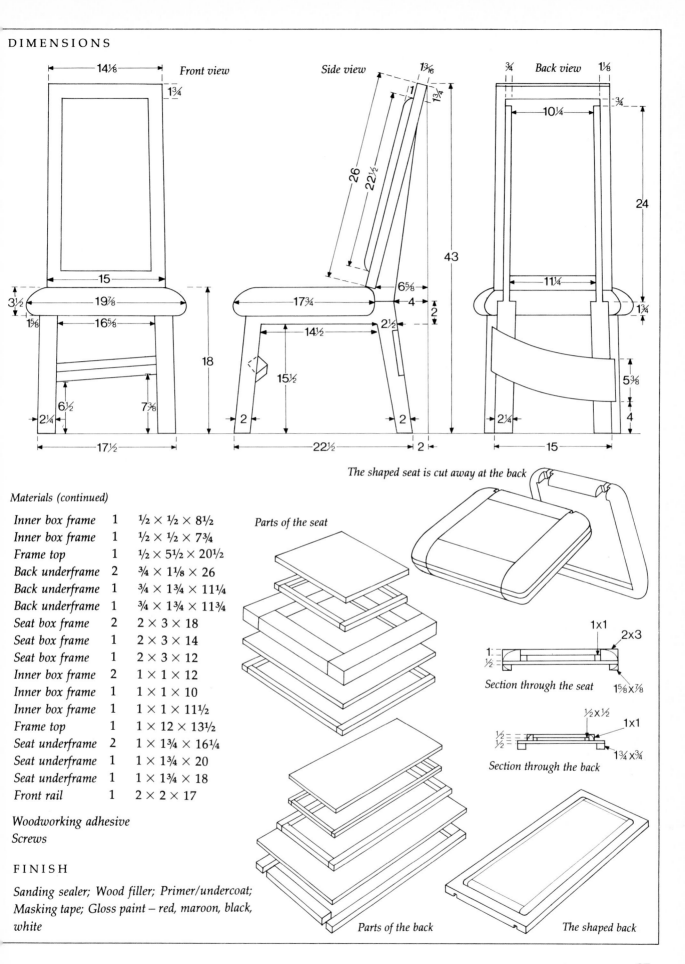

DIMENSIONS

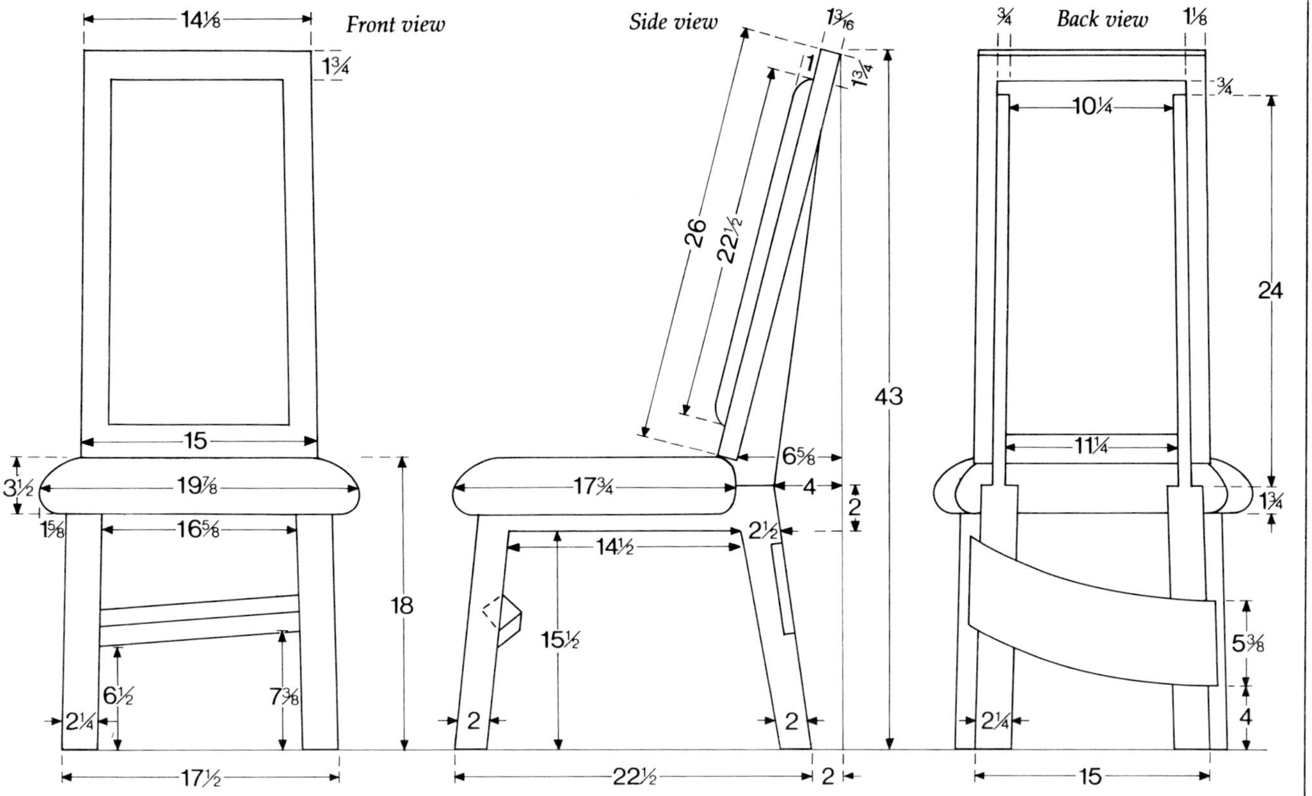

Front view
Side view
Back view
14⅛
1¾
15
3½
19⅞
1⅝
16⅝
6½
7⅜
2¼
18
17½
1³⁄₁₆
1
1¾
26
22½
6⅝
17¾
4
2
2½
14½
15½
43
2
2
22½
2
¾
1⅛
¾
10¼
24
11¼
1¾
5⅜
4
2¼
15

The shaped seat is cut away at the back

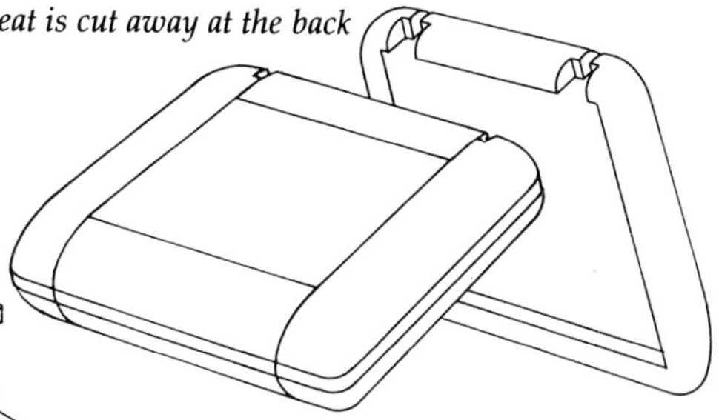

Materials (continued)

Inner box frame	1	½ × ½ × 8½
Inner box frame	1	½ × ½ × 7¾
Frame top	1	½ × 5½ × 20½
Back underframe	2	¾ × 1⅛ × 26
Back underframe	1	¾ × 1¾ × 11¼
Back underframe	1	¾ × 1¾ × 11¾
Seat box frame	2	2 × 3 × 18
Seat box frame	1	2 × 3 × 14
Seat box frame	1	2 × 3 × 12
Inner box frame	2	1 × 1 × 12
Inner box frame	1	1 × 1 × 10
Inner box frame	1	1 × 1 × 11½
Frame top	1	1 × 12 × 13½
Seat underframe	2	1 × 1¾ × 16¼
Seat underframe	1	1 × 1¾ × 20
Seat underframe	1	1 × 1¾ × 18
Front rail	1	2 × 2 × 17

Woodworking adhesive
Screws

FINISH

Sanding sealer; Wood filler; Primer/undercoat; Masking tape; Gloss paint – red, maroon, black, white

Parts of the seat

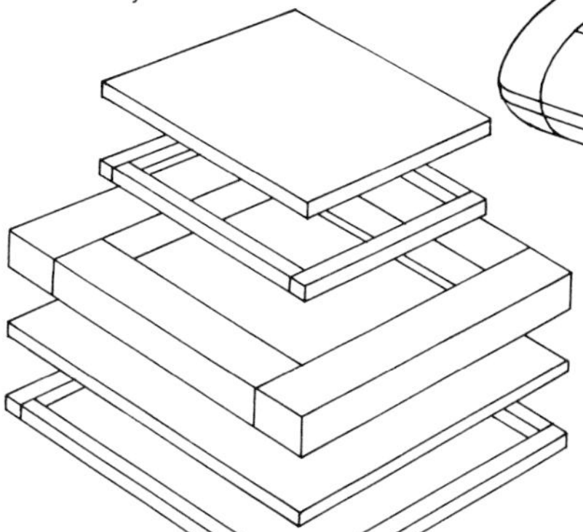

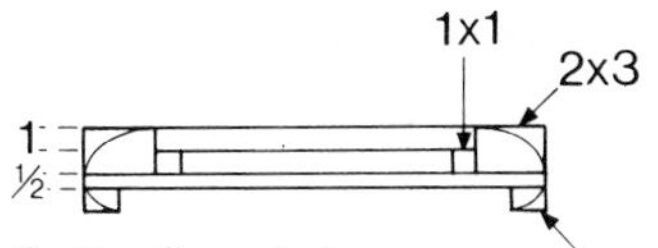

1x1
2x3
1
½
1⅝x⅞

Section through the seat

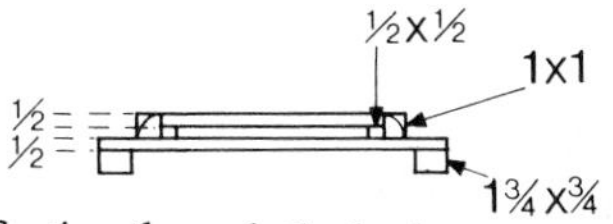

½x½
1x1
½
½
1¾x¾

Section through the back

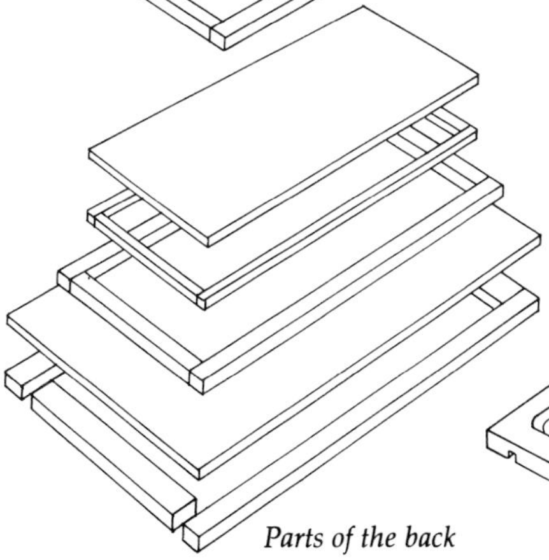

Parts of the back

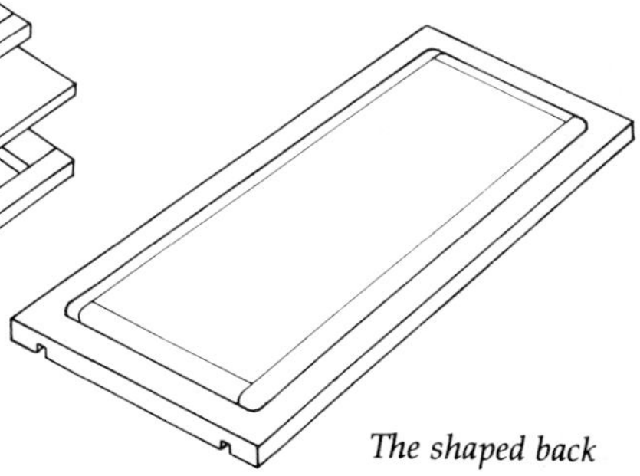

The shaped back

The Proverbial Stool

by Patrick Daw

from *Sitting Between Two Stools* by Pieter Bruegel (*c.* 1525-1569)

Museum Mayer van den Bergh, Antwerp

Bruegel's befuddled peasant is shown falling between two enormously popular pieces of medieval furniture. Such triangular stools, made of turned wooden spindles, were a northern European specialty throughout the Middle Ages. They appear in countless paintings from the fifteenth to the seventeenth century and were acceptable at all levels of society. They provided both a sturdy seat for peasants carousing in grubby taverns and a small table for dignified Madonnas and the infant Jesus.

Bruegel painted the world of the Flemish peasant in the violent, diseased and war-torn Europe of the sixteenth century. He enjoyed going to village weddings, dances and taverns. His paintings document the games played by the children of Flanders and the pastimes of their parents. The panel of *Twelve Proverbs* illustrates traditional peasant wisdom. Our picture from the panel shows its unhappy hero *Sitting Between Two Stools*. The text painted on the panel describes the hero's fall in these words: "In the past I was the greatest glutton of all. Now I have lost everything and I am left sitting in the ashes between two stools."

Designing the proverbial stool

The popularity of the triangular chair faded long ago, yet it remains a surprisingly comfortable type of seat, particularly when used in the common medieval manner with a cushion. It is a pleasingly straightforward job for the furniture maker.

The two most popular forms of the triangular chair appear in Bruegel's painting – the simple backless type and the one Patrick Daw recreated, in which one leg is extended upwards and fitted with a rail to provide a back. This type is sometimes called a "night watchman's chair," the idea being that the watchman on the medieval city walls would straddle the seat, leaning his arms, head and musket on the back rail.

The chair would originally have been assembled by

The Archangel Gabriel appears to Mary in The Annunciation *by the Master of the Brunswick Diptych (detail). The painting shows that cushions were used to improve the comfort of the chair. The Burrell Collection, Glasgow*

the same craftsman who turned the parts to shape. Turning the necessary pieces is a simple job for anyone equipped with a lathe. However, our designer worked out the shapes he needed and sent measured drawings of their profiles (as on p. 102) to a professional wood turner, who did the job speedily and economically. All the parts were turned in pine.

By designing the seat as an equilateral triangle, he avoided complex calculations and drilling angles. All three sides are the same length and they all meet at an angle at 60°.

Making the stool

The side rails are glued into 1in-deep sockets drilled in the legs. Four sockets are needed in each leg. To mark the drilling points, draw a vertical line down the entire leg. At each end of the leg continue the line along the end grain as far as the center point. (This point will be marked where the leg was held in the lathe during turning.) Using a protractor or adjustable bevel, measure and mark a line on both ends at 60° to the first lines. Draw a second line along the entire leg joining the points where these marks touch the circumference.

Grip the leg horizontally in a vice with one of the lines uppermost. Center a brace and bit on the line 8in and 17in from the base of the leg and drill down to cut a pair of 1in-diameter sockets, 1in deep. Turn the leg through 60° and drill a similar pair of sockets centered on the second line. All three legs are drilled in this way.

Although the sockets can be drilled at any point on the circumference – as long as they are at 60° to each other – their positioning determines which part of the leg will form the front face of the stool. Draw the lines so that the most pleasing grain pattern will be seen.

Where two rails enter the leg, their ends will meet, and the inside face of the spindles must be chiseled away until they can be pushed right home. This is a matter of trial and error.

The pair of sockets in each of the six horizontal rails is drilled in the same way, but in this case using a ¾in diameter bit. The sockets are drilled 2⅜in each side of the middle of the rail on a line drawn along the whole spindle. On the upper rails the line is continued on the end grain of the rail at each end to the center point. At each end measure and mark a second line on the end grain at right angles to the first and draw a line along the side of the rail joining these points. This line is a reference point for the seat rebate.

The edges of the seat are rabbeted and housed in a groove ⅜in wide and ½in deep cut in the three top rails. To prevent the seat appearing too low in its frame the line on the rails at right angles to the sockets marks the lower edge of the groove, not the center (see drawing). The grooves were cut with a circular saw – a router or a handsaw and chisel are sound alternatives.

The seat could be made of a single panel, but the designer preferred to use some ¾ × 3in tongue and groove maple boards salvaged from an ancient granary, where they were used as flooring because they impart no smell to the grain. To make the seat, five boards 12in long are glued together to make a rectangle some 12 × 14in. The boards are held until dry by a pair of strap clamps (sash cramps). Any uneven joints are then planed and sanded smooth.

Rather than relying on mathematics to calculate the seat's precise dimensions, assemble the seat rails and legs without glue, and measure the finished seat size.

Allowing for a ½in rabbet all round, saw the triangular seat out of the rectangular panel, with corner angles of 60°. Rout out the lower edge of the panel to leave a ⅜ × ½in tongue all round. The tongue could be cut with a handsaw, while the panel is held in a vise.

When the seat fits, assemble the entire stool up to seat level without glue. The pieces are hammered into position (and knocked apart) with a rubber mallet, which will not bruise the wood. When you are satisfied that the parts fit together and line up as they should, dismantle the stool, glue the spindle and rail ends and hammer the whole piece together using the rubber mallet.

The first step in assembly is to make up the complete front elevation – the two front legs, the upper and lower rails and the vertical spindles. Now join the two sides to the back leg. At this stage slide the seat into position. Finally, push home the front elevation.

Assembly can be a frustrating procedure, as the designer discovered. He found to his despair that as soon as he knocked one pair of upright spindles parallel, the blow threw something else out of square. Correct alignment is important to the look of the chair. It was some two hours before he could get all the uprights parallel at the same time.

The last stage is to make and fit the top section of the chair back. Mark the outline of the horizontal rail on a 2in-thick piece of softwood. For maximum strength the wood grain should run along the rail rather than across it. Cut out the shape with a bandsaw or saber saw (jigsaw), round off the ends with a shaping tool and sand it smooth.

The wood turner's skill, displayed at its simplest in Bruegel's painting, reaches extremes of technical virtuosity in this English armchair in turned ash and oak, c. 1620. Victoria and Albert Museum, London

Drill a 1in-diameter hole 1in deep in the bottom of the rail.

Angled holes must be drilled into both the top rail and the post to house the pair of supporting dowels. To establish the drilling angles push the top rail into position on its post without glue, place a ruler across the corner where the spindle will be fitted and mark the drilling angle on the side of the wood. A flat bit tends to drift when drilling at an angle, so the designer used a twist bit to drill ¾in-diameter holes 1½in deep into both the post and the rail. They were held firm in a vise during drilling.

The depth of these sockets allows some room for maneuver during assembly, which can be quite a struggle. You will have to take advantage of the flexibility of the pine to push the glued spindles home.

When the whole stool was glued together the surfaces were sanded clean of mallet marks and covered in a coat of wax polish.

A turned and rush-seated armchair in ash, maple and pine. New England, 17th century. Henry Francis du Pont Winterthur Museum

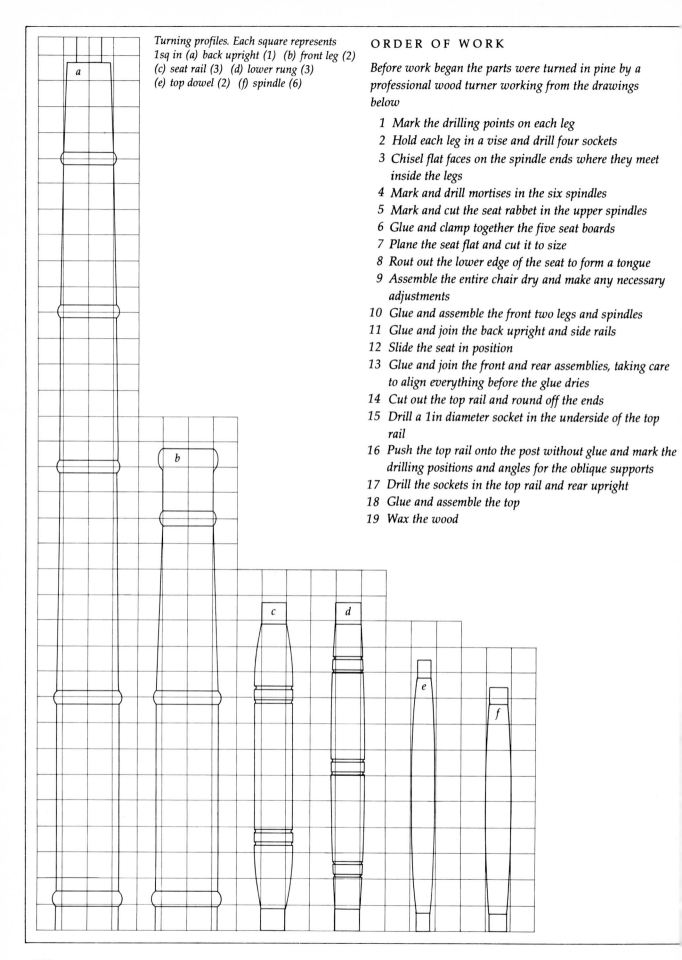

Turning profiles. Each square represents
1sq in (a) back upright (1) (b) front leg (2)
(c) seat rail (3) (d) lower rung (3)
(e) top dowel (2) (f) spindle (6)

a

b

c

d

e

f

ORDER OF WORK

Before work began the parts were turned in pine by a professional wood turner working from the drawings below

1 Mark the drilling points on each leg
2 Hold each leg in a vise and drill four sockets
3 Chisel flat faces on the spindle ends where they meet inside the legs
4 Mark and drill mortises in the six spindles
5 Mark and cut the seat rabbet in the upper spindles
6 Glue and clamp together the five seat boards
7 Plane the seat flat and cut it to size
8 Rout out the lower edge of the seat to form a tongue
9 Assemble the entire chair dry and make any necessary adjustments
10 Glue and assemble the front two legs and spindles
11 Glue and join the back upright and side rails
12 Slide the seat in position
13 Glue and join the front and rear assemblies, taking care to align everything before the glue dries
14 Cut out the top rail and round off the ends
15 Drill a 1in diameter socket in the underside of the top rail
16 Push the top rail onto the post without glue and mark the drilling positions and angles for the oblique supports
17 Drill the sockets in the top rail and rear upright
18 Glue and assemble the top
19 Wax the wood

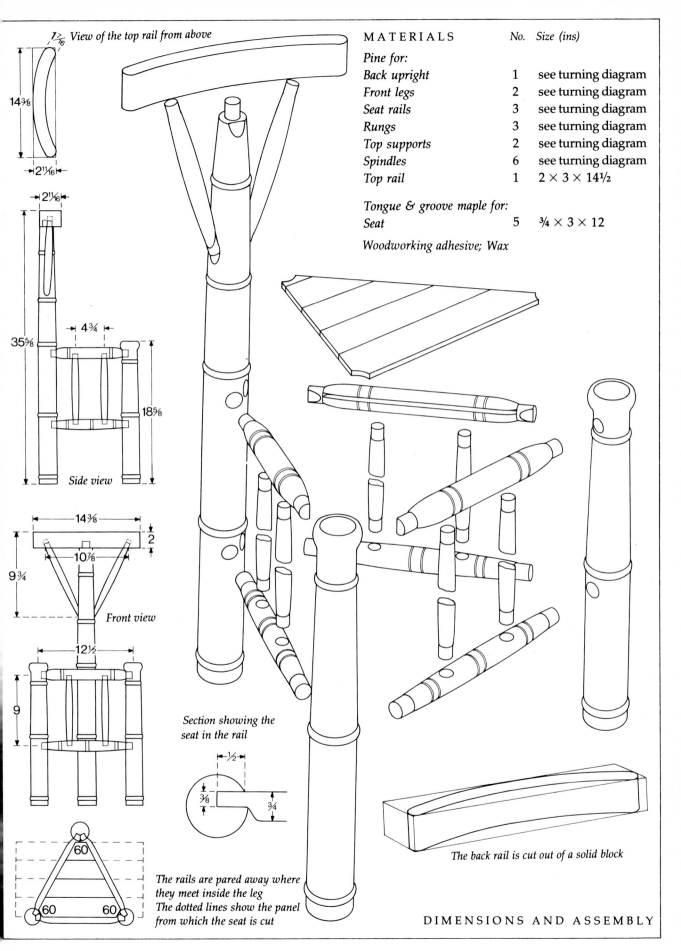

View of the top rail from above

14³⁄₈

2¹¹⁄₁₆

1⁷⁄₁₆

2¹¹⁄₁₆

35⁵⁄₈

4³⁄₄

18⁵⁄₈

Side view

14³⁄₈

10⁷⁄₈

9³⁄₄

2

Front view

12½

9

Section showing the
seat in the rail

½

³⁄₈

³⁄₄

60

60   60

The rails are pared away where
they meet inside the leg
The dotted lines show the panel
from which the seat is cut

The back rail is cut out of a solid block

MATERIALS	No.	Size (ins)
Pine for:		
Back upright	1	see turning diagram
Front legs	2	see turning diagram
Seat rails	3	see turning diagram
Rungs	3	see turning diagram
Top supports	2	see turning diagram
Spindles	6	see turning diagram
Top rail	1	$2 \times 3 \times 14\frac{1}{2}$
Tongue & groove maple for:		
Seat	5	$\frac{3}{4} \times 3 \times 12$

Woodworking adhesive; Wax

DIMENSIONS AND ASSEMBLY

103

Raisins in the Cabin;

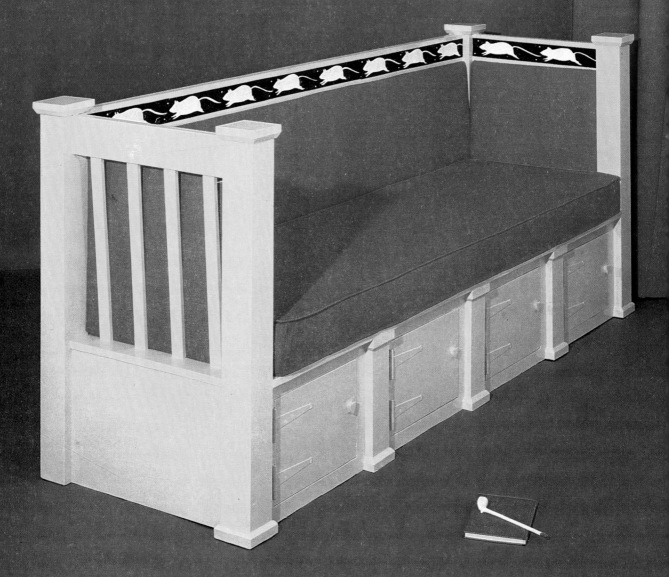

Captain Duck's Settee
by Jim Partridge
from *The Fairy Ship* (1870) by Walter Crane (1845-1915)

Captain Duck sits at ease on the seas aboard The Fairy Ship. His suitably ship-shape cabin reflects Walter Crane's enthusiasm for the design ideas of the Arts and Crafts Movement. This was an attempt to revive standards of craftsmanship and design in a Victorian England swamped by shoddy mass production. The movement's early mentor was William Morris, and Crane its main propagandist.

Crane turned his artistic talents to the design of textiles and wallpapers, many of which appear in his illustrations for children's books. Although he complained about the low pay for his illustrations, he admits that "I had my fun out of them and often made them the vehicle for my ideas in furniture and decoration."

Crane's books were a major influence on English interiors during the Queen Anne revival of the late 1800s. In 1875 he was commissioned to design a series of nursery wallpapers based on his book illustrations, and soon Crane tiles and wallpapers were seen throughout the average Queen Anne house, with Crane friezes running around the walls. The frieze of mice scurrying along the back of the captain's settee is typical, as is the shield with its crane motif – the artist's signature.

The picture is a colored wood engraving from *The Fairy Ship*, published in 1870 in Routledge's Sixpenny Toybook series, the most successful children's books of the time. It tells the story of the duck captain and his crew of white mice, and there were

> Raisins in the Cabin;
> Almonds in the hold;
> The sails they were of satin
> The mast it was of gold.
> . . . . .
> There were fifty little sailors
> Skipping o'er the decks;
> They were fifty little white mice,
> With rings around their necks!
> The Captain was a Duck
> With a jacket on his back.

And when the ship set sail
The Captain he said Quack!
Quack, quack, quack!

The illustration gives no clues about the corners of the seat, all of which are hidden. The designer therefore had to invent them. He looked at Arts and Crafts furniture for ideas, adding corner posts and ends to make the piece free-standing. He gave it a suitable height and depth for sitting in, and for practical reasons made the depth half the width of a standard sheet of particleboard (blockboard). The piece is long enough to sleep on. This is nursery furniture with a pedigree.

Making the settee

The construction of the settee is solid but simple. The four corner posts are slotted – at the bottom to house the front, back and sides of the cupboard (which occupies the space under the seat), and at the top to take the back and side rails. The seat rests on the cupboard walls and is cut away at the corners to fit snugly round the posts. The bottom edge of the rails is slotted – and the seat mortised – to hold the slats that support the back and side cushions. Doors are cut out of the front panel and hinged back in position. The caps on the posts and the pilasters between the cupboard doors are decorative additions. Finally the whole piece is painted.

First plane the four $3\frac{1}{8} \times 3\frac{1}{8}$in pine corner posts smooth and square and cut them to length ($32\frac{1}{2}$in). Mark out the mortises – or to be more exact the slots – that run from the top and bottom of the posts. The top slots will later be covered by caps to give a neat appearance. The slots are a time-saving feature, avoiding the need to cut more complex and precise mortise and tenon joints. The method also hugely simplifies assembly: without this simple device of slotting rather than mortising, the whole seat would have to be assembled in a single operation rather than piece by piece.

The 1in deep slots which take the $\frac{3}{4}$in particleboard panels of the sides, back and front of the cupboard are set in 1in from the outside edge of the posts. They are all 12in long. The slots for the rails are $1\frac{1}{8}$in wide (the width of the rails) and they run $3\frac{1}{2}$in down the centers

ORDER OF WORK

1 Cut the four corner posts to length
2 Mark and cut the slots in the corner posts
3 Mark and cut out the front, back and side panels
4 Mark and cut out the cupboard doors
5 Saw and glue battens inside the front and back panels
6 Glue and clamp the posts, front, back and sides together
7 Cut and attach the central divider
8 Mark and cut out the seat
9 Screw the seat to the battens
10 Cut the back and side rails to length
11 Groove the bottom edge of the rails
12 Mark and chisel out the mortises for the slats in the seat
13 Cut and shape the 24 slats
14 Glue the slats in position
15 Cut and bevel the four corner post caps
16 Dowel the caps on top of the posts
17 Hang the cupboard doors
18 Cut and fit the cupboard door handles
19 Cut, glue and clamp the pilasters between the doors
20 Shape, cut and glue the moldings around pilasters and posts
21 Chamfer the front edge of the seat

Finish

1 Fill imperfections in the surface
2 Sand the whole piece smooth
3 Paint on a coat of wood primer and resand
4 Mask off the frieze area on the top rails
5 Paint on yellow undercoat

6 When dry, resand
7 Repeat steps 5 and 6 until a smooth surface of even color is achieved
8 Paint on yellow gloss coat
9 Apply the frieze of mice
10 Make the cushions

MATERIALS	No.	Size (ins)
Particleboard (blockboard) for:		
Front panel	1	$\frac{3}{4} \times 12 \times 75\frac{1}{8}$
Back panel	1	$\frac{3}{4} \times 12 \times 75\frac{1}{8}$
Side panels	2	$\frac{3}{4} \times 12 \times 20\frac{1}{4}$
Base panel	1	$\frac{3}{4} \times 21 \times 75\frac{7}{8}$
Divider	1	$\frac{3}{4} \times 21 \times 10\frac{1}{4}$
Seat	1	$\frac{3}{4} \times 24\frac{1}{2} \times 78\frac{3}{8}$
Pilasters	3	$\frac{3}{4} \times 3 \times 12$
Softwood for:		
Corner posts	4	$3\frac{1}{8} \times 3\frac{1}{8} \times 32\frac{1}{2}$
Battens	2	$1 \times 1 \times 73$
Back rail	1	$1\frac{1}{8} \times 3\frac{7}{16} \times 75\frac{1}{8}$
Side rails	2	$1\frac{1}{8} \times 3\frac{7}{16} \times 20\frac{1}{4}$
Slats	24	$\frac{1}{2} \times 1\frac{1}{4} \times 17\frac{1}{8}$
Caps	4	$1\frac{1}{4} \times 4 \times 4$
Door stops	4	$1 \times 2 \times 2$
Door handles	4	$\frac{1}{2} \times 1 \times 1$
Molding	1	$\frac{1}{2} \times 1 \times 72$
Hardwood dowels for:		
Corner posts	16	$2\frac{1}{4} \times \frac{1}{4}$dia
Doors	8	$1 \times \frac{1}{4}$dia

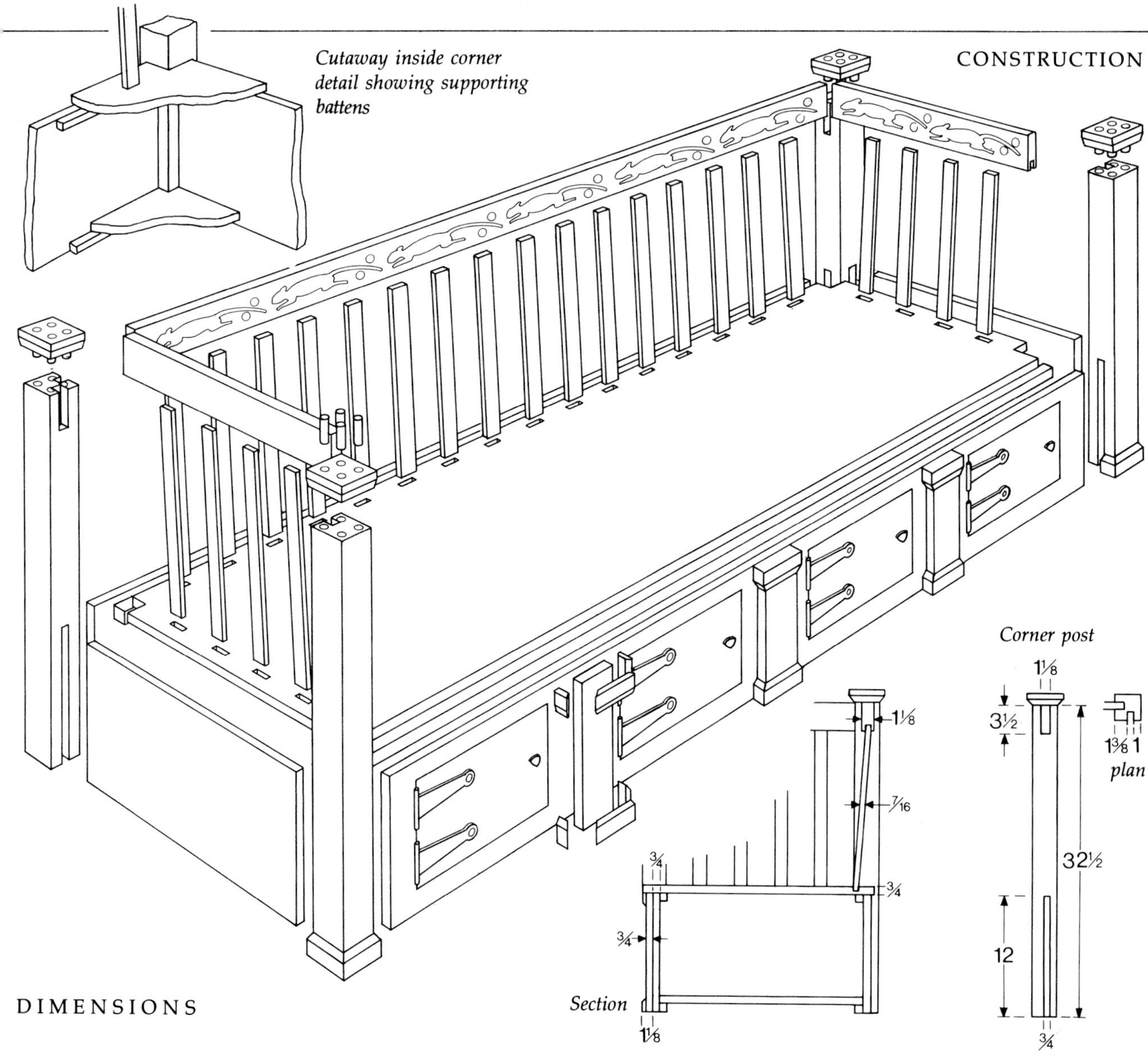
1⅛
7⁄16
¾
¾
¾
1⅛
1⅛
3½
32½
12
¾
1⅜ 1
plan

Cutaway inside corner detail showing supporting battens

DIMENSIONS

Section

Corner post

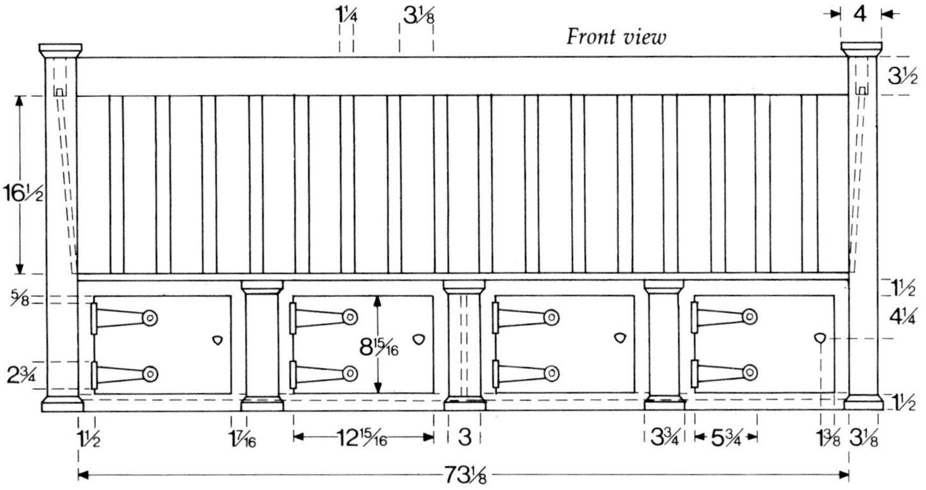
1¼
3⅛
4
3½
16½
⅝
1½
4¼
8 15⁄16
2¾
1½
1½
1 7⁄16
12 15⁄16
3
3¾
5¾
1⅜
3⅛
73⅛

Front view

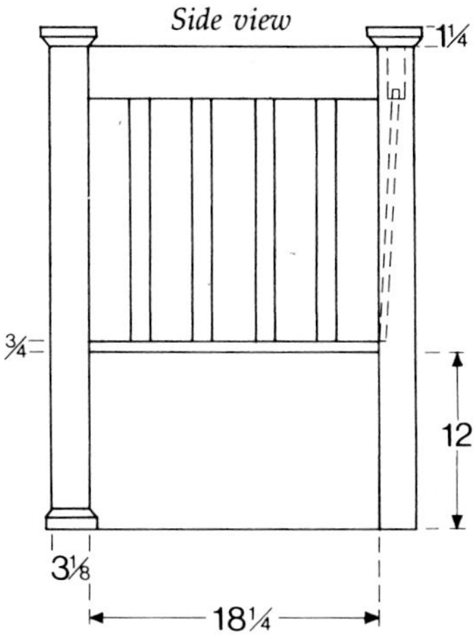
1¼
¾
12
3⅛
18¼

Side view

6in gate hinges (8)
Magnetic door catches (4)
1½ finishing nails (panel pins); Screws; Casein glue

FINISH

Wood filler; Wood primer; Yellow undercoat; Gloss paint – yellow, white, black

Fashionable Arts and Crafts furniture is ably mocked in this cartoon from "Punch" (11 March 1903). The tub chair is similar to one designed by Baillie Scott

THE LATEST STYLE OF ROOM DECORATION. THE HOME MADE BEAUTIFUL.
According to the " Arts and Crafts."

of the faces in which they are cut. It is important at this stage to have the front and rear right and left posts clearly marked. It is easy and infuriating to cut a slot in the wrong face. The slots can be drilled and chiseled out; alternatively the wood can be removed by a router or a number of short cuts with a circular saw, and the end of the groove cleaned out with a chisel.

Now mark out the front, back and sides of the cupboard on a sheet of ¾in particleboard, and saw them to size. Clamping a block of wood alongside the cutting line can help guide the saw. The four 9 × 13in cupboard doors are marked out on the front panel, 1½in from top and bottom, and cut out with a saber saw (jigsaw). To provide access for the saw blade, drill ¼in diameter entry holes in the top left and bottom right hand corners of the door panel, taking care to drill on the door side of the lines. These holes are later plugged with ¼in dowels, which will be hidden under the paint.

Glue and screw 1 × 1in softwood battens along the inside face of the front and back panels, flush with the top and bottom edges. A base panel will sit on the lower battens, and the seat will be screwed onto the top battens – driving screws into the edge of the particleboard panels is harder and less reliable.

The posts and the sides, back and front of the cupboard can now be assembled. These are glued and clamped. Make sure that the base is square and the posts upright before the glue dries.

If you do not have clamps long enough to span the long edges, the front panel can be clamped to the legs using the inside of the door openings – protect the edge with a block of waste wood. At the back a block of wood

could be glued to the panel near each end to provide a grip for the clamps, and sawed and planed off later.

Cut out the 21 × 75⅞in base panel of ¾in particleboard. At each corner of the panel cut out a 1⅜ × 1⅜in notch for the legs, and lay the panel in position on the battens. Cut out a 10¼ × 21in rectangular panel to act as a central divider, providing extra support for the seat. Cut out 1 × 1in rectangles in the top two corners to allow it to fit around the battens, position it centrally in the cupboard and glue and nail it in position. The 1½in finishing nails (panel pins) are driven through the front and back panels into the edge of the divider – the nailheads will later be hidden behind the central pilaster glued onto the front panel.

Now mark out the seat and cut it from ¾in particleboard. Measure it against the base and cut out the notches from each corner that allow it to fit around the posts. It is now dropped down onto the base and held by screws at 12in intervals driven through countersunk clearance holes of the same diameter as the screw shank into the battens inside the front and back panels.

Choose the pine for the back rail with care; it should be knot-free to withstand the pressure of a person leaning back on it. Mark out and cut the back and side rails to length, allowing for the 1in "tenons" at each end.

The rails have a groove 7/16in wide and ½in deep running along the entire bottom edge, which holds the ends of slats that join seat and rail at back and sides. This can be routed, cut with a circular saw or grooving plane, or sawed and chiseled. Cutting such a continuous groove is far simpler than chopping out a series of individual mortises for the slats and allows for some adjustment so that the slats will all stand vertically. Top and bottom mortises do not have to be matched up painstakingly if you use this technique. The groove is cut square to the face of the rail.

At 3¾in intervals, mark out on the seat the position of the twenty-four ⁷⁄₁₆ × 1¼in mortises that hold the ends of the slats and chisel them out, ⁵⁄₁₆in deep.

Cut the twenty-four slats 17¼in long. As the mortises are cut square and the slats set at an angle, it is necessary to pare away wood from the front of each slat at the bottom, and from the back at the top. Assemble slats, rails and base dry, and check that all the slats are properly housed.

Remove the top rails and slats, glue the ends of the slats and the ends of the rails, and assemble. Start at one end and push the rail down on the slats one by one. There is time to adjust the slats before the glue sets.

Cut 4in square caps for the top of each post, 1¼in deep. Mark and plane a ¼in bevel around the lower half of each cap. Drill four ¼in diameter holes through each cap and 1in into the top of the corresponding post. Join caps to posts by gluing ¼in diameter dowels in position. With a chisel pare the protruding ends of the dowels off flush with the top.

Each cupboard door is held by a pair of standard 3 × 6in surface hinges, which are simply screwed onto the face of door and frame with 1in screws. Hinges precisely matching Crane's could not be found, but it was a simple matter to file the edges of standard hinges to shape. Attaching the doors after assembling the seat proved to be difficult, and the designer recommends mounting them as soon as they are cut out of the panel, while it can still be laid flat.

The doors close against wood blocks glued under the top batten inside the front panel. They are held closed by magnetic catches fixed to the door and the block.

Captain Duck's cupboards can be locked to keep out inquisitive crew. This feature seemed an unnecessary detail to the designer, who replaced locks with shield-shaped softwood handles. These are sawed out with a saber saw and beveled slightly around the edge to provide a finger grip. They are glued in position.

The pilaster strips between the cupboard doors are 3 × 12in panels of the ¾in blockboard, glued in position and held by C-clamps until the glue sets. The beveled molding at head and foot of the pilasters and around the base of the front legs can be made as a single strip of ½ × 1in softwood. The bevel is formed by planing away one corner. The strips are then cut into mitered lengths to fit around the pilasters and posts and glued in position. No molding is used on the rear legs, so that the seat can be pushed up flush with a skirting board.

Glue ¾in long ¼in diameter dowels in the corners of the doors to fill the drill entry holes made at the cutting stage and chisel off any protruding ends.

Finishing the settee
Fill any obvious imperfections in the surface of the settee with wood filler. Sand the whole piece smooth. Chamfer the sharp front edges of the seat slightly to avoid the risk of splinters. This chamfering also reduces the risk of paint chipping off the corners.

Paint on a coat of wood primer. This will normally reveal more imperfections, which should be filled and sanded before painting on the undercoat.

Mask off the area occupied by the frieze of mice. Paint yellow undercoat over the rest of the piece. For a smooth and tough finish use at least three layers of undercoat, rubbing down with fine sandpaper between applications. Finally apply a coat of bright yellow gloss paint.

A cardboard mouse is used as a template to trace the outline of the mice on the frieze; the mice are then painted in by hand and the surround painted black.

The settee can be used without upholstery, but a 4in foam cushion brings the seat level up to a comfortable height, and converts the settee into a bed. The foam is covered in cotton fabric with piping sewed inside the edges. To make the back cushions, ½in thick foam pads are placed on hardboard panels. An envelope of fabric is slipped over, turned under at the open edge and hand-sewed in place.

In the Corner *from "At Home", illustrated by J.G. Sowerby and Thomas Crane in 1881*

The Red Studio Chair

by Mark Dunhill

from *The Red Studio* (1911) by Henri Matisse (1869-1954) oil on canvas, 71¼ × 86¼in
The Museum of Modern Art, New York; Mrs Simon Guggenheim Fund

Matisse's red studio was blindingly white. The painting is a transformation of his garden studio in the green Parisian suburb of Issy-les-Moulineaux. Matisse and his wife moved there in 1908 from their city center studio with its view over the Seine to Notre Dame. The new studio was built in the garden at Issy four years later, and there Matisse painted *The Red Studio*. An American visitor to Issy has described the room:

"The studio, a good-sized square structure, was painted white, within and without, and had immense windows (both in the roof and at the side), thus giving a sense of out-of-doors and great heat. A large and simple workroom it was, its walls and easels covered with large, brilliant and extraordinary canvases . . . my main recollection is a glare of light, stifling heat, principally caused by the immense glass windows, open doors, showing glimpses of flowers beyond, as brilliant and bright-hued as the walls within."

Matisse, usually so articulate about his painting, said he did not know why he transformed this hot, white room into a hot, red canvas. But the use of color for emotional effect, and a love of saturated reds, blues and greens, mark his work.

Matisse's work was his life, so it is natural that his studio should occupy an important place in his world. Matisse's paintings, like those of his contemporaries Bonnard and Braque, are full of references to the rooms in which they were painted.

Some pieces of furniture went with him from place to place and appear in picture after picture. When he painted this comfortable, often rather ornate furniture, he transformed its complexity into shapes as simple as signs. When Mark Dunhill came to make the chair in *The Red Studio* his task was to take one of those simple signs and give it a full three-dimensional existence. It was a difficult and stimulating task, because the painting leaves so many options open. In the end he made two versions (see photograph on p. 113). The first was a smaller, neater red chair. The second, which is described here in detail, is unpainted, further from the look of the painting, but closer, perhaps, to its feeling. It also has some affinity with the Dutch *de Stijl* group and the tall, thin-membered chairs made for the Scottish architect Charles Rennie Mackintosh.

Designing the Red Studio chair

The first and most important decision about the design of the chair was to keep the geometry as it appears in the painting. The angles at the front of the seat and the top of the high back could be read as distortions due to perspective, but the designer decided to reproduce them and make an asymmetrical chair. The logic of the piece follows from the decision to place the two uprights in different planes.

The chair was built by clamping, or temporarily gluing, pieces in position. When they were judged to look right, the designer cut lapped joints, mortises or dadoes (housings) to fix them more permanently. The joinery is bizarre by any traditional criterion but is a straightforward reflection of the method of work. The process of making the chair can be compared to making a drawing – trying a line in one place and then rubbing it out and putting it in another – or adding and subtracting lumps of clay when modeling. Even in following Dunhill's design, rather than completely inventing the piece, the *ad hoc* approach has advantages.

Like the more extreme pieces of *de Stijl* furniture, this is a chair for the stoic. Rietveld, the most famous of the *de Stijl* furniture designers, thought that sitting was an active occupation, and that resting should be done in bed. The painter Theo van Doesburg – leader of the *de Stijl* movement – spoke of Rietveld's furniture as "the abstract sculptures of the future interior." Dunhill's chair is in this tradition.

Making the chair

The chair is constructed in three stages. First each of the uprights is joined to a front leg by the side and seat rails. Next the two side assemblies are joined by back and front seat rails, a central stretcher and back rails. Finally the seat is added.

The uprights, legs, seat rails, side rails and slanting top rail are all made from 1×2 in mahogany. This was cut "freehand" with a bandsaw. The designer wanted a hand-drawn look, and preferred the slight irregularities of timber cut by eye to the precise lines of carefully squared wood. The lower rails and the stretcher between the two uprights are $1 \times 1\frac{1}{4}$ in mahogany cut in the same way.

Cut the uprights: at this stage they are both the same length and stand about 1in higher than the top of the

Baby chair (1920/21) by Dutch de Stijl *designer Gerrit Rietveld. It is held together by pegs and nails. Stedelijk Museum, Amsterdam*

tenon on what will be the taller of the two. In the positions shown on the drawing, and measuring from the base, mark and cut (working upwards) the 1in square notch, $\frac{1}{2} \times 2$ in lap joint and $\frac{3}{4} \times 1$ in through mortise in what will be the shorter upright, and the $\frac{3}{4} \times \frac{3}{4}$ in through mortise, $\frac{1}{2} \times 2$ in lap joint and $1 \times 1\frac{1}{4}$ in notch in the taller. Note that the shorter upright presents its narrow face to the front of the chair, the taller one its broad (2in) face.

Draw a full-scale plan of the rails, legs and uprights at seat level (see diagram on p. 114). Mark out the side seat rails. These meet the back uprights at 90°. The seat rails have a 2in end-lap on the shorter upright, a 1in end-lap on the taller. These are marked precisely by holding the rails against the uprights. A notched joint and a ¾ × ¾ in tenon join the lower rails to the shorter and taller upright respectively. Saw the lower rails to length and cut out the end-laps and tenons with a tenon saw.

To reinforce all the mortise and tenon joints in the chair, a thin mahogany wedge is hammered into the tenon after assembly. To accommodate this, a groove is cut down the center of all the tenons before fitting the chair together.

The upper and lower rails do not enter the front legs at a right angle. Read the angle from the drawing with a sliding bevel, and set the bevel at that angle. Mark the angled inner faces of the half joints and ¾ × ¾ in tenons using the bevel. Cut these tenons and joints.

Cut the front legs to length. As the rails meet the front legs off-square, the mortises and lap joints in the legs must be cut at an angle. It is worth making wedges of the correct angle, and clamping these behind the leg so that when it is laid flat the mortises can be made with a vertical drill fitted with a ¾ in bit. Chisel the corners of the mortises square. The half joints at the top of each leg must also be cut at an angle: check this angle both against the drawing and against the shaped ends of the seat rails before cutting the joint with a tenon saw.

At this stage you will have uprights, legs and side rails cut to length and jointed. The front legs are still rectangular in section. Before the sides are glued up a slice of triangular section must be taken off the outside of each. A plane or shaping tool is the most suitable way of paring away the waste. Plane the outer face of each leg until it is parallel with the side rails. Finished dimensions are shown in the drawing.

Assemble side rails and legs without glue to check the fit. Mark the protruding ends of the tenons, dismantle the piece and saw or plane away these protrusions.

Glue and clamp up the side assemblies of upright, two rails and front leg. When these are dry, prop them up the distance apart shown on the full-scale drawing you have made of the chair at seat level. You will now be able to check that the angles of the front legs are indeed following the oblique line of the front of the seat. If they are not, adjustments can still be made by shaving a little off the front leg or by putting the two side assemblies a little closer together or further apart. Having determined their final position, cut the back and front seat rails to length. Mark and cut the ½ × 1in end-lap joint on the right end of the back rail. Drill ¾in-deep holes in each end of the front rail and the left end of the rear rail to take a pair of ¼in dowels, 1¼in long. Cut and joint the 1 × 1¼in central stretcher and back stretcher. Drill the side assemblies for the seat-rail dowels and glue and clamp the whole job.

Cut the top rail to length and lay it against the uprights. When you find the correct position (you can follow the measurements in the drawing on p. 115) mark the slanting line of the top rail on the uprights. Use this line to saw the uprights to length, at the same angle, and to mark and cut out the tenons at the top of the uprights.

Mark the angle of the mortises to be cut in the top rail by holding it against the uprights and penciling the line they make on the side of the rail. Cut the mortises and glue the rail in position, cutting or paring away the projecting ends of the tenons.

The seat is made up from ¾in-thick tongue and groove boards. Glue and clamp together four pieces 3¾ × 11¼in to make the central panel. Cut ¼ × ¼in rabbets on top and bottom of the two outer edges of the seat panel to form a ¼in tongue – a router or circular saw simplifies the job. Cut a corresponding ¼ × ¼in groove in the edges of the 3⅞in and 3¼in boards which form the sides of the seat. Glue the sides onto the seat panel and clamp them in position until the glue sets.

Cut the entire seat panel obliquely to match the angle of the front rail, allowing for a ¼in tongue. Cut a ¼in tongue on the front edge as before, and rout out a ¼in groove in the edge of the board forming the front of the seat. Glue the front board in place and clamp it until the

Mark Dunhill's two versions of the Red Studio *chair*

113

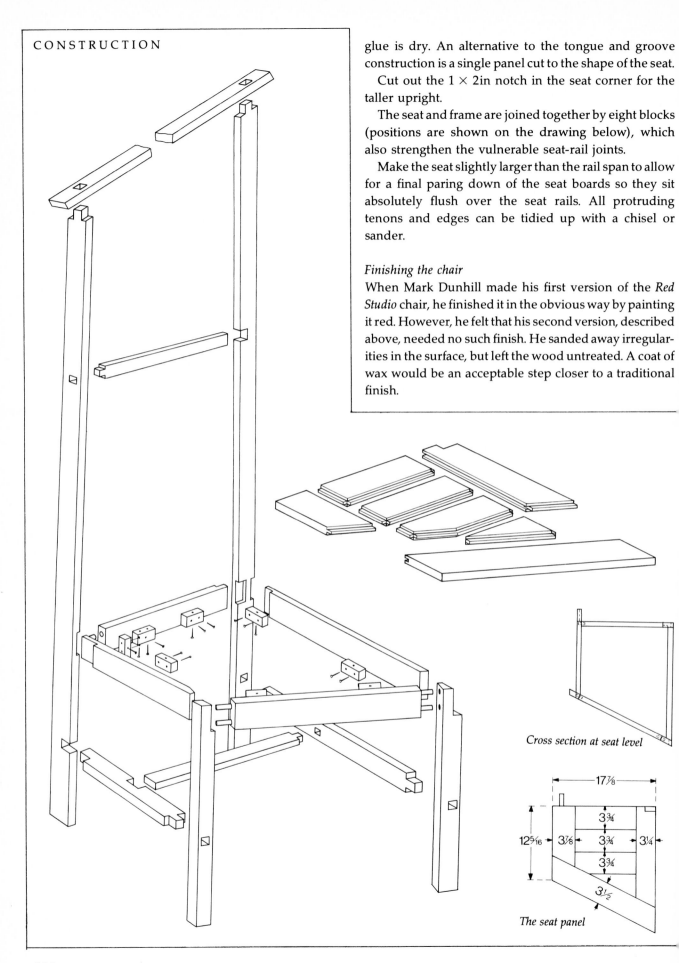

glue is dry. An alternative to the tongue and groove construction is a single panel cut to the shape of the seat.

Cut out the 1 × 2in notch in the seat corner for the taller upright.

The seat and frame are joined together by eight blocks (positions are shown on the drawing below), which also strengthen the vulnerable seat-rail joints.

Make the seat slightly larger than the rail span to allow for a final paring down of the seat boards so they sit absolutely flush over the seat rails. All protruding tenons and edges can be tidied up with a chisel or sander.

Finishing the chair

When Mark Dunhill made his first version of the *Red Studio* chair, he finished it in the obvious way by painting it red. However, he felt that his second version, described above, needed no such finish. He sanded away irregularities in the surface, but left the wood untreated. A coat of wax would be an acceptable step closer to a traditional finish.

Cross section at seat level

17⅞

12⁵⁄₁₆   3⅞   3¾   3¾   3¼   3¾   3½

The seat panel

ORDER OF WORK

1 *Cut the two back uprights*
2 *Mark and cut the joints in the uprights*
3 *Draw a full-scale plan of the frame at seat level*
4 *Measure, mark and cut the side rails*
5 *Cut the front legs to length*
6 *Mark and cut the mortises and lap joints in the front legs*
7 *Plane the outside face of each front leg parallel with the rear uprights*
8 *Assemble without glue, check the fit and make adjustments*
9 *Glue each back upright to its two side rails and front leg*
10 *Cut the back and front seat rails to length*
11 *Mark and cut an end lap joint on the back rail*
12 *Fit two dowels at each end of the front seat rail and the left end of the rear rail*
13 *Cut and joint the central stretcher and back stretcher*
14 *Drill the legs to take the seat rail dowels*
15 *Glue and clamp all the pieces together*
16 *Mark the position of the slanting back rail on the rear uprights*
17 *Cut the uprights to length*
18 *Mark and cut the tenon on top of each upright*
19 *Mark and cut mortises in the top rail*
20 *Glue the top rail in position*
21 *Pare off the projecting ends of the tenons*
22 *Glue and clamp together the tongue & groove boards to make the central seat panel*
23 *Mark and cut a tongue on the outer edges of the seat panel*
24 *Cut a corresponding groove in the side panels*
25 *Glue side and seat panels together*
26 *Cut the seat panel obliquely to shape*
27 *Rout out a tongue and groove in seat panel and front panel*
28 *Glue seat and front panel together*
29 *Cut out a notch in the seat corner for the right upright*
30 *Join seat to frame by seven fixing blocks*

MATERIALS

	No.	Size (ins)
Mahogany for:		
Uprights	2	$1 \times 2 \times 69\frac{1}{2}$
Seat rail	1	$1 \times 2 \times 20\frac{3}{4}$
Seat rails	2	$1 \times 2 \times 15$
Seat rail	1	$1 \times 2 \times 16\frac{1}{8}$
Lower rail	1	$1 \times 2 \times 20\frac{3}{4}$
Lower rail	1	$1 \times 2 \times 14$
Top rail	1	$1 \times 2 \times 19\frac{7}{8}$
Legs	2	$1 \times 2 \times 21\frac{3}{8}$
Lower stretcher	1	$1 \times 1\frac{1}{4} \times 17$
Back stretcher	1	$1 \times 1\frac{1}{4} \times 16$
Seat	4	$\frac{3}{4} \times 3\frac{3}{4} \times 11\frac{1}{4}$
Seat	1	$\frac{3}{4} \times 3\frac{1}{4} \times 16$
Seat	1	$\frac{3}{4} \times 3\frac{7}{8} \times 16$
Seat	1	$\frac{3}{4} \times 3\frac{1}{2} \times 20$
Two-part fixing blocks	8	
$\frac{1}{4}$ dia hardwood dowels	6	
Woodworking adhesive		

DIMENSIONS

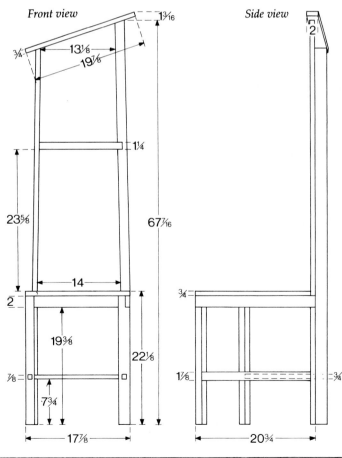

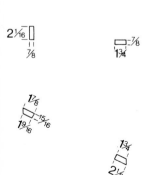

The dimensions and relative positions of the legs, from above

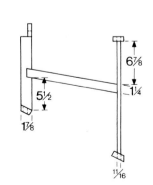

The position of the cross rails, from above

The Madonna's Lectern

by David Knight

from *The Annunciation* by Domenico Ghirlandaio (1449-94)

San Gimignano

Ghirlandaio's Florence was the rich Renaissance city of the Medici. Under the rule of Lorenzo the Magnificent, artists and craftsmen were thriving. By 1474 there were 85 silk factories, 44 goldsmiths and silversmiths and 84 furniture workshops supplying the fashion-conscious Florentines.

Florentine fashion gave Ghirlandaio his name. According to Vasari's epic sixteenth-century *Lives of the Artists,* he earned his name by inventing and promoting "ghirlande" (garlands), which became a fashionable form of headdress among the girls of Florence.

Ghirlandaio is now remembered as Michelangelo's first teacher, but during his lifetime his paintings were ranked alongside those of his great contemporaries Botticelli, Filippino Lippi and Perugino. His finest works were frescoes, among them *The Annunciation* at San Gimignano, which can still be seen in the courtyard where it has stood for five hundred years. The picture shows the archangel Gabriel, the messenger of God, appearing before the Virgin Mary to predict the birth of her son. He holds his attribute, a lily, the symbol of purity.

The Madonna's simple lectern is Florentine in style, as surviving examples show. Lecterns are rare in domestic use today, when the armchair has taken over as the average reader's chosen furniture. Standing up to read or work is not without appeal, and the lectern remains an admirable way of displaying a large, open book at home.

Designing the Madonna's lectern

The proportions of the lectern are not clear from the painting. The designer interpreted the evidence of the kneeling figure and took the width of a useful bookrest into account. He concluded that the piece should be square in plan, like many Tuscan Renaissance originals.

The weighty column and bookrest present problems, as they need secure support. He realized he could house the column between a pair of central dividers in the shelving

Florentine craftsmen of the 15th century were famous for their skill at intarsia *(marquetry). This stunning example of pictorial* trompe l'oeil *woodwork made by Baccio Fontelli (c. 1450-1492) includes a pleasing lectern. Metropolitan Museum of Art, New York; Rogers Fund, 1939*

unit, thereby creating a piece with shelves on both sides. The bookrest stands firm on its column, but it is free to rotate to face in any direction. A pair of doors could be fitted on the hidden side of the shelving unit to convert the open shelves into a closing cupboard. This feature would also

be faithful to Renaissance models. The spacing of the shelves can be varied to improve the unit's versatility.

Walnut was the usual choice of the Italian Renaissance cabinet maker, but it is expensive today. Rustic Renaissance pieces were often made in pine, and as this wood is cheaper and more freely available, David Knight chose pine.

The main problem facing the modern maker is the carving on the column. This was a specialty of fifteenth-century Florentine craftsmen, but experienced hands are needed for such intricate work. We therefore made a plain pine turned post. The bookrest and column remain the hardest parts to make, and it would be perfectly possible to construct only the shelving unit below.

Making the lectern

The Ghirlandaio lectern is designed as an exercise in dado (housing) joints. Dadoes cut in the underside of the top hold the sides in place, and stopped dadoes in the two side panels receive the shelves. Dadoes hold the central partitions, and dadoes in the faces of the bookrest take the triangular panels at each end. Making the piece involves careful, neat but straightforward carpentry. The principle is simple – if you cut all the shelves the same length and all the dadoes the same depth, they will all fit together.

There are three distinct parts to the job – shelving unit, column and bookrest. They are not attached to one another, so the piece can be dismantled in seconds for storage or transport.

The shelving unit
The base of the lectern is essentially a double-sided shelving unit with a central divider. On one side the divider is double above the top shelf, providing a sandwich for the base of the column. It is constructed entirely from 1in-thick pine planks, with $\frac{1}{2} \times 4$in tongue and groove boards in the center. The sides and top are made by planing and gluing together two 9in-wide planks and one 5in, all 84in long, to make a single plank $22\frac{3}{8}$in wide. Three 8in planks would create a plank of the same width, but the designer preferred 9in wood because the quality of softwood is likely to be better in larger sizes, which must be cut from bigger and less knotty logs.

To minimize the risk of distortion, the annual rings visible on the end grain of the planks should run in opposite directions on adjoining planks.

The edges of the planks are planed square, glued and clamped together. No dowels or tongues are necessary. When the glue has set, any slight cusp at the joints can be planed off. The piece is then sanded.

The plank can now be sawed into three pieces to form the sides and top – 28¾in for one side, 24in for the top, 28¾in for the other side. Cut them out of the plank in this sequence (side, top, side) so that the grain pattern of the wood will carry over the top of the piece.

The edges of the top are rounded off with silicon carbide paper (glasspaper), working down from a coarse grade to fine. A molding plane would also do the job, though end grain is difficult to plane.

Saw ¾in off the width of the two sides.

Mark out the position of the dadoes for the shelves and dividers. Remember that the matching dadoes in the left and right sides will be the opposite of each other. These grooves can be routed out or cut in the traditional way by first chiseling out a mortise about 1in long at the stopped end of the dado (see below), then cutting along a scribed line with a tenon saw and finally clearing the joint with a chisel or plough plane. A block of wood clamped alongside the cutting line keeps the saw cutting straight.

The width of the dadoes must be precisely the thickness of the timber – in this case ⅞in for the shelves and sides, ⅜in for the tongue and groove dividers. All grooves are ¼in deep. The dadoes for the four upper shelves are set back (stopped) ¾in from the outside edge of the plank; this is approximately the thickness of the timber, a useful rule of thumb for stopped dadoes. The dadoes for the two shelves forming the base are not stopped, nor are the dadoes for the main dividers; these run the entire length of the sides.

The shelves can now be cut. On the four shelves with stopped dadoes saw out a ¼ × ¾in notch on the two outside corners to take the stopped end of the dado. On the side of the divider with the deeper shelves, the top face of the top shelf and the underside of the top itself have a ⅜in-wide groove, ¼in deep, to take the short divider of tongue and groove boards.

It is now possible to construct the main body of the unit – sides, shelves and top. First assemble it dry to make sure the parts fit. Top, shelves and sides are glued up and clamped in one operation. The short divider of tongue and groove boards between the top and the first shelf must also be inserted before the top is glued on. (The main divider will be slid in from underneath, board by board, after assembly.) Place waste wood between clamps and workpiece to prevent damage. Clamping so many pieces at once can be a problem. You will need strap clamps (sash cramps) pulling the sides onto each shelf and at the same time squeezing the top down. Six will do the job. If you are short of clamps, fit the top later.

Now add the moldings around the top and bottom of the piece. A ⅝ × ⅞in fillet molding runs under the projecting edge of the top on all four sides. The corners of the fillets are mitered, and they are glued in place. At the front and back – where the fillet is unsupported – a second thickness of the same ⅝ × ⅞in fillet is glued behind the first inside the cabinet to reinforce it.

The base molding is made from three pieces (see drawing) – a quarter-round held in the angle of two softwood strips, the vertical one ⅜ × 1¾in, the horizontal ⅜ × 1⅜in. It would have been hard to match the wood color if a ready-cut molding had been used, so the designer turned it from pine. To do this he made a turning block 2½ × 2½ × 30in, made up of four pieces of 1¼ × 1¼in, carefully planed square and glued together

Locking cupboard doors are a feature of this late 15th-century lectern from Siena

119

ORDER OF WORK

DIMENSIONS

The shelving unit

 1 Plane the edges of the three 84in planks square
 2 Glue and clamp them together
 3 Plane joints flat
 4 Saw the 84in plank into three to make the sides and top
 5 Round the edges of the top with silicon carbide paper (glasspaper)
 6 Saw ¾in off the width of the two sides
 7 Mark out dado (housing) positions on sides and top
 8 Cut the dadoes (housings)
 9 Cut shelves to length and saw out the notch on the two outside corners of each shelf
10 Cut dadoes for the short dividers in the top shelf
11 Glue together sides, shelves, top and short tongue & groove divider. Clamp until dry
12 Cut the mitered molding which runs under the top edge
13 Glue the molding in position
14 Cut and glue the reinforcing battens behind the molding at front and back
15 Make the base molding
16 Glue and clamp the base molding to the unit
17 Drill a 2in diameter central hole in the top
18 Drill a 1½in diameter hole through the softwood block
19 With the post in position, glue the drilled block to the short tongue & groove dividers
20 Slide the long tongue & groove boards in position

The bookrest

 1 Make a full-scale drawing of the triangular face of the bookrest
 2 Mark the cutting lines on the spine
 3 Saw out the two rabbets in the spine
 4 Glue and clamp together the two boards to make the side panels
 5 Plane the joints level
 6 Mark and cut dadoes in the side panels and spine
 7 Mark and cut out the two triangular end panels
 8 Glue and clamp the spine, sides and ends together
 9 Glue and clamp the two ledges in position
10 Plane the ends smooth and round off the corners of the ledges
11 Cut and attach the locating blocks for the post
12 Assemble bookrest, post and shelving unit

Finish

The entire piece is sanded and waxed

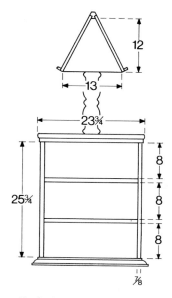

Back view

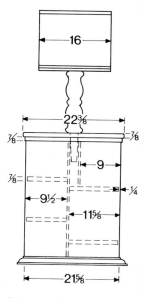

Side view. The dotted lines show the positions of shelves and dividers

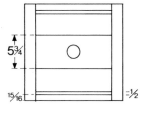

View of the bookrest from below

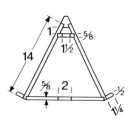

Cross section through the center of the bookrest

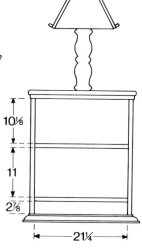

Front view

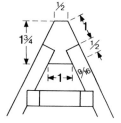

Cross section through the center of the bookrest's apex

Cross section of molding around base

120

CONSTRUCTION

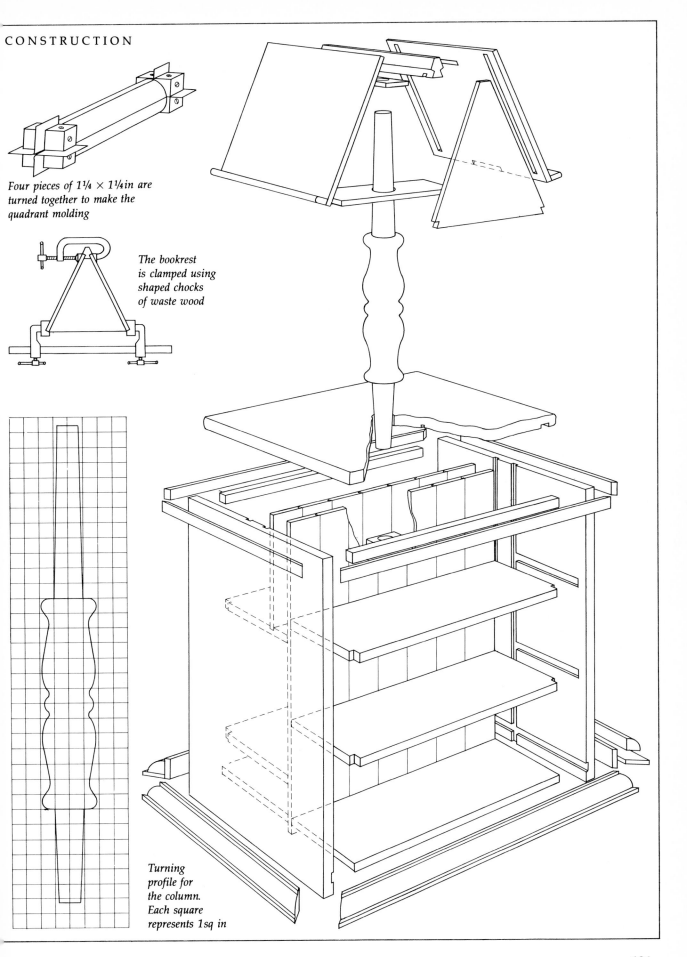

Four pieces of 1¼ × 1¼in are
turned together to make the
quadrant molding

The bookrest
is clamped using
shaped chocks
of waste wood

Turning
profile for
the column.
Each square
represents 1sq in

MATERIALS	No.	Size (ins)
The Shelving Unit		
Pine for:		
Top and sides	2	$1 \times 9 \times 84$
Top and sides	1	$1 \times 5 \times 84$
Shelves	2	$1 \times 11\frac{3}{8} \times 21\frac{3}{4}$
Shelf	1	$1 \times 11\frac{5}{8} \times 21\frac{3}{4}$
Shelves	2	$1 \times 9\frac{1}{4} \times 21\frac{3}{4}$
Shelf	1	$1 \times 9\frac{1}{2} \times 21\frac{3}{4}$
Top edging	1	$\frac{3}{4} \times 1 \times 144$
Lower edging	1	$\frac{3}{8} \times 1\frac{3}{4} \times 96$
Lower edging	1	$\frac{3}{8} \times 1\frac{3}{8} \times 100$
Lower edging	4	$1\frac{1}{4} \times 1\frac{1}{4} \times 30$
Column housing	1	$2 \times 2\frac{1}{4} \times 5$
Tongue & groove pine for:		
Divider	7	$\frac{1}{2} \times 3\frac{1}{2} \times 11\frac{1}{2}$
Divider	7	$\frac{1}{2} \times 3\frac{1}{2} \times 28$
The Bookrest		
Pine for:		
Spine	1	$2 \times 2 \times 16$
Sides	4	$\frac{3}{4} \times 8 \times 14$
Faces	2	$\frac{1}{2} \times 12\frac{1}{4} \times 13\frac{1}{2}$
Ledges	2	$\frac{1}{2} \times 1\frac{1}{4} \times 16$
Housing block	1	$\frac{3}{4} \times 5\frac{3}{4} \times 13$
Housing block	1	$\frac{3}{4} \times 2\frac{1}{4} \times 5\frac{3}{4}$
The Column		
Pine	1	$4 \times 4 \times 32\frac{3}{4}$

Casein glue; 1in finishing nails; Wax or polyurethane

with paper between the joints. In this way they can be separated easily later. To construct the block, glue a piece of paper to two adjacent sides of one of the $1\frac{1}{4} \times 1\frac{1}{4}$in pieces. Glue and clamp on a second piece. When the glue has set add another piece of paper and glue and clamp the other two pieces to form the block. If you try to glue all four at once the block is unlikely to remain square and cannot then be centered on the lathe. The pieces are reinforced by screws 1in from each end (see drawing), which stop the considerable torque exerted during turning from splitting the pieces apart. The 2in at each end are not turned.

The block is held in the lathe at the point where the four pieces meet. This produces a cylinder $2\frac{1}{4}$in in diameter. Sand this smooth, remove the screws and separate the pieces by inserting a chisel in the joints. You should have four perfect quarter-round strips. These are glued to the two softwood strips to make the complete foot molding. Cut each side to length with a mitered

corner. The moldings are then glued to the unit and clamped until the glue sets.

Now drill a 2in-diameter hole through the center of the top. It is important to drill precisely through the center, which can be located by finding the point where the two diagonals cross.

The short divider conceals a softwood block in which the column sits and which is fitted now. Before gluing it in place, drill a $1\frac{3}{4}$in-diameter hole through the block to take the end of the column. Glue the block centrally to the back of the short divider. The fixing can be reinforced at each end by countersunk screws. These must not be driven more than $\frac{1}{4}$in into the tongue and groove board. It is best to fit the block with the post in position, to make sure it is in the correct place.

Slide the long tongue and groove boards up from underneath. Push them all into position except the last one, then measure the remaining space and cut the last board to width, allowing $\frac{1}{4}$in for the housing. As it is quite likely than something will drop down the posthole at some time, leave the pins holding the central board showing, so they can be removed easily.

The bookrest
The bookrest is constructed from two boards, housed in rabbets in a spine running along the top ridge of the lectern. They are held apart by triangular boards which slot into rabbets on the inside of the side boards at either end. A strip glued along the base of each board forms a ledge on which a book can rest. The open base of the bookrest is crossed by a board drilled with a central hole to take the column. The top of the column is located in a hole drilled in a block which is fitted hard under the center of the ridge.

Draw up the job to full scale. It is easier to take angles from a drawing than to calculate them. The dimensions of the triangular ends can also be taken from the drawing. Allow $\frac{1}{4}$in at the sides and top where the panel will sit in its housings.

The spine begins as a 2in square batten, 16in long. Wood from a timber yard is unlikely to be truly square, and must be checked. Plane it square.

Mark the angles of the rabbets on the ends of the top spine, and continue the lines along the long sides.

The two rabbets are sawed out with a tenon saw. To simplify sawing in at an angle, make an angled template. This is just a piece of waste wood planed – or sawed – down to the correct angle and clamped to the workpiece to act as a saw guide. The projections can be planed down later, after the bookrest is assembled.

The two 14×16in side boards are made by gluing together two $\frac{3}{4} \times 8$in planks and planing the joint level.

The boards are then grooved vertically: dadoes ½in wide and ¼in deep are cut 1in from the ends of each board, and stopped 1in from the base at both ends. These dadoes carry across the base of the top spine to form a continuous slot, so that the triangular end piece locks the whole construction together when it is fitted in the slots.

The triangular end pieces are now marked and cut out. The apex of the triangle is sawed off to allow it to slot into the spine. A notch ¼ × 1in is sawed out of the two base angles to fit the stopped dado which prevents the triangles being squeezed out during clamping.

Assemble spine, sides and triangular panels to check the fit. Glue and clamp together. The odd angles make clamping a problem. A useful tip is to keep the two strips of wood which were removed when the rabbets were sawed out of the top spine, and to glue them onto the boards at the top. C-clamps screwed onto these will not slide off. Four C-clamps will be needed along the top to guarantee a tight fit. Notched pieces of waste wood along the bottom of the side panels will give secure footings for strap clamps spanning from side to side. The glued-on strips and the projecting "ears" of the spine block are planed away when the glue has set. It is easier to plane off these projections after assembly than to rely on complete precision at the cutting stage.

Cut the two ledges to length. Glue and clamp them in position. Plane off any uneven joints on the ends and round off the corners of the ledges with silicon carbide paper (glasspaper).

Now chisel out shallow depressions 5¾in long in the boards inside the bookrest, centered 1in below the spine. Cut a piece 2¼ × 5¾in out of ¾in softwood. Use a Forstner bit or hole borer to drill a 1½in-diameter hole through the center of this piece (the center is the point where the two diagonals cross). Glue the piece in the chiseled grooves. The peg of the column, which is pushed up through the hole, is tapered to avoid catching on the edge of the hole as you push it up. This feature also gives a very positive lock without any further fixing.

The column requires a second location point in the bookrest to hold it securely. A similar 5¾in board runs from side to side at the base of the bookrest. A locating hole 2in in diameter is drilled through its center. Chisel out shallow depressions 5¾in long and ⅝in deep in the backs of the side boards at their base. The holes in the two boards must align squarely if the bookrest is to be properly supported, and the whole should be assembled dry to test this. When they align, glue the board in position.

The column

The column is turned from a piece of 4 × 4in pine. The job called for a 1in gouge, a skew chisel, a flat scraper and glasspaper. Choose the wood with care: finding a piece of softwood of this dimension without knots and shakes can be hard. Alternatively four pieces of 2 × 2in timber can be glued together to build up the block. Hardwood would be more suitable if any attempt is to be made to match the carved detail in the painting. It is also easier to turn; the skew chisel tends to bite into softwood, making frequent recourse to scrapers and silicon carbide paper necessary.

The turning diagram on p. 121 shows the profile – if a full-sized template of the outline is cut in card it can be used to check the progress of the turning. It is also easy to adapt if you are forced to alter the shape of the column because you remove too much wood in one place.

When the turning is finished, the column is sanded. This is easy with hardwood – the paper is held under the piece as it turns in the lathe. But softwood scars easily, so finishing must be done working in the direction of the grain. The turning can be entrusted to a local wood turner.

To finish, all three parts of the piece are sanded, waxed and assembled.

The Annunciation was a popular subject with Renaissance painters, and contemporary furniture figures in many Annunciation paintings. The low rush-seated chair behind the Archangel Gabriel in this version of the biblical episode from the S. Lucy Altarpiece by Domenico Veneziano is a common Italian design of the 15th century. Fitzwilliam Museum, Cambridge

Still Life Sideboard

by Patrick Daw

from *Still Life on a Sideboard* (1920) by Pablo Picasso (1881-1973)

Musée Picasso, Paris

The cubists show what the intellect knows, not what the still eye sees. They renounced the 3-D illusions of traditional perspective in an attempt to show the complete structure of objects on the flat canvas. They took simple, recognizable things – guitars, bottles, human figures – broke them down and reassembled them in a two-dimensional image. Picasso and Braque led the way.

Still Life on a Sideboard is one of Picasso's own Picassos, part of the artist's personal collection, which was acquired by the French nation after his death in 1973. It belongs to a series of small gouaches executed at Juan-les-Pins in 1920, during a summer holiday on the French Riviera with his wife Olga, whom Picasso had met when she was dancing with the Ballets Russes.

Designing the still-life sideboard

Picasso's rigorously 2-dimensional picture defies the designer's 3-dimensional imagination. The original sideboard at Juan-les-Pins was no doubt a simple rectangular structure with plain paneled doors, a pair of ordinary drawers, and an assortment of objects on top. Yet this is not what the painting shows. The sides are both visible, and the doors do not match – although the right-hand one is straightforward, the line of the left-hand door continues down to floor level. The designer was determined to play the cubist game and to make a faithful 3-dimensional version of the picture. He therefore decided he must incorporate both these features.

From the complex and apparently contradictory information in the painting, Patrick Daw designed a simple, symmetrical, trapezoid cupboard with splayed sides and a flat top. The height of the top makes the piece suitable for use as a kitchen cupboard or a cocktail cabinet. The top overhangs the base equally on all three sides. At the front and on the left-hand side, triangular fillets add variety and confuse the planes. The logical insertion of two shelves inside the sideboard improves stability and practicality.

At the design stage Daw worked from a black and white photocopy of the painting. By cutting out the color he reduced the problem to one of volumes. Only when he had constructed the entire piece did he finally switch on the color. The impact of the cubist illusion relies heavily on the care with which the paint is applied. The drawers are false, a mere painted outline, but the doors are hinged; they open to reveal the two usable shelves inside.

A flat top is necessary if the piece is to be functional, yet the designer did not want to lose the shapes of the still life at the top of the piece in the painting. He resolved the dilemma by creating a flat but irregular rising back which projects above the flat top. But in solving one problem, he immediately created a second – that of establishing the point in the painting where the vertical and horizontal planes meet.

He was dissatisfied with his first solution, which seemed to destroy the intriguing confusion of Picasso's original. When the piece was constructed he decided it was crucial to avoid a simple right angle between the back and top. He took what proved to be the key decision, an elegant and functional resolution of the difficulty. He referred back to the painting and decided to make part of the still-life pattern 3-dimensional. He added a trapezoid shelf projecting from the back panel and supported at the front by a triangular block matching the shapes in the painting. The result is best seen in the photograph on page 127.

Making the sideboard

Most of the difficulties occurred at the design stage. Construction is comparatively simple. The piece is made almost entirely from ½in particleboard (blockboard). The back is strong ½in plywood, the shelves ¾in laminated chipboard and the shelf on top ¾in particleboard. Battens are fitted in the front inside angles to reinforce the joints. The pieces are pinned, glued and screwed together.

The major construction problems occur because many of the pieces have to be joined at unusual angles. The designer's own approach did not involve reading angles from a measured drawing – in fact he worked only from sketches. He would cut the pieces roughly to size, then place them together without glue, adjusting their relative positions until they looked right. He would then read off the angle between two pieces with a protractor, bisect the angle, set his bench saw at that angle and saw the angled edge on both pieces. A bench saw is clearly a great aid in this process, though most power saber saws (jigsaws) and circular saws can also be set to any angle. It is wise to measure the angle of the saw blade with a

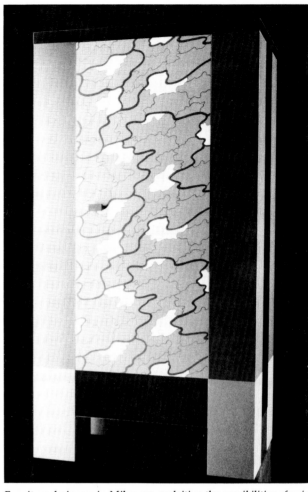

Furniture designers in Milan are exploiting the possibilities of paint and plastic laminates. The paintwork in the "Luxor" closet in laminate and wood by George James Sowden for Memphis (1981) is reminiscent of Joseph H. Davis's work (p. 26)

protractor: relying on the saw's own gauge can lead to errors. A trial cut on a piece of waste wood will determine whether the angle is correct. In the absence of power tools the edges can be cut square and planed down to the desired angle.

The trial-and-error method was used to cut the beveled edges on the triangular fillet underneath the overhanging top on the left-hand side. He cut the fillet roughly to shape, tried it in position and took off more and more until he achieved a perfect fit.

Although at the most basic structural level the piece is a plywood back with the particleboard elements attached, construction does not begin at the back. Access from the rear is needed to fit the shelves.

Mark out the L-shaped door surround on a sheet of ½in particleboard and cut it out. All edges are right angles at this stage. A notch is cut out of the inside face at floor level to form the right-hand leg.

Mark and cut out the two side panels, leaving them slightly oversize at front and rear. Place the three pieces together without glue. When they look right, measure off the angle between each pair, divide it by two and set the bench saw or saber saw at a corresponding angle. Saw the sides exactly to size with angled edges at the front and back, and miter the edges of the L-shaped piece at the same angle to match.

The back panel will sit in a rabbet in the side panels. Cut out this ½in-deep rabbet. This can be done with a circular saw.

Mark and cut out the particleboard top. All its edges are cut at right angles at this stage.

The joints between the sides and the front L are reinforced by 1 × 1in battens. Two edges of these must be sawed or planed to the inside corner angle.

Pin and glue the L-shape, sides, battens and top together, using woodworking adhesive and 1½in finishing nails driven through the battens into the sides and the L.

Mark and cut out the two interior shelves. Note that the upper shelf is not as deep as the lower one and projects forward at the right-hand side to meet the front panel. Cut a 1 × 1in notch out of the front right hand corner of both shelves, so they will fit around the batten. Draw horizontal pencil lines on the inside of the cupboard sides to mark the lower edge of the upper shelf at each side. Cut ½ × ½in battens to support the shelf at the sides. The left-hand batten is shorter than the right. Angle the ends of the battens to match the shelf. Drill three countersunk clearance holes through each batten and corresponding pilot holes in the cupboard sides. Drive ¾in screws through the clearance holes into the cupboard sides. Put the top shelf in position on the battens. Glue a white plastic edging strip to the front edge of the shelf.

Mark the position of the lower shelf on the outside of the cupboard sides. Drill three countersunk clearance holes for screws through each side, place the shelf in position and drive screws through the sideboard sides into the shelf edges.

Mark and cut the panel which supports the lower shelf. At each end the edge is sawed at the same angle as the shelf sides. It is glued along top and side edges and pinned in position through the lower shelf and the cupboard sides, using 1in finishing nails at 4in intervals.

When the piece was assembled so far, the designer thought it looked too regular with its uniformly projecting top. He decided to blur the planes by adding a triangular molding underneath the top at the front and on the left hand side. The simpler front molding is attached first. To calculate the angle at which the molding's upper and lower edges must be cut, place a ruler across the overhang at the side, so that the ruler touches the top leading edge of the overhang and meets

the side spanning a 3½in gap. This fixes where the bottom of the molding will be fixed to the door surround. Read off the angles with a protractor or sliding bevel; as the top meets the front at right angles, the two readings should add up to 90°.

Cut out the molding with the bench saw or saber saw set at these two angles. Alternatively, cut the edges square and plane them down to the correct angles. Set the molding in position under the overhang (see drawing). The edges of the molding are glued, and it is clamped in position until the glue dries.

Cut a small triangle of particleboard to fit in the gap between molding, top and L at the right-hand side. Glue it in position. Plane the front edge of the top to continue the line of the molding.

Before the left-hand molding is made the plywood back is cut to shape and fitted. A pattern for the top section is given on p. 128. The 1in-square grid pattern on the drawing can be drawn full scale on the plywood sheet and the shape of the back plotted by reference to the drawing. Cut out the back with a saber saw.

Bevel the two side edges of the back to fit the rabbet in the sides. This can be done with a bench saw, circular saw or plane, although plywood is not easy to plane. Do not bevel the right-hand edge where it projects over the top. Glue and screw the back in position, driving 1¼in

The 2-D illusion breaks down in this view of Patrick Daw's sideboard

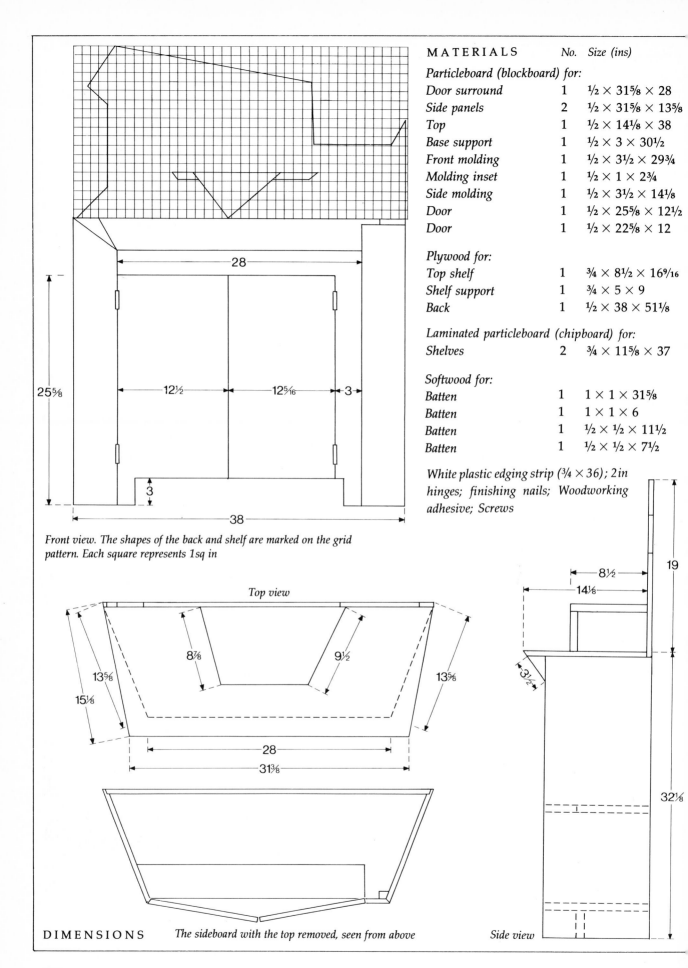

MATERIALS

	No.	Size (ins)
Particleboard (blockboard) for:		
Door surround	1	½ × 31⅝ × 28
Side panels	2	½ × 31⅝ × 13⅝
Top	1	½ × 14⅛ × 38
Base support	1	½ × 3 × 30½
Front molding	1	½ × 3½ × 29¾
Molding inset	1	½ × 1 × 2¾
Side molding	1	½ × 3½ × 14⅛
Door	1	½ × 25⅝ × 12½
Door	1	½ × 22⅝ × 12
Plywood for:		
Top shelf	1	¾ × 8½ × 16⁹⁄₁₆
Shelf support	1	¾ × 5 × 9
Back	1	½ × 38 × 51⅛
Laminated particleboard (chipboard) for:		
Shelves	2	¾ × 11⅝ × 37
Softwood for:		
Batten	1	1 × 1 × 31⅝
Batten	1	1 × 1 × 6
Batten	1	½ × ½ × 11½
Batten	1	½ × ½ × 7½

White plastic edging strip (¾ × 36); 2in hinges; finishing nails; Woodworking adhesive; Screws

Front view. The shapes of the back and shelf are marked on the grid pattern. Each square represents 1sq in

Top view

DIMENSIONS   The sideboard with the top removed, seen from above

Side view

128

FINISH

Acrylic primer/undercoat
Flat enamel (eggshell) paint –
black, white, blue, pink, light
brown and dark brown

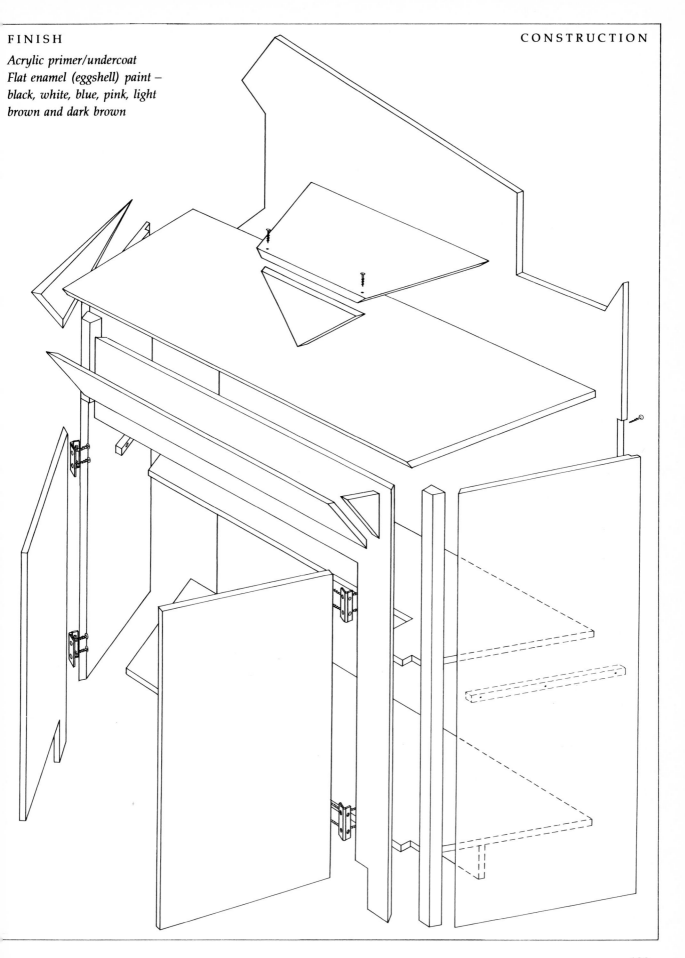

ORDER OF WORK

1 Mark and cut out the L-shaped door surround
2 Mark and cut out the two side panels
3 Angle the front and back edges of the side panels and the L-shaped surround
4 Rabbet the side panels to house the back
5 Cut out the top
6 Shape the battens between front and side panels
7 Glue and nail front, sides and top together
8 Mark and cut out the two shelves
9 Cut and attach shelf support battens
10 Fit shelves
11 Cut and attach the panel supporting the lower shelf
12 Mark and cut out the front molding
13 Glue the molding in position under the top
14 Cut and fit the triangular block at the right hand end of the molding
15 Plane the front edge of the top to match the molding
16 Mark out the back panel using the squared grid
17 Cut out the panel
18 Bevel the panel's sides to fit the rabbets in the side panels
19 Glue and screw the back in position
20 Cut the triangular molding to shape
21 Glue and clamp the molding in position
22 Plane the edge of the top to continue the line of the molding
23 Mark and cut out the two doors
24 Hang the doors
25 Mark out and cut the plywood shelf and support
26 Glue and screw the two together
27 Plane the edges to create the illusion of a continuous line
28 Screw the shelf in position

Finish

1 Sand all surfaces to be painted
2 Paint on a coat of primer/undercoat
3 Pencil in the pattern
4 Paint in the large areas of colour
5 Paint in the stripes

screws through countersunk clearance holes in the back drilled to continue the line of the side.

The left-hand molding is complicated. It is a triangle beveled along every edge. This is a fussy job, too complex to work out from drawings. Trial and error is the only sure route to success. Cut the molding slightly oversize, try it in position, mark the angles, cut them roughly with a saw or plane, and try again, repeating the process until the correct shape is achieved. The designer needed eight fittings before he was satisfied. Glue and clamp the fillet in position. The edge of the top is planed

to continue the angle of the molding.

Cut out the two particleboard doors. The right-hand door is a straightforward rectangle with edges cut at right angles. However, the hinged edge of the left-hand door is angled to meet the side. Saw the edge at the same angle as the corresponding edge of the L-shaped section above it.

Mark the position for the two hinges on doors and sides. Chisel out recesses for the 2in hinges and screw them in place. At first the designer found the left hand door edges pinched together before it was fully open. He overcame this by removing the door and chamfering both edges.

There are no drawers, but the addition of wood blocks cut to create 3-dimensional versions of the handles in the painting would make the doors easier to open. The bottom could be undercut to provide a finger grip.

The top shelf

The shelf is, for visual reasons, made of ¾in plywood, rather than the ½in sheets used for the rest of the piece. Patrick Daw established the shape by making a mock-up out of insulation board, cutting it down until a satisfactory form was made. The two-part structure was then cut in plywood, assembled and shaped as a unit on the bench before being fixed in position. If you follow the drawings based on Daw's construction, the mock-up stage is unnecessary. However, the process is described below.

For the mock-up he cut the trapezoid shelf roughly to shape and propped it up on books on the sideboard top. To establish the position for the shelf the final pattern of the painting was penciled in roughly on the back panel.

The sides of the shelf (and later the triangular support) are angled, and the edges planed away to create the illusion of a continuous plane from the tip of the triangle to the vertical surface of the back. This illusion is utterly convincing from only one fixed viewpoint, which was first established by making a mark on the floor 10 feet in front of the piece. The viewpoint was fixed at eye level above this mark, and was used as the reference point for the shaping of the shelf and the final painting of the entire piece. From now on the job involved constant journeys between reference point and piece; much time could be saved by two people becoming involved, one directing operations from the reference point, the other working on the piece.

He sawed away the shelf sides bit by bit until the illusion worked, and repeated the operation with the triangular support. In this way the final shapes and angles for the shelf and support were established. He then marked and cut the shapes out of ¾in plywood, ready to fix on top of the sideboard.

Drill two countersunk clearance holes in the shelf centered ⅜in from the leading edge. Glue the top edge of the triangle and join the two pieces by driving 1½in screws into the triangle before the glue sets. Fill the screw holes with plastic filler.

It is now a question of planing away the edges of the shelf and support – use the mock-up as a guide if you have made one – to create the illusion of the continuous line, with no thickness of timber showing. The plane blade must be sharp to allow a cut to be made across the junction of shelf and support without damaging the corners. If accidents occur, gaps can be filled with plastic wood filler – this will later be hidden under the paint.

The happy result of the planing is to leave a small foot at the base of the triangle, providing a plane of surface contact with the sideboard top. Drive a single ¾in screw up through a clearance hole in the top and into the tip of the triangle. Three 1¼in screws are driven through clearance holes drilled in the back panel to fix the shelf to the back.

Painting the sideboard

The piece is painted to confirm the illusion of lines running up the back. From the viewpoint 10 feet in front of the piece the illusion is complete – the color photograph on p. 124 is taken from slightly below eye level to indicate some separation of the elements.

The piece is sanded smooth and painted with a coat of acrylic primer/undercoat. The outline of the large areas of color is drawn in lightly in pencil. Paint the large color areas. Six unmixed colors were used – light brown, dark brown, blue, pink, black and white.

The stripes are added last. Like signs on a road surface, they have to be painted very wide on the horizontal surfaces to appear as thick as those on the vertical plane. Strips of black paper can be cut to experiment with widths.

The stripes on the sideboard's sides are radial, with the viewpoint as the center of the circle. The lines are established by stretching a piece of string between the viewpoint and the piece and ruling off the stripes. This is ideally a job for two people. The lines are painted on freehand, without masking off the edges, to give an irregular look true to the painting.

An alternative sideboard

Having made the piece, the designer thought it would look even more dramatic if instead of using paint he had created the colored areas by applying plastic laminates. The limited range of colors, used in large flat areas, makes it ideal for such treatment. Laminates would also hide all surface joints. The black and blue lines can be created by scoring into the plastic surface with an engraving tool and filling the grooves with dyed epoxy grout.

The trapezoid plan of the still-life sideboard appears again in Picasso's Still Life on a Table *(1919). Musée Picasso, Paris*

Saint Augustine's Armchair

by Mark Dunhill

from *St. Augustine in his Study* (1502-8) by Vittore Carpaccio (*c.* 1460-1523)

Scuola di S. Giorgio degli Schiavoni, Venice

Carpaccio's painting shows St. Augustine startled in his study at Hippo by a vision of St. Jerome streaming through the window. The Golden Legend tells the tale of Augustine sitting down to write a letter to St. Jerome, asking for his advice on a thorny theological problem concerning souls in Paradise. As he wrote, Jerome lay dying in Bethlehem, and appeared as a sweet, indescribable light, accusing Augustine of vanity in trying to understand Paradise and asking him enigmatically if he thought he could put the sea in a bottle.

The picture is one of a series of nine painted by Carpaccio for the Scuola di S. Giorgio degli Schiavoni in Venice between 1502 and 1508. The Scuole were an important feature of Venetian life for hundreds of years. They were charitable Christian institutions, often assembling the members of a particular trade or a group of foreign nationals living in Venice. Many carried out social services, running hospitals or caring for widows and orphans. The few Scuole which survived into the nineteenth century were suppressed by Napoleon's decree of 1806. Yet S. Giorgio carried on, and Carpaccio's paintings still hang there in the position they have occupied for over 400 years.

S. Giorgio was founded in 1451 to serve the city's seafaring Dalmatian community. It was dedicated to the Dalmatian saints – George, Tryphon and Jerome. Carpaccio's paintings show the three saints' miracles.

St. Augustine's room reflects Carpaccio's interest in science and learning, typical of the Renaissance humanist. The saint sits at his extraordinary cloth-clad desk raised on a fabric-covered platform, surrounded by books and objects both scientific and religious, the whole scene bathed in magical light. There are astronomical instruments, scissors, a bell, an hour glass and an open book of hours. On the shelf behind the *prie-dieu* stands Augustine's collection of Roman antiquities – antique collecting was a popular hobby among Renaissance men. Above them is a row of forty books. In the back room nautical and astronomical instruments – a quadrant and astrolabes – hang above a lectern. And looking on keenly there's the little dog.

Designing St. Augustine's armchair

The red chair recalls the curule chairs of ancient Rome, in which a magistrate would sit, and which led to the design of the medieval X-chair. The existence of a model for Carpaccio's extraordinary chair seems unlikely, yet a unique survivor from fifteenth-century Venice bears a remarkable likeness to St Augustine's (p. 138). It is made entirely of wood and decorated with copper studs. The chair in the painting appears to be upholstered in red leather, with tassels dangling below. It stands on a similarly covered kneeling platform behind a scrolled lectern.

Making the chair

The Carpaccio chair was made by a sculptor, who has a sculptor's attitude to the shaping and joining of wood. He built up the chair by gluing together pieces which were oversize, but roughly cut to shape. He then carved the piece by sawing, grinding, rasping and sanding away excess material. Before the chair was painted, this patchwork of carved, glued blocks showed. What was obtained was strength, a flexible method of work, and a good surface for paint. The technique allows complex curves in three dimensions to be formed. Wood is used as the raw material for carving and shaping, rather than as a material to be assembled into a construction of finely jointed sticks and planks. As paint will cover the whole surface, errors can be concealed. If you grind away too much wood, an additional block can be glued on and reground.

The wooden "tassel" under the seat and the cone beneath the tassel are turned on a lathe. Those without access to a lathe can give the job to a local wood turner. Alternatively – and less satisfactorily – they could be ground to shape from a solid block.

The chair is made in two parts: the seat (that is to say everything above the inverted cone into which the legs are mortised) and the base (the cone itself and everything below it). Finally the seat and base are screwed together. Mark Dunhill chose screws only after rejecting the idea of a swivel seat, which would have created a sort of office throne. Surprisingly, a swivel seat is a feature of the fifteenth-century original in Milan, where the independence of seat and base is exploited. He also considered building a couple of universal joints into the rising rear section and placing a reading light on top, thereby making an early Venetian angle-poise lamp. The candle on top is all that survives of this appealing idea.

The Seat

The seat of the chair is made of two 18in diameter discs of ¾in plywood. Draw the circles on the plywood sheet and cut them out with a bandsaw, a bowsaw or a saber saw (jigsaw). The two discs are glued together with PVA woodworking adhesive and clamped or screwed to hold them tight while the glue sets. The rim is then rounded off to the shape seen in the photograph (p. 132), using a rasp, shaping tool or hand-held electric grinder.

The U-shaped members that form the supports for the arms are fixed to the front and back of the seat. The discs are squared off front and back to receive them by sawing two parallel faces. To mark the cutting lines, draw a line through the center of the double disc and draw two parallel lines at right angles to the first line – these mark the segments to be sawed off.

The arm supports are, like the seat, made of plywood. The curves are cut out of the flat sheet of plywood and glued together. Two thicknesses of ¾in ply are used for the front; three pieces make the back – two ¾in thick plus one ½in. Dunhill flattened the curve of the front arc dramatically from the semicircle in his original drawing to allow room for the sitter's legs.

As the curve of the back support is narrower and higher on the side away from the seat, the profiles of the pieces that are glued together to make it are stepped in and back (see drawing p. 135). In the end the supports will be glued and doweled to the seat. Clamping or screwing them in place temporarily will give you the chance to judge the progress of the work. It is easier to do most of the shaping before the supports are finally attached.

Mark and cut tenons in the top of the front U at each side, using a tenon saw. The tenons are 2¾in deep on the outside, but only 1½in deep on the inside (see drawing). This is because the underside of the arms is stepped back.

Now the time has come to build up the curved piece that makes the back and arms. The curve of the arms is worked out by reference to the drawing and cut with the two U curves temporarily held to the seat with screws. This proved to be the most difficult part of the construction, as the curve of the arms moves both inwards and upwards.

The curve of arms and back is again built up with stepped pieces of ¾in ply which are clamped and glued together before being fitted to the seat. No single piece of ply runs the full half circle from arm to arm. Concentrate on establishing the lower edge of the curve, leaving the top ragged – it can be shaped later. Begin by cutting the shape crudely, then refine it. Where the arms meet the rear U cut a tenon on the U and a matching

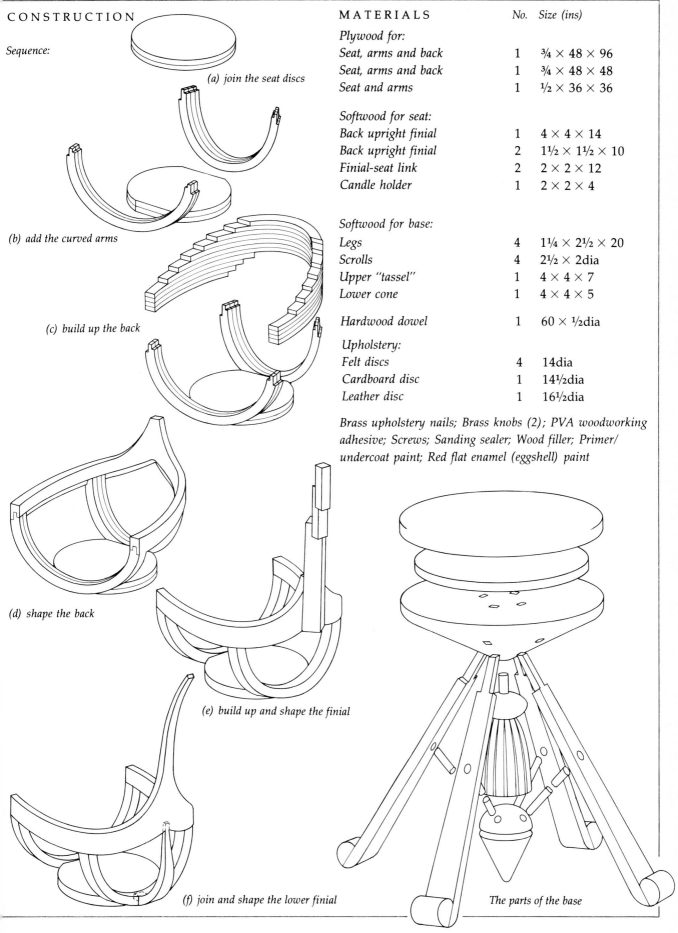

CONSTRUCTION

Sequence:

(a) join the seat discs

(b) add the curved arms

(c) build up the back

(d) shape the back

(e) build up and shape the finial

(f) join and shape the lower finial

The parts of the base

MATERIALS	No.	Size (ins)
Plywood for:		
Seat, arms and back	1	¾ × 48 × 96
Seat, arms and back	1	¾ × 48 × 48
Seat and arms	1	½ × 36 × 36
Softwood for seat:		
Back upright finial	1	4 × 4 × 14
Back upright finial	2	1½ × 1½ × 10
Finial-seat link	2	2 × 2 × 12
Candle holder	1	2 × 2 × 4
Softwood for base:		
Legs	4	1¼ × 2½ × 20
Scrolls	4	2½ × 2dia
Upper "tassel"	1	4 × 4 × 7
Lower cone	1	4 × 4 × 5
Hardwood dowel	1	60 × ½dia
Upholstery:		
Felt discs	4	14dia
Cardboard disc	1	14½dia
Leather disc	1	16½dia

Brass upholstery nails; Brass knobs (2); PVA woodworking adhesive; Screws; Sanding sealer; Wood filler; Primer/undercoat paint; Red flat enamel (eggshell) paint

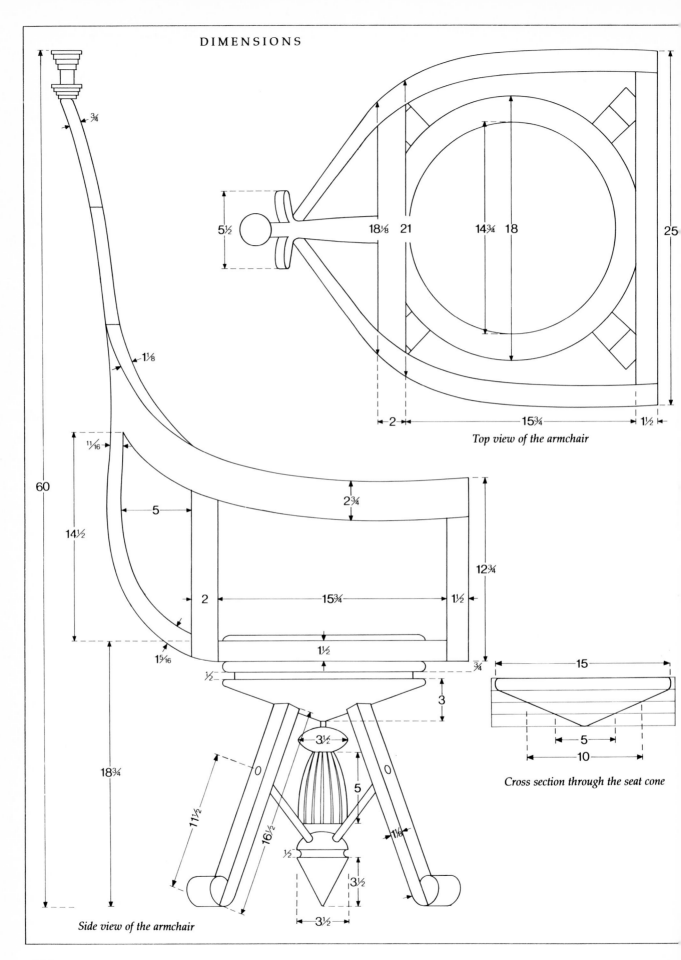

¾

1⅛

60

11/16

5

14½

2¾

12¾

2

15¾

1½

1½

¾

15⁵/16

½

3

½

15

5

10

Cross section through the seat cone

3½

0

5

11½

16½

1⅛

½

3½

3½

18¾

Side view of the armchair

5½

18⅛ 21

14¾ 18

25

2

15¾

1½

Top view of the armchair

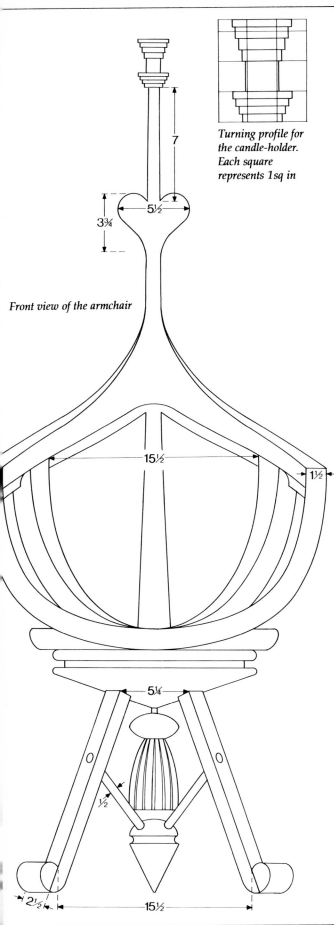

Front view of the armchair

Turning profile for
the candle-holder.
Each square
represents 1 sq in

ORDER OF WORK

The seat

1 Cut out the two plywood discs which form the seat itself
2 Glue and clamp them together
3 Round off the rim
4 Square off two parallel faces on the disc
5 Cut out and glue together plywood arcs to form the front and rear U-shaped arm supports
6 Carve the rear U to shape
7 Mark and cut tenons at each side of the front U
8 Build up the stepped layers of plywood to make the arms and back, gluing and clamping the pieces together
9 Shape the arms and back
10 Cut tenons on each side of the rear U
11 With the U curves temporarily in position, mark and cut matching mortises in the arms
12 Glue and dowel the U supports in position
13 Glue the arms to the U supports
14 Build up the back upright
15 Build up the rear curve down from the back to the seat
16 Cut a half lap joint to fix the rear curve to the seat
17 Shape the rear upright and lower curve
18 Glue and dowel the "ears" to the upright
19 Cut and fix the candle holder on top

The base

1 Cut out the four plywood discs to make the seat cone
2 Glue and clamp them together
3 Grind the cone to shape
4 Cut the legs to length and shape
5 Mark and cut shouldered tenons on top of the legs
6 Mark and drill the four mortises in the cone for the legs
7 Mark the dowel positions on the legs
8 Drill dowel holes in the lower cone
9 Dowel the wooden "tassel" to the tip of the seat cone
10 Glue and wedge the legs in position in the seat
11 Glue the dowels linking the legs and lower cone
12 Shape and glue the scrolls to the bottom of the legs
13 Round off the bottom of the legs
14 Cut and shape discs to fit between seat and base
15 Screw base and seat together

Finish

1 Fill all flaws in the wood and sand the whole piece
2 Paint on sanding sealer and sand smooth
3 Paint on primer/undercoat
4 Resand
5 Repeat steps 3 and 4 until the surface is immaculate
6 Paint on the top flat enamel (eggshell) coat
7 Cut discs of felt padding for the seat
8 Attach a leather disc around the cardboard disc
9 Decorate the chair with upholstery nails and knobs

mortise in the arms. This is not easy on the curve. However, mistakes can be filled in and painted over later.

A mortise is also cut to join the arms to the front U. This is drilled and chiseled out to match the tenon. A sharp blade is needed, as plywood is not easy to chisel.

With the U supports and arms glued in position and held by dowels for additional strength, the next stage is to build up the finial. First a 90° V-shaped notch is cut into the center of the back curve on the rear side. A length of 4 × 4in softwood is glued into the notch and further pieces of softwood spliced in above it. These are half-lapped and glued (and could also be doweled for extra strength). The depth of the first notch – and the dimensions of the spliced-on pieces – must be calculated by eye. The curves already begun in the crest will carry on up through the finial, and a big enough block must be built up for these curves to be realized.

The curve down to the seat is constructed in the same way, with a half-lapped joint linking it to the rear U section.

The process of reducing the blocks of wood to a slender curved shape involves a sequence of drawing, cutting, drawing and cutting until you achieve the right line. Use the abrading tool of your choice.

The "ears" that make the heart-shaped motif half way up the finial are now cut and shaped from softwood. They are held in place by PVA adhesive and dowels, as is the candle-holder on top. A turning pattern for this is given on p. 137. It could be built up by threading discs of different sizes, cut with a set of hole borers, onto a central dowel.

The base
The base is, in constructional terms, very similar to one of the crudest of stool and chair designs, seen for example in the illustration on p. 139. The legs are wedged firmly into mortises cut through the inverted cone of the base. The strength of the design depends on the seat being thick enough to give good support to the legs.

All the other parts are essentially decorative, and if Carpaccio had a real chair in mind they were probably cords and tassels rather than wood. Dunhill turned the two tassels from softwood – profiles can be seen in the drawings. It is a simple turning job for anyone with a lathe. Those without turning equipment can hand the job over to a local wood turner. The detailing in the top tassel is cut with a gouge.

When the seat cone has been built up by gluing together four discs of ¾in plywood (the top and second 15in in diameter, the lower ones 10in and 5in), it is

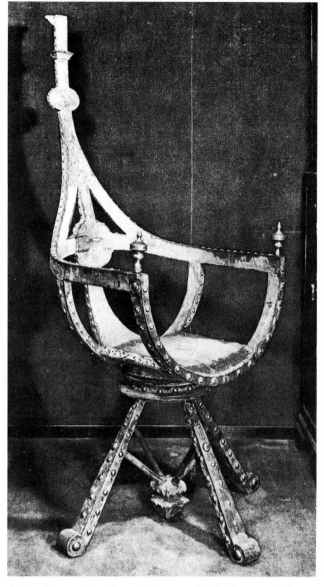

This unique survivor from 15th-century Venice bears a striking resemblance to the armchair in Carpaccio's painting. It features a swivel seat. Palazzo Morando, Milan

ground down to shape. A bandsaw that allows bevels to be cut will make the job easier.

The four softwood legs taper from 2½in at the ground to 1½in where they meet the cone. A tenon 1in wide, and long enough to go through to the base of the cone, is cut 16½in from the foot of each. As the length of the legs through the cone can be very hard to calculate precisely, cut the legs a couple of inches overlong until final fitting.

The designer first cut the legs straight, but they displeased him. He was much happier after putting a slight curve on them, which also made them slightly springy.

This deep mortising of the legs overcomes the potential problem of the legs splaying outward under the weight of a person. The great problem with the chair base is cutting the mortises for the legs and drilling the holes for the dowels which join the lower conical "tassel" to the legs, at the right angle. The glued plywood sandwich into which the mortises are being cut is an intractable material, which does not take kindly to chiseling, so there are practical problems as well.

Draw a square cross on the flat face of the cone and carry the lines to the point of the cone. Mark out the four 1×1 in mortises centered on these lines and 4 in from the apex of the cone. The angle between leg and cone is established by holding the legs up to the cone and reading off the angle with a bevel.

Clamp the cone – point upwards – at an angle which, if the legs were in place, would have the one on the upward-facing curve of the cone standing vertical. A block of wood cut to meet the cone at the correct angle can be used to guide your drill as you drill vertically through the cone to cut the mortise. Clean out the corners with a chisel.

When all the mortises have been cut and the legs are in place (but not yet glued) the position of the holes for the dowels joining legs to lower "tassel" can be marked. This can be done by eye or with a sliding bevel. Line up dowel, leg and lower "tassel." Pencil in the angle on the edge of the leg – be sure that all the dowels enter the legs at the same distance up from the base, in this case 11½in. Remove the legs from the cone while they are drilled.

When the ½in diameter holes have been drilled through the legs, those on the block can be marked in a similar way. Checking the angle is more difficult on a curved surface. A jig can be made to support the drill at the correct angle and hold the block in place.

The turned wooden tassel is now doweled to the point of the cone. Drill a ½in diameter hole 2 in into the point of the cone and the center of the tassel's top section, to take the linking dowel. Glue it in position. Glue the legs in position. Hardwood wedges hammered into the top of the tenons make the joints absolutely firm. Glue the dowels and lower cone in place.

The scrolls at the bottom of the legs are 2½in lengths of 2in diameter doweling, sawed flat on one side and glued in place. The base of the leg is rounded with a shaping tool to continue the curve.

Base and seat are finally joined by screws that go down through the center of the seat into the cone. They should be countersunk but will, when the chair is complete, be covered by a padded leather cushion.

Two plywood discs are fitted between the seat and base. The upper one is ½in thick, and its edges are rounded off before it is glued to the lower ¾in disc. This in turn is glued to the base. Clamp or screw the discs in position until the glue sets.

Finishing the chair

The designer thought that color was the most important element in the finish, whether he used leather or paint. Paint was chosen as the more practical alternative. The more time is spent filling and sanding the surfaces, the better the final paint job will be.

After sanding the chair, paint on a coat of sanding sealer. This will no doubt reveal flaws in the wood surface. As a smooth surface is wanted, fill and sand these before painting on the first undercoat. This sequence of painting, filling and sanding is repeated several times. Only when a surface of even texture and color is achieved should the final coat of flat red enamel be put on.

The padding on the seat consists of four discs of felt. These are cut to approximately 14in diameter, a little smaller than the disc of cardboard around which the leather cover is wrapped. The color of the leather matches the paint exactly. A circle of upholstery nails fixes cardboard and leather to the wood of the seat. Brass upholstery pins are hammered into the wood for decorative effect. These, and other brass embellishments, are standard upholsterer's or brass founder's stock. The pair of brass knobs on the arms are door knobs with a central screw on the base. This is driven into a pilot hole drilled into the arm.

The base of St. Augustine's armchair is similar to the commonest type of medieval stool, seen in this engraving by Burgkmair. The three splayed legs are driven through a thick slab of wood.

Chair in the Valley
by Jim Partridge
from *Furniture in the Valley* (1927) by Giorgio de Chirico (1888-1978)

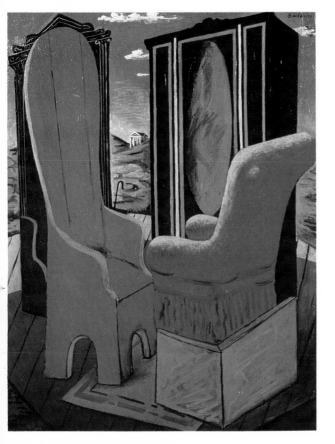

Years before the surrealists announced their arrival, Giorgio de Chirico had created a world as strange as any imagined by Dali or Magritte. It was a quiet world of classical ruins, peopled largely by statues, where long shadows and black silhouettes were the sole occupants of silent Mediterranean squares.

Even a piece of ordinary furniture becomes enigmatic when it stands in de Chirico's landscape. The artist's wife, Isabella Far, has told the story of de Chirico's encounter with furniture in the valley. Driving along a country road he spotted some furniture junked in a field, with no one in sight. The scene pleased him and was to appear in several paintings.

The massive seat standing theatrically on its stage in the classical landscape of *Furniture in the Valley* is no ordinary chair. It has echoes of thrones, settles or the traditional draft-proof porter's chair, but it is a chair of the imagination.

Designing the chair in the valley
The chair is massive but straightforward. The first step was to fix its dimensions. The designer assumed the seat would be at a normal height for seated humans and that it must be flat, even though it appears to slope forward in the painting. He also thought it should not be too shallow for comfort. The chair's other dimensions followed from these decisions, and it became clear that the piece would stand some six feet tall. As the planks in the painting are clearly thick, such unusual height implies a very heavy chair. Nevertheless Jim Partridge remained faithful to the solid de Chirico plank, rejecting lightweight substitutes for timber such as cardboard-cored panels.

It is important to design the base of the chair with stability in mind. The chair's side panels are positioned so that the tall and heavy top does not overhang them at the back. This prevents the chair toppling backward as soon as a sitter relaxes in it.

The back of the chair is hidden in the painting. The

141

designer decided to leave it open below seat level to reduce the weight. He gave the hidden side panel the same arched cutout as the visible one.

Pine planks would be both easy to work with and easy to buy, but the designer chose beech because of good local availability. Boards eight and nine inches wide proved faithful to the painting. The thickness throughout is 1¼ in.

Making the chair

De Chirico's chair has a loose-jointed look, giving the amateur a reassuring margin for cutting errors. The only point where accuracy is crucial is at the awkward joint between back and sides, where the designer's approach makes satisfactory results easy to achieve. Elsewhere it is important that the lines and curves of the chair should be closer to the imprecision of a pencil sketch than the mathematical accuracy of compass-drawn lines. Construction is also straightforward, the basic structure being held together by screws or by battens screwed inside the seat. No complex joints are used.

Construction begins by gluing boards together to make five rectangular panels. These are then shaped individually to make the front, sides, seat and back. The planks are thick enough to be joined by glue alone. Dowels would be needed with thinner planks.

The seat, front and sides are all made in the same way. Three 1¼ × 8in boards are planed along the edges until they butt perfectly together. Wood glue is then applied to the edges, and the boards are held together by strap clamps (sash cramps) until the glue sets. Ridges on the joints are then planed flat.

Saw out the front panel, putting 45° miters along the top edge and down both sides. The front edge of the seat panel is also mitered at 45° where it meets the front panel. Mitering can be done with a handsaw, but an angled blade on a saber saw (jigsaw) or circular saw makes the job far simpler.

With a pencil, draw the shape of the side panels on two of the rectangles, and draw the arched cutout on the front panel. When the drawn shapes look right, prop the three panels up to check the effect and saw them out roughly with a saber saw. The final shaping and rounding of the rear edges is done with a shaping tool after the chair is assembled.

Marking and cutting the miter on the front edge of each side panel is more difficult, as it stops short of the top of the panel. However, only two saw cuts are necessary. Begin by drawing a horizontal line joining the outside and inside edges of the side panel at seat level (the point where the side panel begins to curve). Continue the line on the inside face of the side panel to a

ORDER OF WORK

1 *Make the rectangular panels from which the front, sides and seat will be cut. Three 8in planed boards are glued and clamped together to make each panel*
2 *Plane joints flat*
3 *Saw out the front panel with mitered top and sides*
4 *Saw out the seat panel with mitered front edge*
5 *Saw the side panels roughly to shape*
6 *Mark and cut out the arches in front and side panels*
7 *Miter the front edge of the side panels*
8 *Chisel out the leading edges of the miters on front, sides and seat*
9 *Glue and screw on battens connecting front and side panels*
10 *Screw on the battens supporting the seat*
11 *Fit the softwood block connecting the seat to the front panel*
12 *Glue and clamp together three 9in planed boards to make the back panel*
13 *Plane joints flat*
14 *Saw the lower section of the back panel to shape and put it in position on the seat*
15 *Pencil in the finished outline on the back panel*
16 *Saw the back panel to shape*
17 *Mark and drill countersunk clearance holes in the side panels*
18 *Screw the back panel in place and plug screw holes*
19 *Shape the joints between sides and back*
20 *Shape the rear edge of the left side panel*

Finish

1 *Paint white pigmented primer (emulsion) around the chair edges*
2 *Fill open joints with flexible plastic filler*
3 *Apply a coat of wax*

MATERIALS	No.	Size (ins)
Beech (or pine) for:		
Front panel	3	1¼ × 8 × 19
Seat panel	3	1¼ × 8 × 19
Left side panel	3	1¼ × 8 × 34
Right side panel	3	1¼ × 8 × 34
Back	3	1¼ × 9 × 53
Softwood for:		
Battens	4	1 × 1 × 16
Batten	1	1 × 1 × 6
Woodworking adhesive		
Screws		

FINISH

White pigmented primer (emulsion) paint; Black plastic wood filler; Wax

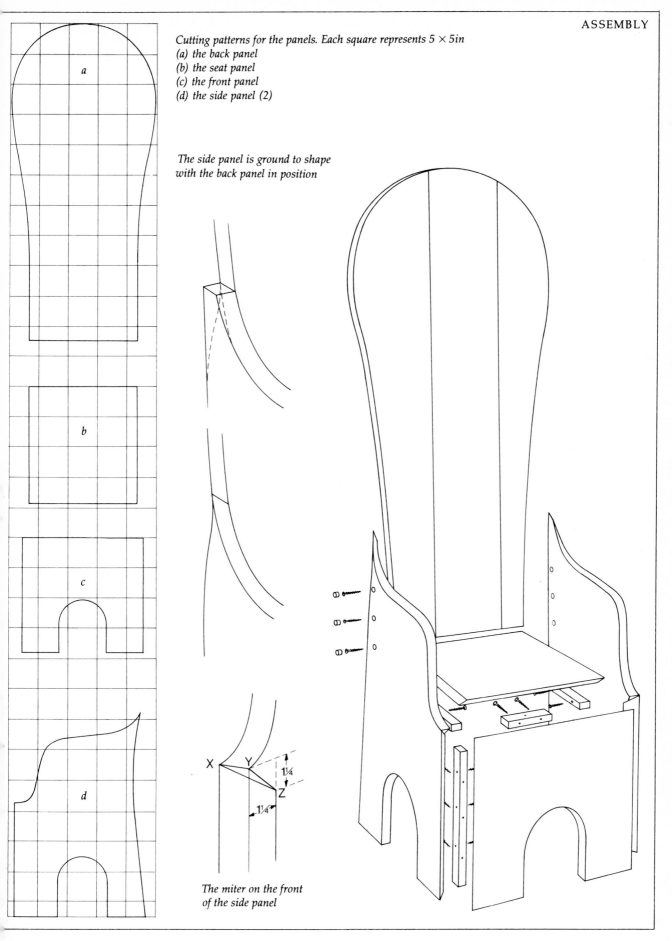

Cutting patterns for the panels. Each square represents 5 × 5in
(a) the back panel
(b) the seat panel
(c) the front panel
(d) the side panel (2)

The side panel is ground to shape with the back panel in position

The miter on the front of the side panel

point 1¼in below the first line. Make a short angled saw cut along the line, joining points X, Y and Z in the drawing on p. 143. Now draw a vertical line on the inside face of the panel 1¼in from the front. Starting at the base of the panel, saw a 45° miter up to the point X, completing the cut with the saw held at an angle to join points X and Z. It is not disastrous if the top of the miter drops out – the gap can be filled later.

The designer wanted to imitate the heavy lines in de Chirico's painting where front, sides and seat meet, but without affecting the strength of the structure. He overcame the problem very simply. He chiseled out the leading edges of the miters between front, side and seat panels. The effect is to open the front of the joint slightly in imitation of the painting. Behind the gap the mitered joint remains firm.

The sides and the front panel are connected by screwing 1 × 1in wooden battens 16in long inside the joint. Three screws are driven through clearance holes in the battens into corresponding pilot holes in each panel to hold the battens in place.

The seat panel sits on two similar 1 × 1in battens screwed onto the side panels. The screws are driven into ½in-long slots drilled in the battens; this allows the wood to shrink and expand with changing temperature and humidity without tearing the screws loose. At the front the seat is joined to the front panel by a 6in-long batten of 1 × 1in softwood screwed to seat and front.

Three 9in-wide planks are used to construct the high back. They are glued, butt-jointed, clamped together and planed as before. De Chirico's rough brushwork gives the impression that the planks in the back panel are as ill-fitting as the joints between the sides, front and seat. To recreate this open-jointed look, the designer used a disc sander to put an irregular chamfer on the front face of the planks. He then glued the planks tightly together and when the glue was dry filled these shallow ruts with black plastic filler.

The designer found that fitting the back to the base was the hardest part of the construction. A smooth curve is necessary where back and side meet. To simplify construction he kept this curve shallow, so it fits within the thickness of the plank and does not therefore demand complex carving. The lower part of the chair's back, from the point where the sides meet it down to the seat, is straight-sided. He knew the distance between the two side panels of the chair and the distance from the seat to the highest point of the side panels. Using these measurements he marked out the rectangular lower back on the glued-up back panel and sawed out the rectangular blocks on each side of it. This left a shoulder on each side which will overhang the side panels. He

then pushed the back in place, drew in the tongue shape of the rest of the back with a pencil and cut the panel to shape with a bandsaw. The shape he arrived at is shown in the scale drawing on p. 143, which can be used to cut the panel to its finished shape at this stage.

The back is held in place by three screws driven through the arms on each side. Lay a straight edge on the side panel along the line of the back to establish the screw positions. Drill holes ½in deep, slightly wider than the screw heads – these will later be filled with wooden plugs. At the bottom of each hole drill shank-wide clearance holes for the screws.

With the back panel in position, mark the screw entry points on its side and drill pilot holes as deep as the screw. This will prevent the screws splitting the wood. When the screws are driven in, cover the heads with wooden plugs and chisel them flat.

The joint between back and sides can now be rounded to shape with a hand grinder or shaping tool. The designer used a disc sander to round off the rear edge of the side panel to produce a roughness reminiscent of de Chirico's brushwork.

Irregularities in the surface can be sanded down by hand or less laboriously with a drum sander attachment on an electric drill. These are preferable to a disc sander as they can be run in the direction of the grain and will not therefore scar the wood.

A pale line runs around the edge of the chair in the painting. This was imitated by painting on a coat of white pigmented primer (emulsion). The dark open joints were emphasised like the joints in the back by filling the gaps with a flexible plastic filler. Finally the whole chair was waxed.

Furniture in the Valley *(1927) by de Chirico.*